PN2430.G6C5

P9-DXM-669

The Types of English Literature

EDITED BY

WILLIAM ALLAN NEILSON

THE LITERATURE OF ROGUERY

BY

FRANK WADLEIGH CHANDLER

VOLUME I

BURT FRANKLIN BIBLIOGRAPHICAL SERIES

1. Burt Franklin & G. Legman. David Ricardo and Ricardian theory. A bibliographical checklist. New York, 1949.
2. Francesco Cordasco. A Junius Bibliography. With a preliminary essay on the political background, text and identity. A contribution to 18th century constitutional and literary history. With eight appendices. New York, 1949.
3. Burt Franklin & Francesco Cordasco. Adam Smith: a bibliographical checklist. An international record of critical writings and scholarship relating to Smith and Smithian theory, 1876-1950. New York, 1950.
4. Edmund Silberner. Moses Hess: an annotated bibliography. New York, 1951.
5. Francesco Cordasco. The Bohn Libraries. A history and checklist. New York, 1951.
6. Jan M. Novotny. A Library of Public Finance and Economics.
7. Andrew George Little. Initia operum latinorum, quae saeculis XIII, XIV, XV, attribuuntur, secundum ordinem alphatbeti disposita. 13 + 275 pp. 8vo., cloth. (Manchester University Publications, n. 5 - 1905). New York: Burt Franklin, 1958.
8. John William Bradley. Dictionary of miniaturists, illuminators, calligraphers and copyists with references to their works, and notices of their patrons, compiled from sources, many hitherto inedited, from the establishment of Christianity to the 18th century. 3 volumes, lg. 8vo., cloth. (London, 1887-89) New York: Burt Franklin, 1958.
9. Frank Wadleigh Chandler. The literature of roguery. 2 vols., 8vo., cloth. (The Types of English Literature, ed. by W. A. Neilson). (Boston, 1907). New York: Burt Franklin, 1958.
10. Robert Huntington Fletcher. The Arthurian material in the chronicles, especially those of Great Britain and France, 9 + 313 pp., bibliography, 8vo., cloth ([Harvard] Notes and Studies in Philology 10, 1906) New York: Burt Franklin, 1958.
11. John Alexander Herbert. Illuminated manuscripts. 10 + 355 pp., 51 plates; index of manuscripts, scribes and illuminators; bibliography, lg. 8vo., cloth. (London, 1911). New York: Burt Franklin, 1958.

THE LITERATURE OF ROGUERY

BY

FRANK WADLEIGH CHANDLER, 1873–
PROFESSOR OF ENGLISH IN THE POLYTECHNIC INSTITUTE OF BROOKLYN; SOMETIME LECTURER IN COMPARATIVE LITERATURE IN COLUMBIA UNIVERSITY; AUTHOR OF "ROMANCES OF ROGUERY"

Humani nihil a me alienum puto

IN TWO VOLUMES
VOL. I

Burt Franklin Bibliographical Series IX

BURT FRANKLIN
New York 25, N. Y.
1958

Reprinted by
BURT FRANKLIN
514 West 113th Street
New York 25, N. Y.

Published October 1907

Printed in U.S.A. by
NOBLE OFFSET PRINTERS, Inc.
400 Lafayette Street
New York 3, N. Y.

CONTENTS

VOLUME I

PREFACE

This book presents a detailed study of a large, complex, and important tract of literature. In the main it deals with what has hitherto escaped classification, or considers familiar matter from a new angle. Such types as the anatomy of roguery and the criminal biography are here for the first time defined and displayed in their development and connection with imaginative letters. Other types, like the jest-book, the drama, and the detective story, are now first correlated with the genre. Authors never before ranged in this camp are accorded honors there, and the credentials of those long enrolled are subjected to revision. If the English novel in a few specimens has already received attention as exemplifying the picaresque strain, no endeavor has before been made to discuss it from this standpoint as a whole. Nor has any rigorous criticism of individual works sought, as here, to determine their exact dependence upon foreign sources or the degree of their resemblance to and divergence from models of the type in other lands.

In the broadest sense, this history follows the fortunes of the anti-hero in literature. More narrowly, it is a study of realism, for it investigates the rôle enacted in literary art by the observation of low-life. Specifically, it traces in English letters a notable series of gradations from the first crude records of actuality to the complete reshaping of experience by the imagination, and in this process it points a constant tendency toward romanticism, counteracted at times by fresh returns to fact. It aims therefore to do a threefold service: first, to exhibit in its origins and organic growth a body of literature of considerable extent and intrinsic interest; secondly, to trace the development of anti-heroism in letters as reflecting the disintegrating play of the forces of evil in society; and thirdly, to exemplify a significant process and tendency in art.

The opening chapter, after defining the genre, is devoted to a rapid survey of its progress in Spain, France, Germany, and Holland. Since this is intended merely as an outline map of the foreign field to serve the uses of the scholar, the general reader may well avoid it by proceeding at once from the definition of the type to the account of roguery in England.

It has been my purpose to make this study authoritative, not only in the main, but in matters of detail. To this end the conclusions of the standard monographs dealing with its various phases have been embodied in the text, and such works of reference, as well as the best editions of originals, are noted in bibliographies appended to each chapter. In every case, however, I have worked at first hand with the sources themselves and can confess to little immediate debt to books about books.

To friends my obligation is greater. Professor G. R. Carpenter of Columbia University first called my attention to this subject ten years ago. Professor G. E. Woodberry directed my earlier investigations in the field and personally supervised the issue of my "Romances of Roguery," dealing with the picaresque novel in Spain. To Sr. Menéndez y Pelayo and the late Professor Jan ten Brink, as to Professor J. E. Spingarn of Columbia University, I am indebted for valuable suggestions; while to Professor W. A. Neilson of Harvard University I owe the thanks of one who has benefited by the kind offices of an admirable editor and a generous friend. F. W. C.

NEW YORK, September, 1907.

THE LITERATURE OF ROGUERY

THE LITERATURE OF ROGUERY

CHAPTER I

SCOPE AND FOREIGN SOURCES

1. *The Type Defined*

HE literature of roguery occupies a peculiar place in the history of letters. Determined by subject-matter rather than by form, and depending upon observed actuality rather than ideals, it presents low life in lieu of heroic, and manners rather than conscience and emotion. It prefers prose to verse, descriptive narrative to the drama, and is therefore primarily associated with the novel. Yet works as various as "Eulenspiegel," the "Fourberies de Scapin," the ballades of Villon, the "Beggar's Opera," a felon's confession, and a sociological study of criminals may fall within the genre. From jest-book to cantata, from criminal pamphlet to character sketch and essay, from Jonsonian comedy to the "Newgate Calendar," its range is surprisingly catholic. And within the scope of prose fiction proper, it can boast of narratives as unlike as "Guzman de Alfarache" and "Moll Flanders," the "Roman Comique," "Dead Souls," "Vanity Fair," and the "Amateur Cracksman." In English alone its cultivators include such dissimilar talents as Greene, Godwin, Dickens, Nash, Fielding, and Borrow; Head, Defoe, Bulwer, Smollett, Johnstone, and Lever; Marryat, Ainsworth, Thackeray, and Reade.

At the outset roguery must be distinguished from villainy. The latter is the creature of malice, if not of pathological conditions; its evil proceeds to extremes. The former is less vicious; it regards rascality with humor, or explains it as the result of social environment. Between the two no hard and fast line can be drawn; for the rogue may vary from the practical joker bent on mere mischief to the swindler and the highwayman; while the villain, like Hamlet's uncle, may smile and smile, or with Iago carol a drinking song. Nevertheless, the distinction remains generally perceptible. Falstaff is not to be mistaken for Iago, and the contrast between them, as between every rogue and villain, hinges less upon the relative venality or atrocity of deed committed than upon the rascal's and the author's point of view.

Criminologists have remarked five types of moral delinquent: the insane, the instinctive, the impassioned, the occasional, and the habitual criminal. Of these but two types figure largely in literature before the Renaissance, — the criminal by instinct, and the criminal by passion. The latter has ever been the darling of art, for crime done under great provocation, or in response to a sudden emotional stimulus, by no means precludes in the doer noble or heroic traits. Moreover, he offers unique opportunities for contrasting virtue with wickedness, the intoxication of passion with the pangs of remorse. His deed, although only an incident in what may otherwise be a blameless life, is momentous and dramatic as revealing through action the crisis of a soul. Such a criminal is more often social than anti-social in impulse; he attracts rather than repels; to him alone can attach the sublimity of wrong-doing.

The instinctive or congenital criminal, on the other hand, although far more difficult of recognition in life because of his complexity, has long been accepted in art as a simple and useful abstraction. He appears in drama and fiction as the born villain, that incarnation of moral perversity who without adequate motive is predetermined to the pursuit of all evil. As a matter of fact, the congenital criminal is rarely the unrelieved villain that the traditions of literature paint him. But, whether the conventional Barabas of Marlowe or the elaborately studied Jacques Lantier of Zola, he alienates sympathy, and in art can live only to be worsted and destroyed.

Neither of these types includes the rogue. He is even further removed from the insane delinquent, and so must be sought in the other two categories, — the occasional criminal and the habitual. The former is the child of circumstance. Given favorable conditions, he lives a normal life. Under stress of temptation, he yields, not to great and revolting crimes, but to petty. The temptation may be removed, or he may gather strength to oppose it. In either case he returns to a career of virtue in appearance or in fact. But if repetition of the crime breeds indifference, and circumstances favor a continuance of delinquency, the occasional criminal is transformed into the habitual, and the character of his crimes grows blacker. Thus, the famished boy who steals a loaf is an occasional criminal. By following the line of least resistance he may come to subsist upon pilferings from the baker. Then, under the influence of fresh opportunities and bad associates, he may sink through the grades of pickpocket, sneak thief, burglar's apprentice, and housebreaker, to the desperado who bludgeons the victim he robs.

Now the literature of roguery, born of the later Renaissance, deals essentially with the occasional criminal who is tending to become professional, or with the professional criminal who stops short of villainy. It depicts the occasional criminal lured farther and farther into the mazes of habitual crime, or else turning back ere confirmed in iniquity. Gil Blas, for example, is merely an occasional criminal who, achieving a competency, lives thereafter as honest as you please. But his acquaintance, Don Raphael, from occasional cheating falls to cheating habitually, and dies by the hand of the law, a hardened professional. Lazarillo de Tormes, the first Spanish rogue, commences picaro because he must thieve from his masters, the priest and the blind man, or die of starvation; yet he has scarcely attained professional rank when the wind of prosperity blows his bark into port, and he turns from rascality. Defoe's Colonel Jack, setting forth under similar conditions, becomes an habitual criminal, and reforms only when transported. Others, like Fielding's Jonathan Wild, the prince of professionals, or Thackeray's Barry Lyndon, a scoundrelly free lance, die in their sins.

As the typical crime of the villain is murder, so the typical crime of the rogue is theft. To obliterate distinctions of *meum* and *tuum* is the rogue's main business. He aspires to win by wit or dexterity what others have wrought by labor or received of fortune. He may cheat at cards or snatch purses. He may forge a check or a will. He may beg with a painted ulcer, or float a commercial bubble. He may scheme for title and fortune by means of a worldly marriage, or pocket his hostess's spoons. He may prey on the government as smuggler, illicit distiller, or counterfeit utterer. He may play the quack, levy blackmail, crack a safe, or even rob on the highway. But the use of personal violence usually ends his career as rogue and stamps him the villain. Thus the brigand and the pirate stand without the pale of roguery proper, unless, like other desperate characters, they be admitted on the score of earlier crimes of mere cunning.

It is not enough, however, that the rogue should be distinguished from the villain. He must also occupy the centre of the stage, or at least with his fellows command attention. So long as the conflict between good and evil is dealt with, so long art of necessity will employ the anti-hero as a foil to the hero. But where the former exists simply to be worsted by the latter he cannot be claimed for the literature of roguery. Distinguished rascals like those of a Dickens or a Shakespeare may deserve consideration, however slight their part upon the scene, but the true test of the genre is roguery's preponderance. If this shibboleth excludes rascality that is incidental, it also admits the virtuous hero,— an Oliver Twist, a Lavengro, or even a Sherlock Holmes, although the detective story approximates a separate genre, the outgrowth and complement of this.

Compared to the test of preponderant roguery, the test of form, though more precise, is less generally applicable. If the literature of roguery includes many types, one alone is perfectly definite. This is the picaresque novel. As conceived in Spain and matured in France, the picaresque novel is the comic biography (or more often the autobiography) of an anti-hero who makes his way in the world through the service of masters, satirizing their personal faults, as well as their trades and professions. It possesses, therefore, two poles of interest,— one, the rogue and his tricks; the other, the manners he pillories. Since the rogue moves from master to master, he is often a traveler, yet that fact offers no excuse for confounding the picaresque novel with the novel of mere adventure.[1] So rigorous, indeed, proved this form that its limits were early overpassed in the land of its birth. First one element, then another fell away from the scheme, and out of Spain other tendencies quickened the process. Thus, the "Roman Comique," like the "Viage Entretenido," dispensed with the service of masters and considered a single profession; "Simplicissimus" dwelt on

[1] A misconception dear to many. Cf. Martin A. S. Hume, *Spanish Influence on English Literature* (London, 1905, chs. v, vi).

adventures; "The English Rogue" forgot satire and manners in assembling mere tricks; and Defoe eschewed humor.

By the middle of the eighteenth century the orthodox picaresque type had been exploited so fully that later novels of roguery were forced, as a rule, to abandon it. Some retained only its humor and irony, some its shifts of condition in service, some its zest for adventure, and others its scenes of low-life. New aims and new methods inspired romancers. Rogue fiction, in fine, for the past hundred years has lived more and more apart from its origins. The picaresque novel proper is to-day little cultivated, and attempts to revive it fall short of the form.[1]

Inasmuch, however, as the literature of roguery is conditioned rather by content, the picaresque novel fills but part of its field, and this study must deal with rogue fiction in its wider development and with such other types as celebrate roguery, — the jest-books, the canting songs, the essays on criminal manners, the biographies of rogues of reality, and the drama. To discuss these matters for English literature entails, moreover, a preliminary survey of foreign picaresque sources.

2. *The Spanish Source*

Historically, the literature of roguery arose in Spain in the middle of the sixteenth century. Earlier than this the Greek New Comedy and its Latin heirs had laughed at the rascal as parasite and witty slave, the Greek novels had exhibited him as valorous robber and pirate, Petronius had shown him a debauched voluptuary, and the "Roman de Renart" had transformed him into a merry beast. But the Spaniards were the first to cultivate preponderant roguery. The *fabliaux* and

[1] E. g., *The Picaroons* (1904), by Gelett Burgess and Will Irwin. Cf. *infra*, ch. xii, sect. 6, p. 520.

novelle might set forth traditional cheats and gallant ruses; the jest-books might assemble such tricks and ascribe them to single rogues; tales of legendary outlaws and Rabelaisian grotesques might contribute to the conception of roguery; and the German "Liber Vagatorum" might paint the manners of thieves and vagabonds from life; but it is "La Vida de Lazarillo de Tormes" (1554) that marks the birth of the genre.

Within Spain itself the satires of the Archpriests of Hita and Talavera, the masterly "Celestina," Jaime Roig's anti-feminine "Libre de les Dones," and the realistic "Lozana Andaluza," prepared the way for this book. In form "Lazarillo" took its method of satirizing professions from the medieval reviews of estates, and its scheme of describing society through the service of masters from Apuleius. Its spirit was due in part to a literary recoil, the hero giving place to the anti-hero, and in part to social conditions. For the Spanish decadence was beginning. Reality everywhere discredited the ideals of chivalry. The disdain for patient labor made room for easy cheating, and the lack of bread more and more enforced it.

The "Lazarillo" bore no author's name, although tradition since 1607 has assigned it on doubtful grounds to the statesman and poet, Diego Hurtado de Mendoza. Its rogue jauntily recounts his rise through service with a blind beggar, a miserly priest, a proud hidalgo, an indulgence-seller, a busybody friar, a painter, a chaplain, and an alguazil, to the dignities of town crier and complacent husband of an archpriest's mistress. Of these upward steps the first four alone are described minutely, but the little volume in smartness of satire and sparkle of narrative has never been excelled.

Notwithstanding the influence it was destined to exert, "Lazarillo" produced no immediate effect beyond suggesting an anonymous continuation. By a lapse into the fantastic this

"Segunda Parte de Lazarillo de Tormes" (Antwerp, 1555) missed the spirit of the first. It met deserved failure, and in the Peninsula was printed only in 1844, although earlier bound with the first part in Flanders. As for the initial "Lazarillo," it was republished in Spain, the Netherlands, and Italy during the sixteenth century, but the trail it had blazed was not further cleared, unless Juan de Timoneda's "Patrañuelo" (1566) may be said in its twenty-two tales to have trod here and there in the steps of the rogue of the Tormes.

The autobiography of Diego García de Paredes, an adventurous boaster, was but mildly roguish; and the description of prison life in Christóval de Chaves's "Relación de la Cárcel de Sevilla" lacked fictional form. It was only in 1599 with the publication at Madrid, Barcelona, and Saragossa of Mateo Aleman's "Primera Parte de la Vida de Guzman de Alfarache" that the continuous development of the picaresque novel began. Here was a fiction of bulk, ambitious design, and complex treatment, which, accepting the plan of the first rogue romance, wrought out in detail what its predecessor had but sketched, and gained in breadth of view what it lost in simplicity.

A second part was promised, and in 1603 a Valencian, Juan Martí, calling himself Mateo Luxan de Sayavedra, attempted to forestall Aleman by issuing a spurious sequel. It followed the first author's design and did not lack merit; but Aleman in 1605 returned to the breach with his genuine and superior second part. This was longer than either of the others, and assailed the impostor Martí by including him among its rogues. So considerable a work, describing with satire the service of masters of every condition in Italy as well as in Spain, cast the die for the success of the genre, and the many editions it underwent attest its popularity.

The chord struck by the "Lazarillo" was now fully vibrant,

and the strain broke up into peals and counterpeals upon the dominant theme. Agustín de Rojas in "El Viage Entretenido" (1603) included much that was picaresque in the prose and verse account of his strollings with three other comedians. A friar, Andrés Pérez, or, as now seems more likely, a Toledan physician, Francisco de Ubeda, published an avowed imitation of the "Celestina," "Lazarillo," and "Guzman," in his long-winded "Pícara Justina" (1603). Cervantes might well condemn it, for the novel's *conceptista* style was pernicious; yet as celebrating an anti-heroine it first proclaimed women's rights in the realm of roguery, and, despite its narrow range of adventure, was amusingly burlesque.

The vein of burlesque, however, was to be wrought to finer perfection by Francisco de Quevedo y Villegas, distinguished for his talents and versatility. Between 1602 and 1607 he composed the "Historia de la Vida del Buscon llamado Don Pablos," published only in 1626. Here Paul the Sharper describes with rare directness and vivacity the humors of boarding-school and university, and life among organized rogues in Madrid and Seville. His accounts of prison miseries, of stageland, and of matrimonial cheats, remain classic in picaresque literature. Quevedo's collection of "Sueños" is scarcely less famous. Of these satirical visions one at least dates from 1608, five were printed in 1627, and the series entire appeared eight years after. Much that was roguish figured also in such minor works of Quevedo's as the "Capitulaciones de la Vida de Corte" and the "Poesías Picarescas," the latter recalling an anonymous versified "Vida del Pícaro" (1601) and Juan Hidalgo's anthology of canting ballads, the "Romances de Germanía" (1609).

Cervantes entered into rivalry with makers of the picaresque when in "Don Quixote" he drew a memorable rascal, Ginés de

Pasamonte, whose autobiography, he declared, if ever written, should excel Lazarillo's and Guzman's. In the delightful "Novelas Exemplares" (1613) he further told such tales of roguery as "Rinconete y Cortadillo," "La Ilustre Fregona," "El Casamiento Engañoso," and the "Coloquio de los Perros;" and several of his pieces for the stage — notably the "Rufian Dichoso" and the farce "Pedro de Urdemalas" — proved their kinship with the genre. Less distinguished authors were inspired by his lead. Francisco Loubayssin de Lamarca's "Engaños deste Siglo" (1615) and "Enriquez de Castro" (1617) bore the stamp of the new rogue fiction. Christóval Suarez de Figueroa's "Passagero" (1617) mingled entertaining autobiography with picaresque satire and adventure. The same year saw the publication of Juan Cortes de Tolosa's "Discursos Morales," among which appeared romances of roguery in miniature. And a year later a long and complicated novel issued from the pen of the poet and priest, Vicente Espinel. His "Marcos de Obregon" (1618) proved, indeed, one of the pleasantest works of the type, for the style was pure, the scene embraced both Italy and captive life in Algiers, and the anti-hero himself was less a rogue than a wanderer of romantic proclivities. Although "Marcos" was immediately done into French, it remained forgotten until Le Sage a century later revived some of its episodes. Similarly influential was the curious "Desordenada Codicia de los Bienes Agenos" (1619), by Dr. Carlos García, the richest account in Spanish of the grades and tricks of professional rogues. This extended beggar-book, although little known at home, was early popularized abroad by translations into French and English, and contributed incidents to foreign picaresque fiction.

The literature of roguery was now in full flower, and in 1620 alone five works of the type were put forth. The more important, like the "Desordenada Codicia," came from the Parisian press. Juan de Luna, an interpreter at the French capital, continued the first "Lazarillo," replacing the fantastic incidents of the sequel of 1555 by exploits more in consonance with the spirit of the original. Juan Cortes de Tolosa produced a dull imitation in his "Lazarillo de Manzanares," and Diego Agreda y Vargas's "Novelas Morales," echoing the tales of Cervantes, were partially picaresque. Better still were the *novelas* that Antonio Liñan y Verdugo, in the "Guia y Avisos de Forasteros," assembled as a warning to the innocent against the wiles of city sharpers. Alonso Geronimo de Salas Barbadillo, in the meantime, had broken the way for his other rogue essays in "La Hyia de Celestina" (1612), singing the triumphs of Ingenious Helen, an amusing anti-heroine. He further wrote for the stage an "Escuela de Celestina," and in imitation of Cervantes's farce composed a semi-dramatic "Subtil Cordovés Pedro de Urdemalas." His comedy, "El Sagaz Marido Examinado," was roguish; and in 1621 he produced two works still more closely affiliated with the type, — "La Sabia Flora Malsabadilla," a drama not intended for representation, and "El Necio bien Afortunado," a novel whose anti-hero remains a cross between philosopher and rogue.

To be ranked with the more important Spanish novels was the long and discursive "Alonso, Moço de Muchos Amos" (1624, 1626), by the physician, Geronimo de Alcalá Yañez y Ribera. This followed the ups and downs of a gossiping adventurer in service, and with no little power pictured his vicissitudes among Mexicans, Algerines, and Gypsies. Another long fiction, the "Soldado Píndaro" (1626), by Gonzalo Cespedes y Meneses, betrayed a romantic ancestry, to which the same author's "Español Gerardo" could lay still larger claim. As a matter of fact, the picaresque field had been fairly well harvested even thus early, and authors were turning elsewhere. The crude realism of the first romances of roguery could no longer satisfy a more polished generation. As fiction gradually recovered from the excess of realism into which by a recoil from idealism it had plunged, less of description for its own sake and more of the story for the story's sake was desired.

In obedience to this need, Alonso Castillo Solórzano, who had already tried his hand at other styles of fiction, undertook to refine the picaresque type without dulling the edge of its wit. The four *novelas* of his "Harpías en Madrid" (1631), exposing the roguish harpies of the capital, were not unlike the tales of the "Guia y Avisos de Forasteros." But Solórzano's first long novel of the class was "La Niña de los Embustes, Teresa de Manzanares" (1632). Holding to a more logical form than most, this "Child of Frauds" was highly diverting. A promised sequel failed to appear, but Solórzano soon issued an independent fiction as the "Aventuras del Bachiller Trapaza" (1634), describing a vivacious picaro, whose jealous mistress cut short his career at its height by procuring his imprisonment in the galleys. The story reflected the incidents of other rogue novels, and contained by way of relief unpicaresque tales and a versified *entremes*. Of all Solórzano's work, however, "La Garduña de Sevilla" (1634), a sequel to "Trapaza," proved the best and most enduring. Its Rufina was the sauciest and cleverest of anti-heroines, and its introduction of romantic *novelas* accorded with the taste of the time, and followed the example set as early as "Guzman de Alfarache." The "Garduña," however, possessed greater unity of plot, and was readier than its forerunners to relinquish detail where it might interfere with the story. It emphasized the anti-heroine rather than the society through which she passed, and eschewed both the coarseness of the "Pícara Justina" and the moralizings of the "Alonso."

In the meantime Diego Tovar y Valderrama's "Raimundo el Entremetido" (1627) had described the typical day of a picaro, and the lives of several rogues of reality had been chronicled. Ordoñez de Cevallos's "Viage del Mundo" (1614), so far as it portrayed the early exploits of its author in Spain and America, was sufficiently picaresque, and gave rise long after to a French tale of adventure by Ternaux Compans (1853). Other roguish memoirs remained two centuries in manuscript, as did the "Comentarios del Desengañado" of Diego Duque de Estrada, written between 1614 and 1646, and the "Historia de la Monja Alférez," which, when published in 1829, furnished the basis for De Quincey's "Spanish Military Nun."[1] The genre was already in decline, and it disintegrated in several ways. Now it succumbed to invasions of the romantic; now it gave the picaresque scheme a fantastic rendering; now it laid emphasis upon the scenes of reality, and forgot the picaro; and again it transformed him into fool or villain.

The "Diablo Cojuelo" (1641) of Luis Vélez Guevara, for example, varied the method of the romance of roguery by untopping, through the magic of a limping devil, all the houses of Madrid, thus revealing the pretensions and deceits of their occupants. The "Siglo Pitagórico" of Antonio Enriquez Gómez (1644) more ingeniously replaced the passage of a servant from master to master by the transmigrations of a soul from body to body. The longest prose section of this partially versified narrative was the "Life" of Don Gregorio Guadaña, a picaro. In the same year Francisco de Navarrete y Rivera brought out his "Casa de Juego" to expose the frauds of gam-

[1] Briefer accounts of the Monja Alférez were printed, however, as early as 1618 and 1625. Cf. Chandler, *Romances of Roguery*, p. 316 n.

ing houses, a work based upon the earlier invectives of Diego del Castillo, Adrian de Castro, and Quevedo.

A reversion to the primitive, helter-skelter type of autobiography was made in "La Vida y Hechos de Estevanillo Gonzalez" (1646). Its anti-hero, a rascally buffoon in the service of Ottavio Piccolomini, related his story of religious and military frauds with the artlessness that characterized the German "Simplicissimus," concerned with the same period and historical events. A mild satire, that in dream-form sought to rebuke the passion of the age for doing all things hurriedly rather than well, was published by Marcos García as "La Flema de Pedro Hernandez" (1657). The "Ardid de la Pobreza," by Andrés de Prado (1663), and the anonymous "Pícaro Amante" (1666) were *novelas* that echoed more closely the romance of roguery. But the "Teatro del Hombre, el Hombre," or the "Life of Count Matisio," written fifteen years before it appeared in 1667 among the prose works of Juan de Zavaleta, took for anti-hero one who was no longer a picaro but an out-and-out villain.

The drama might continue in its *graciosos* and characters of low-life the rogue tradition; but the picaresque novel in Spain was at its last gasp. Francisco de Santos, whose "Dia y Noche de Madrid" (1663) followed the fashion of Quevedo and Guevara in reviewing the metropolitan underworld, brought the picaresque series to a close with his novel, "Periquillo, él de las Gallineras" (1668). Periquillo, who began as a picaro, died a rustic philosopher, and with him, so far as the Peninsula is concerned, died the literature of roguery. For Santos, who might have continued the tradition, deeming the vein worked out, fell to composing allegories; and the novel of manners, born with the rogue, but no longer needing him, was ready to take on an individual existence.

3. *The French Tributary*

In France the literature of roguery opened its career in 1596 with the publication at Lyons of "La Vie Genereuse des Mercelots, Gueuz, et Boesmiens." This is the autobiography of a boy who at the age of nine runs away and joins successively three troops of vagabonds, the last being a tribe of Gypsies. He attends a general assembly of all the rascals of France, and with humor and an eye for detail describes their tricks, orders, manners, and language. Although knavery had earlier figured in the *facéties*, in Rabelais, and in the verse of the poet-laureate of roguery, François Villon, as well as in the "Roman d'Eustache le Moine" celebrating a thirteenth-century rogue of reality, this anonymous little low-life anatomy was unique. Its realism was tempered by art, its aim was entertainment rather than reform, and its satire assailed roguery alone instead of all grades of society.

Undated imitations promptly followed. "Le Jargon, ou le Langage de l'Argot Reformé," with less of fictional interest, proved more specific in regard to canting and rogue orders. A "Responce et Complaincte au Grand Cœsre sur le Jargon de l'Argot Reformé" continued the vein in a cant dialogue. Parisian rogues were shown assembled by night on the Pont Neuf, listening to the promulgation of laws for their band in the "Reigles, Statuts, et Ordonnances de la Caballe des Filous;" and in a French and Latin pamphlet of 1607, "Chimæra seu Phantasma Mendicorum," Parisian beggars hold a conclave to argue governmental reforms.

Just how far Spanish influence was responsible for these tracts remains doubtful. The "Celestina" had been thrice translated in the sixteenth century, Jean Saugrain had done the first "Lazarillo" into French in 1561, and it had been reprinted in 1594 and 1598. In the latter year, also, the fantastic sequel had appeared in French dress, while combined French and Spanish texts of the "Lazarillo" were issued in 1601, 1615, and 1616, and the first installment of "Guzman de Alfarache" was rendered by Gabriel Chappuys in 1600.

Ere long, however, the influx of Peninsular picaresque literature became too obvious to be neglected by French writers. Juan de Luna's second "Lazarillo" was translated in 1620, and the first section of the tale was done into French verse in 1653. "Guzman" was retranslated by Jean Chapelain in 1619 and 1620, and saw eight editions by 1646. Gabriel Bremond in 1695 offered a fresh and equally popular version, although that of Le Sage in 1732 supplanted the others. "Don Quixote" and the "Novelas Exemplares" came into French in 1618, as did the "Engaños deste Siglo" and "Marcos de Obregon." Three years later, versions of "La Desordenada Codicia" and the "Novelas Morales" of Agreda y Vargas appeared, and in 1633 La Geneste rendered Quevedo's "Sueños" and "Buscon." The latter was presented also by Raclots (1699) and by Restif de la Bretonne (1776), who appended a conclusion. The "Pícara Justina" became "La Narquoise Justine" (1635), and the "Garduña" became "La Fouyne de Seville" (1661). Moreover, half a dozen of the Spanish works of the genre first saw the light in France.

It is not strange, therefore, that Frenchmen should have imitated the Spanish model. At first the essays in this kind were feeble. John Barclay, the son of a French mother and a Scotch father, dedicated to King James of Scotland and England his Latin "Euphormionis Lusinini Satyricon,"[1] which depended as much upon the classic satires as upon Peninsular sources, and,

[1] The first edition of the first part was probably published at London, 1603, but it has disappeared. The earliest edition now known was published at Paris, 1605. The *Satyricon* was issued in French at Reims, 1624, and at Paris, 1625.

like its author's "Argenis," contained disguised portraits and political allegory. This was notably the case in the second part (1607); while the third and fourth parts published at London (1610, 1614), and a continuation by Morisot (1625), diverged completely from roguery and realism.

In the meantime Agrippa d'Aubigné's "Avantures du Baron de Fæneste" (1617, 1620, 1630) presented in Fæneste and his valet a brace of Gascon rogues, whose lies and cheats were designed to illustrate the devices of seeming as opposed to the honesty of simple being. But impeccable Enay was less amusing than the rascals who, despite their employment in an allegory, proved creatures of flesh and blood somewhat related to the picaros.

It was not, however, until the publication of "La Vraye Histoire Comique de Francion," by Charles Sorel, that the Spanish rogue tradition was effectively transplanted to France. This memorable fiction contained twelve books issued in three installments (1622, 1631, 1641). Although it borrowed directly from the Spanish novels, it deviated widely from their form. Its plot development was complicated and ambitious; it eschewed the crude realism of its models by suppressing non-essentials; it directed satire against the high as well as the low, and against individuals rather than professions. Its anti-hero, despite his frequent shifts of condition, was no longer the rogue in service, but a person of family and a gallant adventurer, while the erotic element, little emphasized in Spain, was here paramount. "Francion" ranks with the "Roman Comique" and "Gil Blas" as the most notable work of the type produced in France, and its influence was felt in Germany, Holland, and England.

Spanish novels, together with jests, *novelle*, and *fabliaux*, contributed to the "Histoire Générale des Larrons," a classic collection of rogueries early ascribed to the Sieur d'Aubrincourt and later signed with the initials of François de Calvi. To the first part of 1623 were added second and third parts in 1625, and the three were united in 1636. Here were nearly seventy rogue biographies, lacking in satirical purpose and loosely associated, but composing a treasure-house of cheats to be pilfered from by later writers, especially the authors of "The English Rogue."

Low-life love was written of in heroic strain in "Les Amours Folastres et Recreatives du Filou et de Robinette" (1629), and in the slighter "Catherine des Bas Souhaiz" of Jean de la Roche. But Sorel composed the first successful French burlesque, the "Berger Extravagant" (1627), an imitation of "Don Quixote." Its satire was by no means confined to the pastoral, and a successor, "Le Chevalier Hypocondriaque" (1632), by the Sieur du Verdier, introduced ample roguery. The mad Don Clarazel's squire is a thorough-paced picaro, outdone, however, by a *fin matois* meant to echo Ginés de Pasamonte. Cervantes inspired more remotely Clerville's "Le Gascon Extravagant" (1639), which employed the tricks, the realism, the professional satire, and the service of masters, of the picaresque genre.

Two autobiographies of real poets affiliated with the type. The "Fragments d'une Histoire Comique" (1620), by Théophile de Viau, described the events of a single day, and the "Page Disgracié" (1642), by Tristan l'Hermite, gave a fresh and delightful account of a mischievous boy in service. It reviewed many estates, laughed at frequent rogueries, exhibited the sprightliness of the best Spanish tales, and in one love affair, at least, approached the tenderness of a modern romance.

More than quarter of a century after the issue of the first seven books of "Francion," its author reverted to the *histoire comique* in "Polyandre" (1648). But the criticisms passed upon his earlier work had warned Sorel away from seeming to extol rascality. The new venture accordingly proved a forerunner of the *roman bourgeois*, rather than a continuation of the picaresque novel. It was burlesque, however, and, together with such earlier essays as "Euphormio," "Fæneste," "Filou et Robinette," and the imitations of "Quixote," led to the cultivation of a special strain of burlesque in French letters. Italy contributed to this, but Spain was prepotent, — Lope, Góngora, and Quevedo reinforcing the native *esprit gaulois*.

Paul Scarron, chief of the new school, was indebted to Castillo Solórzano and Francisco de Roxas for "Don Japhet" and his two "Jodelet" comedies, to Salas Barbadillo and María de Zayas for picaresque tales in his "Nouvelles Tragicomiques," and to the Peninsular romances of roguery for the plan, spirit, and episodes of his "Roman Comique" (1651, 1657). This amusing account of French strollers, although suggested by the "Viage Entretenido," was no piracy, for it freely acknowledged the tales it borrowed, and its method and subject-matter were original. It mingled romance with realism, abandoned the picaresque form, substituted farcical scenes and tricks for sordid cheating, and narrowed the range of society observed. Scarron exerted considerable influence upon the English novel of the eighteenth century, and in France his unfinished history gave rise to continuations by Offray and Preshac in 1678 and 1679, a conclusion in 1771, another by Barré in 1849, a dramatization by La Fontaine and Champmeslé in 1684, and a poetic version by Le Tellier d'Orvilliers in 1733.

A work much closer to the original type was the "Avantures Tragicomiques du Chevalier de la Gaillardise" (1662), by César Oudin de Préfontaine. Because of its lack of literary merit as well as its servile following of the foreign fashion, this autobiography of an "unfortunate orphan" attracted little attention, although it remains one of the most accurate transcriptions of the Spanish picaresque novel in any language.

The burlesque genre, however, received more noteworthy cultivation at the hands of a merry buffoon, Charles d'Assoucy. He rated himself a disciple of Scarron, and his autobiography of 1677 in two parts, "Les Avantures de Monsieur d'Assoucy" and "Les Avantures d'Italie," displays Scarron's method and spirit. Plunging *in medias res* with a journey from Paris to the south, it introduces several sharp rogues, and then reverts to the author's picaresque youth and his service with various masters. D'Assoucy's page, Pierrotin, recalls Lazarillo de Tormes, though becoming more wicked; and a gamester he meets reveals the wiles of professional thieves quite in the style of "La Vie Genereuse" and the "Desordenada Codicia."

As for the "Roman Bourgeois" (1666) of Antoine Furetière, it was burlesque only in part. The taste for travesty was already in decline, and middle-class realism was tending to displace the extravagant as well as the roguish. In its vignettes of the folk of the Place Maubert the novel owed only its observational method to picaresque fiction, whose other elements survived here, however, in the story of Cupid the trickster with his shifts from master to master.

Burlesque having had its day, satire came to the fore, and the Abbé Olivier's "L'infortuné Napolitain, ou les Avantures du Seigneur Rozelli" (1708) combined this feature with adventure. Priests were Rozelli's special butts, and his rogueries were drawn from Italian *novelle* and Spanish tales rather than observed actuality. A French continuation appeared in 1722, and England offered two others, the first ascribed to Defoe in 1724, the second contained in a short appendix of 1725 done into French in an edition of 1784. The novel itself was Englished in 1709, and it enjoyed some vogue in German and Italian translations.

Stronger in its bias against ecclesiastics was "Les Libertins en Campagne" (1710), written no doubt by a Protestant refugee. The adventures of its anti-hero include love intrigues, thieving, cheating enlistments, and beggary, and he listens to the story of a rascally monk. Similarly in "Les Tours de Maître Gonin" (1713) the amorous intrigues of a monk are set forth, and rationalism speaks in Gonin's attacks upon the supernatural. His career repeats many of the Spanish rogueries, and promises to present "deceits peculiar to almost all estates and professions." But the author's bitterness spoils the humor. Satire more diffused marked a pale imitation of Cervantes, "Le Voyage Forcé de Becafort" (1709). Here a madman determines to speak only the truth, and is sent for his cure on a journey, which affords him opportunities for reviewing the evils of many conditions.

Satire and burlesque having each undergone development alone, it was now the turn of realistic adventure to be separately exploited before the three elements should reunite in "Gil Blas." From the "Caractères" of La Bruyère to J. B. de Rocoles's "Imposteurs Insignes," an account of eminent rogues of reality, the desire for fidelity in portraiture had been uppermost, and amid the swarm of realistic *mémoires* it was natural that some should prove picaresque.

Gentlemen adventurers were especially favored, and the "Mémoires de Mr. d'Artagnan" (1700, 1701), by Gatien Courtilz de Sandras, is a case in point. If d'Artagnan be better known from "Les Trois Mousquétaires," he was here more the rogue; and his companion Besmaux was shown as an out-and-out picaro. Such a narrative as the "Mémoires du Chevalier Hasard" (1703) in its rapid round of exploits foreshadowed the novels of Lever, but the best of this type was the "Mémoires du Comte de Gramont" (1713). Anthony Hamilton, a Scotchman, had shared the French exile of Charles II, and wrote in old age this account of his polished but rascally brother-in-law. With Gramont the picaro entered high life, rubbing elbows with Mazarin and Louis XIV, but his scheming valet remains as a souvenir of the older tradition.

Had the French literature of roguery gone no farther, it would still have remained an item of importance in the history of letters; but its most significant development was yet to come. Alain-René Le Sage, more than a century and a half after its birth in Spain, perfected the genre, and did more than any other to develop out of it the modern novel. He alone of all picaresque romancers attains to universality. Le Sage's early translations from the Spanish drama, and the pseudo "Quixote" of Avellaneda, as well as his original pieces of Spanish stage intrigue, the "Point d'Honneur," "Crispin," and "Turcaret," prepared him for successfully reviving the picaresque formula. His "Diable Boiteux" (1707) adopted the scheme of Guevara's "Diablo Cojuelo," although it made little use of the latter's subject-matter. But "Gil Blas" (1715, 1724, 1735) first fully realized the possibilities of the romance of roguery.

It resembled its Spanish forbears in the adventurous career of its anti-hero, his shifts of condition through the service of masters, his satire at their expense, his progress from poverty to a competence, his survey of actual manners, and the looseness of his story with its interpolated biographies and lack of organic unity. It differed from these in its choice of an anti-hero from respectable, middle-class life, in minimizing his roguery, awakening his conscience, and softening his heart. It varied his changes of masters with more of adventure and intrigue, sharpened his satire to a finer edge, applied it to individual types more often than to mere professions, led its central personage to a higher place in the social scale, and left him more thoroughly convinced of honesty as the best policy.

Moralizations and digressions in the Spanish sense "Gil Blas" avoided, but it achieved an implicit morality, and, while increasing the proportion of inserted episodes and histories, secured by recognitions and cross-references to events and personages past and to come a superior unity of interest. Its manners were less Spanish than French, less French than universal. Its realism, never crass or offensive, was tempered by artistic reserve and occasional gleams of romance. In short, "Gil Blas" outdid the Spanish picaresque tales in art, morality, humanity, and breadth of appeal. It raised to the highest power their merits, and eliminated so far as possible their defects.

This novel has emerged from its trial for plagiarism acquitted of all save petty larceny. Passages here and there it did steal, — the longest from "Marcos de Obregon," — but its spirit and treatment are essentially original. Le Sage in his other novels showed even less immediate dependence upon Spanish sources. His "Aventures de M. Robert Chevalier, dit de Beauchêne" (1732) was a pure adventure romance, its filibustering anti-hero roving from Canada to Brazil, and from Ireland to the Guinea Coast. The study it early afforded of Indian manners was paralleled by pictures of Mexican life in the "Bachelier de Salamanque" (1736). Here Don Cherubin of Ronda, after serving seven masters as tutor, crosses the seas to satirize Spanish rule in the colonies, and to laugh at the church, the theatre, and letters.

The Inquisition and the medical faculty received rough handling in the "Histoire d'Estevanille Gonzalès" (1734), which was as much indebted to "Marcos de Obregon" and the "Siglo Pitagórico" as to its Spanish namesake; yet none of the three contributed to it more than occasional suggestions. Even in translating "Guzman de Alfarache" (1732) the artistic eclecticism of Le Sage led him to suppress the superfluities of that first great exemplar of the type, and to retain the felicities of its earlier translators.

But despite these later labors, Le Sage's best picaresque work had been done by 1724. The last installment of "Gil Blas" showed signs of a decline, more marked in the other fictions. "Beauchêne" stepped outside the genre. "Estevanille" kept to it, but like its predecessors abused the interpolated autobiography; and the "Bachelier" ran over mechanically the stock incidents of the romance of roguery without the vivacity, the certainty of satire and characterization, or the realism that had signalized "Gil Blas." Le Sage, although he had exhausted his theme, wrote on, falling into garrulous duplications. His miscellanies, "Une Journée des Parques" (1735), "La Valise Trouvée" (1740), and "Le Mélange Amusant" (1743), exhibited the disintegration of the type, — even the framework of the first two disappearing in the last.

Le Sage at his worst, however, was superior to most of his imitators. One of the least contemptible of these was Thibault, governor of Talmont in Poitou, who three years after the initial issue of "Gil Blas" published his "Histoire Comique et Galante de Pedrille del Campo" (1718). The scene is Spain, the convict galleys, and Barbary; the scheme and its episodes are picaresque; a love story strives to bestow unity upon the rogue's autobiography, which is constantly broken, nevertheless, by the histories of others. The satire flags, and a first-hand study of life is replaced by the musings of a mind teeming with recollections of Spanish rogue romances. Yet "Pedrille" was translated into German and English, and a zealous Iberian, the Abate Alcino, inspired by Padre Isla's Spanish "Gil Blas" (1787), did it into Castilian (1792) as "a work restored to its original idiom."

Italy was the scene of a similar fiction, "Les Avantures de Don Antonio de Buffalis" (1722), which, like so many of the picaresque family, included an excursion to Algiers. Yet the adventures of its rogues, Buffalis and Fabricio, could boast no novelty. By contrast, the Chevalier de Mouhy in "La Mouche, ou les Espiègleries et Avantures Galantes de Bigand" (1736), did exploit an original conception, but so poorly that the genre which he almost chanced upon found no cultivation for many years to come. Bigand was a rogue of the jest-books, whose main motive was curiosity. His picaresque shifts of condition are crowned with success, the result of his service as domestic spy. In short, he approaches the private detective, and his tale hints at a line of divergence from rogue fiction popular to-day.

In "Gil Blas" the picaresque type had attained such perfection that thereafter its decline or complete transformation could alone be expected. An account of a fraud by lackeys in the "Histoire Comique d'un Chevalier d'Industrie" (1728), of roguish adventure in the "Mémoires de Madame de Barneveldt" (1732), of the vicissitudes of an actress in "La Vie et les Mœurs de Mlle. de Cronel" (1739), or of the tricks of a buffoon in "Le Momus François, ou les Avantures du Duc de Roquelaure" (1739) might amuse; but they stood quite apart from the organic development of the type.

In the meantime "Manon Lescaut" (1731) had exhibited a use of low-life more in sympathy with the novels of Richardson, which its author, the Abbé Prévost d'Exiles, was later to translate. Marivaux's "Paysan Parvenu" (1735, 1736) showed the same tendencies. Passion and sentiment were reinforced by English influence, and Rousseau established a new ideal. Henceforth adventurers like Plancher-Valcour, Dorvigny, and the Chevalier de la Morlière might indite their memoirs, or a Beaumarchais might bring upon the boards his Figaro, but the literature of roguery was destined to lie dormant until revived to new purposes by a Hugo and a Balzac.

4. *The Genre in Germany and Holland*

The German literature of roguery took its rise in the jest-books. These flourished principally in the sixteenth century, but as early as the thirteenth Der Stricker in Austria had ascribed popular jests to a roguish English priest. His "Pfaffe Amis" became the father of a swarm of *Schwänke*, of which the most notable was "Till Eulenspiegel." Till as a peasant in service and a cheater of burghers, churchmen, physicians, and nobles anticipated the picaro, and his feigned stupidity linked him with the fools. Equally roguish were his South German rivals, the Pfarrer von Kalenberg and Peter Leu, the former of whom was well known in England before the reign of Elizabeth.

Another jesting anti-hero was Marcolfus, King Solomon's legendary disputant, who in the German Markolf, as later in the Italian Bertoldo, proved a downright rogue. Æsop, too, as described by Heinrich Stainhöwel of Ulm, was a knavish slave passing from master to master, and setting off with merry common-sense the learning of his lord, the philosopher Xanthus; and with him was slightly affiliated the cynical Diogenes. Trenchant in satire and roguish also were the several reworkings of the "Roman de Renart." Bruder Rausch, the devil in the guise of a monk, played his tricks to good purpose in Low Saxon and High German, as well as in Danish and Swedish. The court-fools of actuality became the patrons of special jests, and many unrelated *Schwänke* tended to roguery, as witness Bebel's "Facetiæ," inspired by Poggio, and Pauli's "Schimpf und Ernst," which drew upon the "Gesta Romanorum." Seven such collections were issued within a single decade (1555–65), while during it, or shortly after, Fischart rhymed "Eulenspiegel" and paraphrased Rabelais; and Jörg Wickram evolved from the *Schwänke* a national fiction.

In the meantime other types had developed. Wernher der Gartenære's narrative poem, "Meier Helmbrecht" (*c.* 1240), had shown a peasant turning highwayman, and two centuries later Heinrich Wittenweiler's "Der Ring" had poked fun at chivalry in its account of a country wedding. The jest-books gave birth also to a satirical fool-literature, best represented by Sebastian Brandt's "Narrenschiff" (1494). This inspired Thomas Murner's "Narrenbeschwerung" and "Schelmenzunfft" (1512), and vied with Grobianism, a phase of satire less directly related to roguery in its ironical praise of the bad and the gross. Friedrich Dedekind's Latin "Grobianus" (1549) was turned into German and added to by Kaspar Scheidt (1551), and, being accepted by the original author in his revised "Grobianus et Grobiana" (1552), caught the popular fancy in England, where the "Narrenschiff" had already found favor. Satire through the lies of travelers in the "Finken-Ritter" (1560), or directed against the incompetent in authority in the "Lalenbuch," "Schildbürgerbuch," and "Grillenvertreiber" (1597, 1598, 1603), was often of a picaresque cast, and to "Die Hummeln" (1605), a continuation of the "Lalenbuch" group, both "Grobianus" and the "Liber Vagatorum" contributed.

The "Liber Vagatorum" itself (1510–16) was, however, the first pure example of German rogue realism. It gave an account of some thirty mendicant orders, as well as amusing *notabilia* and a Rothwelsch vocabulary. Its matter was drawn in part from manuscript accounts of criminal trials at Basel (1475), which may also have furnished lore for the "Narrenschiff." It was versified by Pamphilus Gengenbach (1517), was reissued in prose by Martin Luther (1528), and reappeared in new editions. In Italy it inspired Giacinto Nobili's "Il Vagabondo" (1627), which later came north in a French translation (1644). It contributed likewise to the first English beggar-books, — Awdeley's

"Fraternitye of Vacabondes" and Harman's "Caueat," — and through them to countless works that have used its separate tricks.

All this native literature of roguery was confirmed in the seventeenth century by the naturalization of Spanish picaresque novels. Most were received through French or Italian versions, and the treatment of all was exceedingly free. The "Celestina" not only appeared in German (1520, 1534), but was done into Latin by Kaspar Barth (1624). Ægidius Albertinus translated "Guzman de Alfarache" (1615), altering it, and adding Swiss, German, and French adventures. Martin Freudenhold composed a sequel (1662) devoted to Guzman's rogueries in the East, and Kaspar Ens, with more respect for the Spanish original, Latinized "Guzman" (1623, 1624, 1652), yet included in his version the "Lazarillo de Tormes," which in the meantime, together with the "Rinconete y Cortadillo" of Cervantes, had found a translator into German in Niclas Ulenhart (1617).

Georg Philipp Harsdörffer, an industrious disseminator of Spanish letters, praised and employed in his "Frauenzimmer Gesprächspiele" (1641–49) several of the picaresque novels, besides rendering later two of the tales of Cervantes. The "Pícara Justina" was translated (1627) from the Italian paraphrase of Barezzo Barezzi; and, although Quevedo's "Buscon" did not come into German until 1671, his "Sueños" was much earlier adapted to native manners by Hans Michael Moscherosch, whose "Gesichte Philanders von Sittewald" (1639, 1642, 1650) was powerful in satire and realism.

Nor was Moscherosch the only satirist stirred by the turmoil of the Thirty Years' War. This period, with its intermingling of all classes in a struggle devoid of principle and its quick alternations of fortune, presented social conditions analogous to those that in Spain had given rise to the picaresque novel. It was but natural, therefore, that a German laureate of roguery should appear, and Hans Jakob Christoffel von Grimmelshausen qualified for the office with "Der Abentheurliche Simplicissimus" (1669), the first German novel of manners.

This confused and formless fiction carries its naïve anti-hero as fool, soldier, charlatan, and robber, up and down war-ridden Germany and to Paris. Magic and far journeys more and more invade the story, which concludes with an island shipwreck that foreshadows "Robinson Crusoe." In "Trutz Simplex," a sequel, the dare-devil Amazon, Courage, sets forth her career as vivandière, forager, combatant, wife to five officers, and the mistress of countless privates. In her feminine rivalry with Simplicissimus she doubtless harks back to the "Pícara Justina," while her tricks and her life with the Gypsies, from whose number she picks a sixth husband, are reminiscent of the Spanish "Alonso." In "Der Seltzame Springinsfeld" (1670) one of her victims relates his adventures as juggler and drummer boy, musketeer, robber, dragoon, inn-keeper, showman, and mendicant. Then his wife steals his treasure-trove, a bird's nest that makes its possessor invisible; but her pranks with it end when, taken off guard, she is slain by outraged peasants. The nest reappears, however, in "Das Wunderbarliche Vogel-Nest" (1672), affording in the hands of an honest warrior a means for reviewing the deceits of each rank of society, but when transferred to a wicked merchant becoming an instrument of evil. For this rogue by its aid persuades a Jewish maiden that he is Elias the Prophet and she the predestined mother of the Messias,[1] and having betrayed her robs her father, and enters the army to steal.

All of these narratives, save the "Trutz Simplex," are over-

[1] Developed from Boccaccio (*Decameron*, day iv, *novella* 2) and Massuccio (*Il novellino*, *novella* 2).

weighted with moral reflections, yet in grossness they far outdo any novels of Spain. Their realism knows no subdual of detail, their range of observation is narrower than that of the Spaniards, and their satire is rude. The plots remain loose — travel, magic, and superstition confusing the true issues; and the characters are little removed from those of the jest-books. Nevertheless, Grimmelshausen's novels and his six minor "Simplicianische Schriften" are notable for the freshness and epic quality of their portrayal of life. They are thronged with episodes based upon popular native tradition and literature. They supplement the romance of chivalry, heroic romance, and the tale of adventure with a new genre, and if the form and inspiration for this be derived from Spain and France, its matter and manner are original. It is the glory of the works of this cycle that they are thoroughly national; it is their limitation that they lack the art which alone could have made them universal.

Although Grimmelshausen translated or conceived other satirical fictions,[1] it was left for his disciples to cultivate further the *Schelmenroman*. Yet their works were little more than servile imitations.[2] Only one among them won distinction for roguery. This was the "Ungarischer oder Dacianischer Simplicissimus" (1683). Its anti-hero in his thefts of food and his youthful exploits emulates Lazarillo, plays the wandering student, serves a trumpeter, is captured by Turks, passes from

[1] Cf. *Die verkehrte Welt* (1672), in which a traveler visits the underworld, and *Der fliegende Wandersmann nach dem Mond* (1659), a rendering of Bishop Francis Godwin's *Man in the Moone* (1638) through the French of J. Baudoin (1648). Godwin influenced Cyrano de Bergerac.

[2] A *Simplicianischer Jan Perus* (1672), a French *Simplicissimus* (1681), a *Simplicianischer Hasenkopf* (1683), a *Haspelhaus Simplicien* (1684), an *Abenteurliche Malcomo von Liebendau* (1686), and a series of pamphlets by M. J. Bähr, author of a *Simplicianischer Welt-Kukker sive abenteurliche Jean Rebhu* (1678), sought to perpetuate the type; and as late as 1743 appeared a *Simplicissimus redivivus.*

master to master, and at last reaches Constantinople, and in the "Türkischer Vagant" (1683) travels in Egypt, Persia, and India.

Other fictions attempted to develop the "Vogel-Nest" theme; "Der Goldene Hund" (1675), satirizing the world after the fashion of Apuleius, and "Der Französische Gyges" of "Terpo Mirifando" (1687), using an invisible observer to the same end. In general, however, the exploitation of roguery declined; such an ironical tract as "Don Iro" (1665), with its praise of beggar life, and Hörl von Wätterstorff's "Bacchusia, oder Fasznacht-Land" (1677), which described the travels of three satirical Germans, falling short of the genre.

Except upon Grimmelshausen himself little effect was produced by the translation of the "Histoire Générale des Larrons" (1627, 1669) or by the appearance in German of "Francion" (1668). Dürer's "Tychander" (1668, 1685) showed the influence of "Lazarillo de Tormes," and contributed to Happel's better known "Akademischer Roman" (1690), whose personages are but empty types of students good and bad. Abraham a Santa Clara's "Judas der Ertzschelm" (1686) was allied with heroic romance, and its story served only as an excuse for long-winded homilies. Hunold's "Satyrischer Roman" (1705), exhibiting a love intrigue in Germany and Italy, departed still further from the picaresque, and the imitations of "Robinson Crusoe" supplied the place of the literature of roguery.

A few of the "Robinsonaden," however, still expounded rascality or even adapted foreign rogue fiction. The "Garduña de Sevilla" in translation ranked with this group, as did also the "Avantures de Don Antonio de Buffalis" revamped as the "Italienischer Robinson," or "Gil Blas" rechristened the "Spanischer Robinson" (1726). It was less the island episode than the far wanderings of Crusoe that most of the Germans admired;[1] yet the island remained to be put to new service in the best of this class. For Schnabel's "Insel Felsenburg" (1731–43) pictured an idyllic escape from the ills of civilization, wherein, as elsewhere in letters, the ideal and the sentimental replaced picaresque realism. And so for a time the spirit of Rousseau and Richardson ruled.

Except for the jest-books, the satires, and the novels of Grimmelshausen, the German literature of roguery had been a derivative growth, and its Dutch counterpart proved even less original. Owing to the political relations of Holland with Spain and its geographical and social relations with France, picaresque literature reached the Netherlands in two streams. One came direct from the Peninsula, the other from France; and many a romance of roguery that lacked a Dutch translator was nevertheless well known in Holland in its original French or Spanish. Just before the first picaresque tale was issued, its distinguished prototype, the "Celestina," was done into Dutch (1550). "Lazarillo" itself followed in 1579, but it was not until thirty-eight years had passed that the transplanted novel bore fruit in Brederoo's excellent comedy, the "Spaansche Brabander" (pr. 1617). Hooft's "Warenar" of the same year, a comedy derived from the "Aulularia" of Plautus, localized picaresque scenes in Amsterdam, and Huygens's "Klucht van Trijntje Cornelis" (1659) later described with spirit the rogueries practiced in Antwerp upon the wife of a Zaandam sailor.

Versions of "Amadis" and "Palmerin," however, furnished the chief Spanish models of Dutch literature prior to the fourth

[1] Perhaps because of their antecedent use of such incidents in the second adventure of Gudrun, in the epic *Habsburgischer Ottobert*, in *Simplicissimus*, and in Happel's *Insulanischer Mandorell*, German versions of the Spanish picaresque novels, as well as native tales of the type, had paid especial attention to travel.

and fifth decades of the seventeenth century, when Quevedo's "Sueños" was issued at Leeuwarden (1641) and "Guzman de Alfarache" appeared at Rotterdam (1655, 2d edition). The "Gitanilla" of Cervantes, as dramatized by Antonio de Solis, gave rise to "De Spaensche Heidin" (1643), as well as to other comedies by Verwers (1644) and Geerard van den Brande (1649); Jacob Cats translated the original *novela*; and its companion, the "Ilustre Fregona," was done into Dutch (1645), and served as the basis of van Meekeren's comedy, "De Doorluchtige Dienstboden" (1714). Although the assembled "Novelas" found no translator until 1731, Lambert van Bos stood sponsor for "Don Quixote" in 1657, and stage versions of its separate incidents followed. Thus Soolmans, van der Kruyssen, Cornelia Wils, Langendijk, and van Hoven, each employed episodes in plays produced from 1681 to 1723. In the meantime "Guzman de Alfarache" had been dramatized by Thomas Asselijn (1693).

Thus far, the literature of roguery in Holland had been meagre enough and chiefly dramatic; but in 1695 Nicolaas Heinsius, Junior, doctor of medicine and philosophy, adventurer, and temporary exile from his native land, issued "De Vermakelyke Avanturier." Its anti-hero, after service with a rascal inn-keeper, a miserly advocate, and the son of a Flemish marquis, reviews high society in Paris, and then becomes steward to the French ambassador in London. He is an adventurer rather than a rogue, and his later progress lies within the bounds of respectability. Romantic love is, indeed, his main business; the service of masters declines in importance, and the satire is personal rather than professional. Moreover, Mirandor's story, despite its intercalated autobiographies, possesses unity, and his field of observation is French rather than Dutch. The novel, accordingly, is an exotic rather than a native growth, and fails of national significance. Its very incidents are largely a *rechauffée* of Spanish and French rogue novels. Of the latter, "Francion" and the "Roman Comique" are especially potent; and of the former, "Lazarillo," "Guzman," and the "Buscon." It is probable, also, that Heinsius had read "The English Rogue."

Beyond the eight editions that the "Vermakelyke Avanturier" underwent by 1756, it was translated into French (1729, 1801), and thence transferred to Italian (1748). Mirandor's tricks upon his stingy master reappeared in Jan van Hoogstraten's "De Geleerde Advokaat, of de Bespotte Drüivedief" (1707), and the same author dramatized Mirandor's deceit upon a lovesick servant of the marquis in "De Verliefde Kok," an incident derived in turn from "Francion."[1]

Heinsius's second venture in the picaresque field was made in "Don Clarazel de Gontarnos" (1697). Here, however, he did little more than refurbish a French original, — the "Chevalier Hypocondriaque" (1632) of the Sieur du Verdier. This undoubted imitation of "Don Quixote" Heinsius professed to believe independent of the Spanish masterpiece. The source of both he declared to be a French manuscript of 1617 by Polignac of Grénoble. But since the first part of "Don Quixote" appeared in 1605, the contention was absurd. Heinsius's *refacimento* of Du Verdier achieved scarcely more success than its original, being reprinted only once, in 1712.

Hard upon the heels of these novels followed a translation of Quevedo's "Buscon" (1699), and Solórzano's "Garduña de Sevilla" appeared as "Het Leven van Ruffine" (1725). Original fictions continued to cultivate roguery, from "Het Koddig en Vermakelijk Leven van Louwtje van Zevenhuizen" (1704) to "De Vermakelyke Avanturesse, of de Dienstmaagd

[1] *Vermakelyke Avanturier*, i, 5; *Francion*, i.

van Fortuin" (1754). But such works had little to add to the genre. They were essentially tales of adventure, like the German "Robinsonaden," and even Jeanneton of the "Avanturesse" proves scarcely a rogue, though she serves many masters, travels in Italy and Spain, and is captured by Algerine pirates. Sentimentalism invaded Dutch letters as it had French, English, and German, and Betje Wolff and Aagje Deken came to the fore.

In reviewing what has been said, it will be evident that the direct current of the literature of roguery flowed from Spain through France to England. Germany and Holland could show but eddies in the stream. They received their share of French and Peninsular inspiration, but in this particular they gave little to other lands. "Gil Blas" was the great distributer of picaresque influence, and English fiction of the eighteenth century felt its full effect.

England, indeed, prior to the nineteenth century, drew without scruple upon foreign sources, although its own picaresque matter was rich in extent and variety. But with the rapid rise of the novel, the Spanish impulse has been lost in English currents. For the past hundred years, the genre is almost confined to fiction, in examining which the student ceases to be occupied with questions of foreign influence, earlier of prime importance. He is confronted instead with many fresh developments of the type, to be studied in their relation to characteristic themes, moods, and social conditions.

BIBLIOGRAPHY

CHAPTER I

1

Criminologists have thus far neglected the part played by the rogue in literature, confining their attention to the villain. This is the case with Enrico Ferri's *Les criminels dans l'art et la littérature* (Paris, 1897), translated from the Italian by Eugène Laurent, and Josef Kohler's *Die Verbrecher Typen in Shakespeares Dramen* (Berlin, 1903). From the many studies in criminal sociology and anthropology that throw light upon the classes of the delinquent may be named Cesare Lombroso's *L'uomo delinquente* (Torino, 1896, 5th ed., 3 vols., French tr. by G. Regnier and A. Bornet, Paris, 1887–88, 2 vols.); Lombroso's *La donna delinquente* (Torino, 1894, English tr., N. Y., 1895); Rafaele Garofalo's *Criminologia* (Roma, 1885, French tr., Paris, 1892, 3d ed.); Ferri's *Sociologia criminale* (Torino, 1892, English tr. by W. D. Morrison, N. Y., 1896); Armand Corre's *Les criminels* (Paris, 1889); X. Francotte's *L'anthropologie criminelle* (Paris, 1891); works bearing the same title by Lombroso (Paris, 1891, 2d ed.) and by Émile Laurent (Paris, 1893); Gabriel Tarde's *La criminalité* (Paris, n. d.); together with such briefer treatises in English as Havelock Ellis's *The Criminal* (N. Y., 1890); Arthur MacDonald's *Criminology* (N. Y., 1893); and August Drähm's *The Criminal, his Personnel and Environment* (N. Y., 1900). Still other aspects of the subject are discussed by L. G. Rylands's *Crime: its Causes and Remedy* (London, 1889), and by A. C. Hall's *Crime in its Relations to Social Progress* (N. Y., 1902).

2

Spanish picaresque fiction is most fully discussed in my *Romances of Roguery. Part I. The Picaresque Novel in Spain* (N. Y., 1899). To this the reader is referred for a criticism of individual works, an account of their translations into other languages, and a view of the growth of the genre and the social conditions that gave rise to it. Fonger De Haan's brief *Outline of the History of the Novela Picaresca in Spain* (The

Hague, 1903) considers in addition several works of the eighteenth and the nineteenth centuries, and is especially helpful in its notes. The same author's *Pícaros y ganapanos* in the *Homenaje á Menéndez y Pelayo* (Madrid, 1899) examines the much mooted etymology of the word *pícaro*, upon which Adolfo Bonilla y San Martín in his leaflet *Etimología de "pícaro"* has shed further light, tracing it to Arabic sources. Auguste Vitu's *Le jargon du xve siècle* (Paris, 1884) is less satisfactory on this point. Francisco Javier Garriga's *Estudio de la novela picaresca* (Madrid, 1891) and Albert Schultheiss's *Der Schelmenroman der Spanier und seine Nachbildungen* (Hamburg, 1893) are accurate so far as they go, though deficient in detail. Still briefer treatment of the whole subject may be found in the standard histories of Spanish literature by Ticknor, Lemcke, Baret, Demogeot, Butler Clarke, and Fitzmaurice-Kelly, as well as in Émile Chasles's *Michel de Cervantès* (Paris, 1866), F. M. Warren's *History of the Novel Previous to the Seventeenth Century* (N. Y., 1895), David Hannay's *Later Renaissance* (N. Y., 1898), J. C. Dunlop's *History of Prose Fiction* (edited by H. Wilson, London, 1888, 2 vols.), and in articles in the *Deutsche Jahrbuch für Politik und Litteratur* (Berlin, 1862, iii, p. 411), *The Cornhill Magazine* (vol. xxxi, p. 670), and the *Revue des deux mondes* (vol. lxxxvi, p. 871). The sociological aspects of Spanish roguery are studied by Rafael Salillas in *El delincuente español, El lenguaje* (Madrid, 1896); *Hampa* (Madrid, 1898). The authoritative study of early Spanish fiction is Menéndez y Pelayo's *Tratado histórico sobre la primitiva novela española*, in the *Nueva biblioteca de autores españoles* (Madrid, 1905, vol. i, *Orígenes de la novela*).

The more important of the Spanish novels may be read in volumes iii, xviii, xxiii, and xxxiii of Rivadeneyra's *Biblioteca de autores españoles* (1846–80), and in Eugenio de Ochoa's *Tesoro de novelistas españoles* (Paris, 1847). The 1554 Burgos edition of *Lazarillo de Tormes* is reprinted by H. Butler Clarke (Oxford, 1897), but that it is the *editio princeps* is ably disputed in *Remarques sur Lazarille de Tormès* (*Revue hispanique*, 1900, p. 81) by R. Foulché-Delbosc, who in the *Bibliotheca hispanica* of the same year offers a "*restitución de la edición príncipe.*" M. Foulché-Delbosc has also shown (*Revue hispanique*, 1903, p. 236) that Francisco Lopez de Ubeda was the real name of the author of the *Pícara Justina* and not the pseudonym of Andrés Pérez. *Marcos de Obregon* has been edited with a valuable preface by J. Pérez de Guzman (Barcelona, 1881); the *Viaje entretenido* is reprinted (Madrid, 1901) with a critical introduction by Manuel Cañete in the *Colección de libros picarescos*, which contains also Francisco Delicado's *Retrato de la Lozana Andaluza.* The rare *Don Raimundo el Entremetido* is reproduced by Adolfo Bonilla y San Martín in his *Anales de la literatura española* (Madrid, 1904). The most accessible English versions of *Lazarillo* and *Guzman de Alfarache* are issued together (1881), the former translated by Thomas Roscoe, the latter by J. H. Brady through the French of Le Sage. *Guzman* has also been translated by E. Lowdell (1883). The *Celestina*, Englished by James Mabbe, is edited by J. Fitzmaurice-Kelly (Tudor Translations, 1894). Cervantes's *Novelas* are translated by W. K. Kelly (Bohn Library), and Mabbe's early version of six of them has been reprinted (London, 1900). The best rendering is that by Norman Maccoll (Glasgow, 1902, vols. vii and viii of *Cervantes's Complete Works*). Quevedo's *Don Pablos* may be read in Roscoe's *Spanish Novelists* (London, 1832), in the *Romancist and Novelist's Library* (London, 1841), or in H. E. Watts's *Pablo de Segovia, the Spanish Sharper* (London, 1892), which includes an *Essay on the Picaresque Novel.* Translations of other picaresque works are referred to *passim.* The preface to Alfred Morel-Fatio's *Lazarille de Tormès* (Paris, 1886) and his *Études sur l'Espagne* (Paris, 1888) discredit Diego Hurtado de Mendoza's claim to the authorship of the *Lazarillo.* The *Mateo Aleman* of Joaquin Hazañas y la Rua (Sevilla, 1892), the *Don Francisco de Quevedo* of Rheinhold Baumstark (Freiburg, 1871), and the *Essai sur la vie et les œuvres de Francisco de Quevedo* of Ernest Merimée (Paris, 1886) contain much matter relative to the genre. Cervantes's *Novelas* are discussed by Merry y Colson's *Ensayo crítico* (Sevilla, 1877), by Luis Orellana y Rincón's *Ensayo crítico* (Valencia, 1890), and by Francisco A. de Icaza's *Novelas ejemplares de Cervantes . . . su influencia en el arte* (Madrid, 1901). See, also, Menéndez y Pelayo's *Notas y adiciones* to the *Obras completas de Don Francisco de Quevedo*, edited by Guerra y Orbe (Sevilla, 1897), and Leopoldo Ruis's admirable *Bibliografía crítica de las obras de Miguel de Cervantes Saavedra* (Madrid, 1895–1904), which contains lists of Cervantine imitations.

3

The best account of picaresque fiction in France is given by Heinrich Koerting's *Geschichte des französischen Romans im 17ten Jahrhundert* (Leipzig, 1891, ii, *Der realistische Roman*). Less detailed treatment is afforded by André Le Breton's *Le roman au xviii siècle* (Paris, 1890), and more general by Paul Morillot's *Le roman en France depuis* 1610 *jusqu'au nos jours* (Paris, 1894); Victor Fournel's *La littérature indépendente* (Paris, 1862) and the preface to his edition of *Le roman comique* (Paris, 1857) consider rogue romancers of the seventeenth century; Charles Monselet's *Les oubliés et les dédaignés* (Alençon, 1857) studies minor writers of the eighteenth century; and Ferdinand Brunetière's *Études critiques* (Paris, 1891, 3ième & 4ième séries) notices French cultivators of the genre. Spanish influence in France is discussed in Adolf Puibusque's *L'histoire comparée des littératures espagnole et française* (Paris, 1844), in Philarète Chasles's *Études sur l'Espagne et sur les influences de la littérature espagnole en France et en Italie* (Paris, 1847), in Gabriel Hanotaux's *Études historiques sur le xvi et le xvii siècle en France* (Paris, 1886), in Brunetière's *L'influence de l'Espagne dans la littérature française* (*Rev. d. d. mondes*, Mars, 1891), in Gustav Lanson's *Études sur les rapports de la littérature française et de la littérature espagnole au 17 siècle* (*Rev. d'hist. litt. d. la Fr.* iii, 1 and 3, iv, 2), and in Ernest Martineuche's *La comedia espagnole en France de Hardy à Racine* (Paris, 1900). Picaresque influence receives special treatment in Granges de Surgères's *Les traductions françaises du Guzman d'Alfarache* (Paris, 1886), and in connection with a review of the works of picaresque authors in Eugène Réaume's *Étude historique et littéraire sur Agrippa d'Aubigné* (Paris, 1883), in Gaspard d'Ardenne de Tizac's *Étude historique et littéraire sur Vital d'Audiguier* (Villefranche et Paris, 1887), in Émile Roy's *Étude sur Charles Sorel* (Paris, 1891), in Jules Dukas's *Étude bibliographique et littéraire sur le Satyricon de Jean Barclay* (Paris, 1880), in Paul Morillot's *Scarron et le genre burlesque* (Paris, 1888), in R. Peters's *Paul Scarron und seine spanischen Quellen* (Erlangen, 1893), and in several monographs upon Le Sage. Chief of these are Léo Claretie's *Le Sage romancier* (Paris, 1890), Eugène Lintilhac's *Le Sage* (Paris, 1893), Gustav Haack's *Untersuchungen zur Quellenkunde von Le Sages Gil Blas de Santillana* (Kiel, 1896), and the older *Geschichte der Gil Blas-Frage* (1879), by E. Veckenstedt. G. E. B. Saintsbury's *Essays on French Novelists* (London, 1891) contains a notice of Le Sage, who is more fully discussed by Sainte-Beuve (*Lundis*, ii, ix; *Portraits littéraires*, i). Of less importance are Felix Bobertag's *Charles Sorels Histoire comique de Francion und Berger extravagant* (*Zeitschr. f. neufranzösischen Sprache u. Litt.* iii, 2, 228, 1882), Francis Wey's *Antoine Furetière, sa vie, ses œuvres* (*Rev. contemp.* 31 Juill., 15 Août, 1852), N. M. Bernardin's *Tristan l'Hermite* (Paris, 1895), and J. J. Jusserand's "Paul Scarron" in *English Essays from a French Pen* (N. Y., 1895).

Eustache le Moine is edited by W. Foerster and J. Trost in the former's *Romanische Bibliothek* (1888, vol. iv), and was first published by F. Michel (Paris, 1834). The *Vie genereuse des mercelots* after its appearance at Lyons (1596) saw later editions at Paris (1612, 1618, 1622) and at Troyes (1627). It is reprinted by Techener together with other anatomies of roguery in *Les joyeusetez facecies et folastres imaginacions de Caresme Prenant, Gauthier Garguille*, etc. (Paris, 1831), and by Édouard Fournier in vol. viii of *Variétés historiques et littéraires* (Paris, 1855–59, 9 vols.). Paul Lacroix (Le Bibliophile Jacob) has reproduced the 1644 French translation of *Il vagabondo* (Genève, 1867). Many old novels may be found in the *Bibliothèque universelle des romans* (1775–89, 224 vols.) and in the *Nouvelle bibliothèque des romans anciens et modernes* (1798–1805, 112 vols.). The *Œuvres complètes d'Agrippa d'Aubigné* appeared in 1873–77, and the *Œuvres complètes de Théophile de Viau* in 1855–56 (Jannet). Jules Gay reprinted *Les amours du Filou et de Robinette* (Paris, 1862) with an interesting *Avant-propos* concerning *filoux* by M. P. L. (Paul Lacroix), and *Les libertins en campagne* was issued by J. Gay et Fils (Turin, 1870). *Francion* has been published with notes and introduction by Émile Colombey (Paris, 1858), who has also edited the *Mémoires* of D'Assoucy (Paris, 1858). Editions of the three parts of the *Histoire générale des larrons* appeared at Paris (1639, 1709), at Lyons (1652, 1664), and at Rouen (1657, 1666, and n. d.). The *Roman bourgeois* may be read in the edition of Édouard Fournier and Charles Asselineau (Paris, 1854), and the *Roman comique* in Victor Fournel's edition (Paris, 1857) or in the later redactions of Garnier Frères and Paul Bourget. J. J. Jusserand has written an introduction to the English translation by Tom Brown, John Savage, and others (London, 1892, 2 vols.). The works of Le Sage and his followers are so accessible that they require no special notice here. *Gil Blas* may be read in Smollett's translation edited by Saintsbury (London, 1881, 3 vols.), or in the translation of Henri Van Laun (London, 1885, 3 vols.). J. Townsend has Englished *Estévanille* and the *Bachelier* as *Vanillo Gonzalez* and *The Bachelor of Salamanca* (1881), and Van Laun stands sponsor for the *Diable boiteux* as *Asmodeus; or, the Devil on Two Sticks* (London, 1896, 4 vols.). Gustave Larroumet's *Marivaux, sa vie et ses œuvres* (Paris, 1882), Gaston Deschamps's *Marivaux* (Paris, 1893), and H. Harrisse's *L'abbé Prévost* (Paris, 1896) afford an account of more romantic eighteenth-century fiction.

4 *a*

Spanish picaresque influence in Germany is considered in Arturo Farinelli's *Die Beziehungen zwischen Spanien und Deutschland in der Litteratur* (Berlin, 1892), in Julius Schwering's *Litterarische Beziehungen zwischen Spanien und Deutschland* (in his *Kritische Studien*, Münster, 1902), and in Adam Schneider's painstaking *Spaniens Anteil an der deutschen Litteratur des* 16. *und* 17. *Jahrhunderts* (Strassburg, 1898). Special phases of Peninsular influence are dealt with by J. Fitzmaurice-Kelly's *Caspar Ens* (Paris, 1897), Ed. Dorer's *Cervantes und seine Werke nach deutschen Urtheilen* (Leipzig, 1881) and *Cervantes Literatur in Deutschland* (Zürich, 1877), and in critical essays upon Grimmelshausen and Albertinus noted below. The authority for the German novel of the seventeenth century is Felix Bobertag's excellent *Geschichte des Romans und der ihm verwandten Dichtungsgattungen in Deutschland* (Berlin, 1876–84, 2 vols.). L. Cholevius's *Die bedeutendsten deutschen Romane des xvii Jahrhunderts* (Leipzig, 1866) concentrates attention upon romantic and heroic fiction alone. A general view of the period may be gained from H. Palm's *Beiträge zur Geschichte der deutschen Litteratur des* 16. *und* 17. *Jahrhunderts* (Breslau, 1877). Of the general histories of German literature G. C. Gervinus's *Geschichte der deutschen Dichtung* (Leipzig, 1871–74, 5 ed. by K. Bartsch, 5 vols.) affords the best account of the *Schwänke* and *Volksbücher,* and Karl Goedeke's *Grundriss zur Geschichte der deutschen Dichtung* (Dresden, 1884, 2d ed.) is the most useful for general reference.

For Wickram consult W. Scherer's *Die Anfänge des deutschen Prosaromans und Jörg Wickram von Colmar* (*Quellen und Forschungen*, Strassburg, 1877, 21). Scheidt's *Grobianus* is edited by G. Milchsack (*Neudrucke*, Halle, 1882, 34, 35), and the satirist receives notice in A. Hauffen's *Kaspar Scheidt, der Lehrer Fischarts* (*Quell. u. Forsch.*, 1889, 66). H. Lämbel's *Erzählungen und Schwänke* (Leipzig, 1883, 2d ed.) contains *Der Pfaffe Amis* and *Meier Helmbrecht.* The latter is also to be found in the edition of F. Keinz (Leipzig, 1887, 2d ed.) and in the *Deutsche Nationallitteratur* series (Stuttgart, 4, 1, 2). Here, too, appear selections from the jests and popular tales edited by Bobertag (1885–88, 11, 24, 25), whose *Vierhundert Schwänke des* 16. *Jahrhunderts* (27) with Karl Goedeke's *Schwänke des* 16. *Jahrhunderts* (Leipzig, 1879) supplement such earlier works as C. Simrock's *Die deutsche Volksbücher* (1845) and J. Scheible's *Das Kloster, weltlich und geistlich. Meist aus der ältern deutschen Volks-, Wunder-, Curiositäten-, und vorzugsweise Komischen Literatur* (1845). Although the Low German version of *Eulenspiegel* (1483) is lost, there remains in High German *Ein kurtzweilig Lesen von Dyl Ulenspiegel* (Strassburg, 1515). Till was naturalized in France (1532), and in England (1548–60) through an Antwerp abstract of the original. His influence in England will be noted *passim*. His jests were translated also into Flemish, Latin, Danish, and Polish. More than a hundred editions are noticed in that of J. M. Lappenberg (Leipzig, 1854). Cf. also the editions by H. Knust (*Neudrucke*, 1885, 55, 56). *Reynke de Vos* is edited by K. Schröder (Leipzig, 1872), by F. Prien (Halle, 1887), and by E. Wolff (*Deutsche Nationallitteratur*, 1883, 19); and the *Narrenschiff* is edited in that series by Bobertag (1889, 16), in the *Deutsche Dichter des* 16. *Jahrhunderts* (Leipzig, 1872, 7) by Goedeke and separately by F. Zarncke (Leipzig, 1854). On the *Liber vagatorum* consult the *Weimarisches Jahrbuch* (1856, 10), and on the beggar industry, Heinrich Schreiber in the *Taschenbuch für Geschichte und Alterthum in Süd-Deutschland* (Fribourg, 1839, p. 335).

A selection from Moscherosch's *Gesichte Philanders von Sittewald* may be read in Bobertag's edition (*Deutsche Nationallitteratur*, 1884, 32). *Simplicissimus* is presented in that series by the same editor (1882, 33, 34), as well as by Julius Tittman (*Deutsche Dichter*, 1877, 7, 8), and by R. Kögel (*Neudrucke*, 1880, 19–25). The *Simplicianische Schriften* are edited by Heinrich Kurz (1863–64), by Tittman (*Deutsche Dichter*, 1877, 10, 11), by Bobertag (*Deutsche Nationallitteratur*, 1883, 35), and they appear in the *Sammlung Göschen* (Leipzig, 1901, 138). Adolphe Bossert's *Essais sur la littérature allemande* (Paris, 1905) opens with a study of Grimmelshausen. Ferdinand Antoine's *Étude sur le Simplicissimus de Grimmelshausen* (Paris, 1882) is the best treatment of the subject. Albertinus is discussed by R. von Liliencron (*Deutsche Nationallitteratur*, 1883, 26), and by Rudolf von Payer in *Eine Quelle des Simplicissimus* (*Zeitschrift f. deutsche Phil.* xxii, 93.) The same author considers the *Simplicissimus* imitations in his article *Der Schelmenroman unter besonderer Berücksichtigung seiner Verbreitung in Oesterreich-Ungarn* (*Oesterr. Ungar. Rev.*, vii, 285). Weise is considered by L. Fulda (*Deutsche Nationallitteratur*, 39), and his *Drey ärgsten Ertz-Narren* is edited by W. Braune (*Neudrucke*, 1878, 12–14). *Judas der Ertzschelm* is edited by Bobertag (*Deutsche Nationallitteratur*, 1883, 40). The work and its author are discussed in W. Scherer's *Vorträge und Aufsätze* (Berlin, 1874), and by T. G. von Karajan in a monograph

(Wien, 1867). F. Zarncke's *Christian Reuter* (Leipzig, 1884) deals with *Schelmuffsky* and its author, and the fiction is reprinted (*Neudrucke*, 1885–90, 57–59, 90, 91). Joseph von Eichendorff's *Der deutsche Roman des 18ten Jahrhunderts* (*Vermischte Schriften*, Paderborn, 1866, vol. iii) considers the later development of the novel, special phases of which are studied in A. Kippenberg's *Robinsonaden in Deutschland bis zur Insel Felsenburg* (Hannover, 1892) and in H. Ullrich's *Robinson und Robinsonaden* (Weimar, 1898). The romantic recoil from realism is treated in Erich Schmidt's *Richardson, Rousseau, und Goethe* (Jena, 1875).

4*b*

The principal account of the Dutch literature of roguery is Jan ten Brink's *Dr. Nicolaas Heinsius, Junior, eene studie over den hollandschen schelmenroman der zeventiende eeuw* (Rotterdam, 1885). W. J. Jonckbloet's *Geschiedenis der nederlandsche letterkunde* (Groningen, 1881, 3d ed., and a German version by Wilhelm Berg, Leipzig, 1870) considers Heinsius and Brederoo. Compare also L. Schneider's *Geschichte der niederländischen Litteratur* (Leipzig, 1887) and ten Brink's *Geschiedenis der nederlandsche letterkunde* (Amsterdam, 1897). Ten Brink is the author of the standard monograph upon Brederoo (Rotterdam, 1871), and has also edited his *Werken* (1890). Spanish influence in Holland is discussed in considerable detail by J. te Winkel's *De invloed der spaansche letterkunde op de nederlandsche in de zeventiende eeuw* (*Tijdschrift voor nederlandsche taal-en letterkunde*, Leiden, 1881, vol. i, p. 59). A. Werner's *Humor of Holland* (London, 1893) may be consulted for its introduction and translated selections. The romantic reaction is considered in C. J. Luzac's *De nederlandsche sentimenteele roman* (Amersfoort, 1890).

CHAPTER II

ENGLISH PICARESQUE ORIGINS

1. *Roguery Before 1550*

AWS rather than letters bear witness to the roguery of Saxon and Norman England. As early as the seventh century robbers, fugitive slaves and ceorls, wandering chapmen, beggars, and monks, were subjects of legal restriction. Bede and Ælfric refer to mendicancy as common, and the Church encouraged it by preaching the duty of almsgiving. Canute, in order to check increasing roguery, demanded of every male above twelve years of age an oath that he would neither be a thief nor be cognizant of theft; and the Normans, retaining this vow together with the best of the Saxon edicts against vagabondage and crime, imposed severe penalties upon grave-robbers and offenders against the forest laws. Yet the stringency of the latter statutes so far justified those who defied them that the woodland outlaw caught a glamour which he long continued to reflect in popular song and story.

Seignorial rascality seems to have rivaled, too, that of professed marauders, the Chronicles recounting the spoliation of peasants by their lords throughout the reign of Stephen, as well as such acts of private violence as the plundering of Peterborough minster in 1102 by French and Flemish robbers, emulating the earlier exploits of the Saxon, Hereward the Wake. Edicts of Edward I directed against the vagabonds and wandering bards of Wales could not restrain Welsh rogues from plying their trade in England; and even Englishmen of rank resorted to brigandage. Sir Gosseline Denville with his Yorkshire band terrorized the north, and on one occasion robbed Edward II himself. It profited little that the roads were cleared of underbrush for two hundred feet on either side, and that in the towns the carrying of arms and resort to taverns after curfew were forbidden. Quacks and empirics, thieves and bullies, continued to thrive, and the great forests furnished shelter to Drawlatches, Roberdesmen, and Wastours. Rascals threatened with capture had ever the resource of ecclesiastical refuge. Of ten who escaped from Newgate in 1324, five were successful in claiming sanctuary. Charters of pardon could always be purchased, and it was not unusual for hue and cry to be set by robbers upon honest strangers found abroad after dark.

The fourteenth century with its visitations of the Black Death, its industrial troubles, and growing religious corruption offered fertile soil for the flourishing of roguery. In 1376 the Commons petitioned the King for protection against Ribalds and Sturdy Beggars. Begging hermits haunted highways and churches; lepers sounding their clack-dishes clamored for charity; university scholars traveled and studied on the proceeds of mendicancy and theft. The rising of Wat Tyler inspired not only the worthy downtrodden, but also the evil climbers and parasites.

Chaucer, Langland, and Gower from diverse points of view remarked the roguery about them. Gower in the "Vox Clamantis" cries out upon the social evils of the day. He sees the lower classes as swine and wolves, asses, oxen, foxes, cats, and dogs, wasps, and frogs, broken loose and swarming upon their masters. In the "Confessio Amantis" he looks from low to high, from stubborn servants, cheating merchants, bribe-taking jurors, bailiffs, and sheriffs, to lying men of the law, rapacious soldiers, and a godless, grasping clergy.

So, too, Langland in "The Vision of William concerning Piers the Plowman," with keener sympathy for the poor and greater moral earnestness, laments corruption in high places, especially in the Church. The arts, lies, hypocrisy, wealth, and pride of all that goodly company of archdeacons, summoners, pardoners, monks, and mendicant friars provoke his wrath. He has seen spiritual shepherds forsaking their flocks during the plague to live in sloth and luxury; he has gazed on the pomp of the cardinal legate, and contrasted it with the humility of Jesus; he has noted the rivalry of the Popes of Avignon and Rome, zealous only in extorting contributions from impoverished Englishmen. But though Langland remarks roguery in high places, he is not oblivious to it among the lowly. As a practical reformer he insists upon the saving grace of work, for the sin of idleness to him is the sin unpardonable. This it is that incites his tirades against hermits who whiningly ask alms "in hope to sitten at even by the hote coles," and against shameless beggars, who, bag upon shoulder, jog from house to house in quest of bread and ale. In one rare scene he depicts an assembly of rogues taking their ease at a tavern. Among them are such merry souls as

> Watte the warynere and hus wife dronke,
> Thomme the tynkere, and tweye of hus knaues,
> Hicke the hakeneyman, and Houwe the neldere,
> Claryce of Cockeslane, the clerk of the churche,
> An haywarde and an heremyte, the hangeman of Tyborne,
> Dauwe the dykere, with a dosen harlotes
> Of portours and of pykeporses, and pylede toth-drawers.[1]

The boisterous mirth as Glutton grows drunker is that of a Flemish kermess. Elsewhere the wiles of chapmen and mer-

[1] Skeat's ed., Text C, Passus vii, ll. 363–370.

chants are set forth by Coueytise, who confesses to having learned to lie and wickedly to weigh while serving Symme-at-the-Style as 'prentice. Sent by his master "to Wy and to Winchestre" to the fair, he admits that had he used no guile his wares would have remained unsold this seven years. Rose, the regratour, his wife, has abetted him in roguery, and bad ale of her brewing as well as false cloth of her weaving have helped to fill their pockets.

Langland, like Wyclif and Gower, is intent upon preaching repentance. Chaucer, on the other hand, depicts vice humorously with all the tolerance of a great artist. It speaks for itself and wields its own scourge. The Pandarus of Boccaccio becomes in Chaucer's "Troilus and Crysede" such a vitalized and self-portrayed rogue. The humor of the scenes between this subtle, hard-headed, reverend sinner and the impassioned, idealizing Troilus results from the clash of incongruous characters. Like the Spanish Celestina, Pandarus is both a comic figure and the mainspring of a tragedy. He is Chaucer's most original and complex rascal.

Roguery is more plentifully and variously exhibited, however, in the "Canterbury Tales." The general "Prologue," with its vivid character sketches, includes vignettes of several rascals. Picaros in clerkly clothes are the chief. Chaucer's "gentil Pardoner," whose wallet is "bret-ful of pardoun come from Rome al hoot," is typical of a class accomplished in the forging of papal bulls and in the assumption of strange immunities. He is a coiner of relics, whose stock comprises a piece of the Virgin's veil, a shred of St. Peter's sail, and a glass of pig bones doing duty as those of martyrs. Chaucer's Monk is a sporting man, his mendicant Frere is a lisping dandy, and his Somnour, with scrofulous face and tongue dropping legal Latin, is a cheater of the innocent and a taker of bribes. The drunken Miller is true to the traditions of his trade, for "wel coude he stelen corn, and tollen thryes;" the Shipman is little more than a pirate; and the Doctour of Phisyk is an astrological charlatan.

Among the stories themselves roguery thrives, drawn very largely, however, from foreign sources. The "Freres Tale" relates the outwitting of a vicious somnour by the Devil; the "Pardoneres Tale" describes the murderous quarrel of three Flemish thieves over a treasure-trove; the "Milleres Tale" recounts the beguiling of an Oxford carpenter by his wife and student lodger; and the "Shipmannes Tale" descants upon the merry infidelity of a merchant's wife with a monk. Two Cambridge scholars in the "Reves Tale" are outwitted by a thieving miller, and at night take revenge on the honor of his wife and daughter; and the alchemist of the "Chanouns Yemannes Tale" swindles a priest by ingenious expedients.

In the post-Chaucerian "Tale of Beryn" a naughty youth falls among rogues worse than he, but comes off triumphant through the wit of a pretended cripple, who conquers falsehood by falsehood and guile by guile.

Charlatans like Chaucer's Canon and pretenders like Edward II's court physician, John of Gaddesden, who cured smallpox by wrapping his patients in red cloth, continue the butts of letters and laws down to the day of Ben Jonson. Nor are clerical rogues forgotten. The pardoner in particular suffers in the dramatic compositions of John Heywood, and in Lyndsay's "Ane Satyre of the Thrie Estaitis" (1535). Lyndsay's pardoner carries as relics the jawbone of Fin-Mac-Coull, the horn of Colling's cow, and the cord that hanged Johnnie Armstrong: —

My patent Pardouns ye may se,
Cum fra the Cane of Tartarie,
  Weill seald with oster-schellis.

Thocht ye haue na contritioun
Ye sall haue full remissioun
  With help of buiks and bellis.

Begging friars were attacked by More in "Utopia" (1516); and in his "Dyalogue . . . of the Worshyp of Ymagys" (2d ed. 1530), he tells the story repeated by Grafton, Foxe, and in the Shakespearean "2 Henry VI," of Duke Humphrey's exposing a beggar feigning blindness. Henry VIII among laws against mummers, Gypsies, unlicensed students, rufflers, and shipmen pretending the loss of their vessels, included provisions against pardoners and practicers of crafty sciences. Erasmus in his "Encomium Moriæ" (1511) exposed rascals of the latter type, and as late as 1664 Richard Saunders in "Palmistry, the Secrets Thereof Disclosed," after drawing up a list of "such quallifications as every able Artist ought to be endued with," assails mere sycophants of the black art.

In the meantime beggars had been pilloried by kings and poets. The fifteenth century saw Irish chamber-deacons, or vagrants, banished by acts of Henry V and Henry VI; the laws against Welsh beggars confirmed by the latter; and new reforms enforced by Henry VII. The rebellion of Jack Cade drew into the train of the peasants throngs of vagabonds. Soldiers returning disappointed from the French Wars fell upon their own countrymen's goods by way of compensation. Lydgate, Dunbar, and Skelton point out the wiles of vagabonds; and James V of Scotland, if the ascription to him of the "Gaberlunyie Man" be correct, exposes the tricks while he sings the joys of mendicant life: —

I'll bow my leg and crook my knee,
And draw a black clout o'er my eye,
A cripple or blind they will ca' me
  While we shall be merry and sing.

About the same time Alexander Barclay's rhyming "Shyp of Folys" (1508) and the prose version of its German original, issued by Henry Watson in 1517, furnished fresh satire at the expense of ecclesiastical and lay beggars. Here are pardoners who sell horse hair as the beards of the innocents, and feathers attested to have been plucked from the Holy Ghost. Here are vagabonds begging with children, whose arms and legs they have broken in infancy in order the better to excite compassion. Such rascals go about in gowns patched with a hundred colors and bind "foule cloutes about theyr legges as who say they be sore." Sir John Cheke in his "Hurt of Sedicion" (1549) complains of a similar crew of "vagabonds and loitring beggers and daie sleepers, purse pikers, highwaie robbers, and quarrel makers."

Apart, however, from the poetry of Chaucer and an occasional reflection of social conditions in the works mentioned above, and despite the many laws enacted against the picaresque commonwealth under Henry VIII and Edward VI, the literature of roguery achieved little before the middle of the sixteenth century. Although the early drama included a few pieces of mirth-provoking rascality, and certain legendary rogues became the subject of ballads and chap-books, the great collections of jests, the tales of popular heroes, the characters, and the satires date from the reign of Elizabeth.

2. *The Early Drama*

What little roguery figures in the early drama is associated with the doings of the Devil and the Vice or of comic servants, and with the incidental portrayal of vulgar manners. Among the Miracle Plays, the "Sacrifice of Cain and Abel" in the York Cycle shows a realistic servant in Brewbarret, or Strife-brewer, a sufferer from Cain's irritability. His counterpart in the more comic and naturalistic Towneley Plays is Pyk-harness, the wittily disputatious "Garcio." Here also the two "Shepherds' Plays" approach downright roguery in the drinking bout of the first and in the sheep-stealing incident of the second.

Mak, the thief of the "Secunda Pastorum," rises at night while his companions are sleeping in the fields and makes off with a fat sheep which his wife tucks up in the cradle as a newborn babe. Then he returns to his fellows, who because of portentous dreams accuse him of the theft. He denies the charge, but they search his house, and Mak and his wife are at their wits' end to keep the inquisitive shepherds from the cradle. Just as the guests are leaving, one insists that he must kiss the baby. The knavery thus exposed, Mak receives chastisement by being tossed in a blanket.

In the Chester Cycle the parallel "Play of the Shepherds" opens with a riotous scene presided over by jolly Trowle; and the "Harrowing of Hell" introduces a repentant but erstwhile dishonest hostess, who warns against the cunning of tippling tapsters and false minglers of wine. In the Digby Mysteries the "Killing of the Children" presents Herod's man, Watkyn, whose boasts of prowess and fears of combat foreshadow those of the typical picaresque soldier. Here, too, the "Mary Magdalene" affords a striking representation of tavern life in the passage recording the heroine's temptation.

In the Moralities, realism and roguery are found to centre chiefly in the Vice. As the Devil corresponds to the villain of the later stage, so the Vice anticipates the more modern fool and rogue. Allied in origin, probably, to the domestic jester of actual life, this teasing servant of the Devil was enjoyed as a scoundrel whose tricks merited license because their object was to plague a fiend, yet whose evil doings were paid for at last by a ride to the nether world on the Devil's back. Now and again the Vice became a concrete person, like the Nichol Newfangle in Ulpian Fulwell's "Like wil to Like quod the Devel to the

Colier" (pr.[1] 1568). Here, too, Nichol's associates take on such particular titles as Cuthbert Cutpurse, Pierce Pickpurse, Tom Tosspot, Ralph Roister, and Hankin Hangman. In "Hycke-Scorner" abstract Free-will and Imagination are as great rogues as Hycke himself, and they discuss such matters as craft in stealing, the pains of Newgate, and Tyburn hangings. Other types of low character appear in the Moralities, from Snatch and Catch, the vagabond soldiers of "The Marriage of Wit and Wisdom," or Prodigality, the highway robber in the "Contention Between Liberalitie and Prodigalitie," to the brace of rufflers, Creweltie and Avarice, in the "New Custome." Even the respectable hero of "Mankind" becomes a rogue for the nonce through the machinations of Myscheff and others; and the hero of Skelton's "Magnyfycence" is lured into evil by Crafty-conveyance, Counterfeit-countenance, Cloked-collusion, and Courtly-abusion.

Of the interludes, John Heywood's "Mery Play between the Pardoner and the Frere, the Curate and Neybour Pratte" (pr. 1533) exposes the roguery of a begging friar and a relic-mongering pardoner; and the latter type is again laughed at along with a lying palmer in "The Four P's." But in "The Husbande, Tyb the Wife, and Syr Jhon the Priest" Heywood remains content to draw the merely amorous scamp, and Thomas Ingelend's prodigal in "The Disobedient Child" is only an occasional rascal who eventually repents. The best interlude roguery, indeed, was derived from a famous Spanish source in the adaptation of the first four acts of the "Celestina," printed by John Rastell (*c.* 1530).

When full-fledged comedy appeared, it drew its rogues either from native stock, or more frequently from Latin comedy and

[1] Throughout in giving the dates of plays the abbreviations "pr." and "pl." stand for "printed" and "played" respectively.

its original, the Greek New Comedy. Of the former type is Diccon, the developed Vice of "Gammer Gurton's Needle," a mischief-making "Bedlam," or Abraham Man, who steals bacon and plays practical jests. Of the latter type is Matthew Merygreeke, the parasitical picaro of "Ralph Roister Doister," and the blatant Ralph himself.

The less developed drama lingered on, however, and in it roguery was by no means forgotten. "A Knacke to Knowe a Knave" (pl. 1592), which mingled historical and allegorical characters, introduces the Bailiff of Hexham, carried off by the Devil after having advised each of his cheating sons as to the wiles they are to practice. These worthy children of a worthy father are Courtier, Priest, Farmer, and Cutbert Cutpurse the Coney-catcher. The last is here distinguished as a bearer of false witness, being captured in which offense he is adjudged to stand at the market-cross with his tongue pinned to his breast.

Robert Wilson's "Three Ladies of London" (pr. 1584) presents as the chief of several roguish characters Fraud, who travels up to London to get entertainment of the three sisters,— Lucre, Love, and Conscience. He is recognized by Simplicity as having been a cheating inn-boy at Gravesend, the doubler of all travelers' reckonings, and as the hostler at Ware notorious for greasing horses' teeth that they should eat no hay. Fraud's boon companions are Dissimulation, Simony, and Usury, as well as Lawyer, who boasts his ability to make black white and white black again. When two mendicants, Tom Beggar and Wily Will, have lured Simplicity into their way of life, the three chant, in the vein of Autolycus, the joys of ragged freedom:—

> Our fingers are lime-twigs, and barbers we be,
> To catch sheets from hedges most pleasant to see;
> Then to the ale-wife roundly we set them to sale,
> And spend the money merrily upon her good ale.

Simplicity draws Fraud a coat of arms, which contains two trees rampant surmounted by a sour tree passant, "with a man like you in a green field pendant;" and Tom introduces Wily Will as a good fellow "to go a-fishing with a crank through a window, or to set lime-twigs to catch a pan, pot, or dish," — a reference to the trick of the hooker of the beggar-books.

In Wilson's sequel to this popular play — "The Three Lordes and Three Ladies of London" (pr. 1590) — Fraud reappears to perform several tricks. Disguised as a French artificer he cozens Simplicity into buying copper trinkets for gold. As Fraud is being conveyed under arrest to Newgate he offers his keeper, Diligence, a purse of two hundred angels as a pawn to insure his return when he shall have visited his house. Then he foists upon Diligence a duplicate purse that is empty, and readily escapes. Later, when apprehended by Simplicity, he gets away with Pleasure's connivance. But Simplicity, thinking he has disposed of Fraud, declares that "the tanners will miss him in their leather, the tailors in their cutting out of garments, the shoemakers in closing, the tapsters in filling pots, and the very oystermen to mingle their oysters at Billingsgate."

3. *Legendary Rascals*

A native anti-hero of the early stage especially dear to the May-day pageants was Robin Hood. A "Newe Playe of Robyn Hoode," "for to be played in Maye games," came into print shortly before Shakespeare's birth, but the tradition of the prince of English outlaws and its literary expression were much older. This legendary rogue seems first to have sprung from folklore, then to have assumed definiteness in popular ballads of uncertain date, and only after that to have taken on historical dignities. Before the middle of the fifteenth century he had been labeled as an actual personage of the thirteenth, and later historians assigned him to the twelfth. Thus Richard I, Henry III, and Edward II were each honored as Robin's sovereign, though no contemporary chronicler had deigned to notice him. The association of his name with things and places far apart, the nature of the May-day celebrations, and the popular literature devoted to him, tend to confirm his legendary origin.

In the second half of the fourteenth century Langland remarked upon the people's love for "rymes of Robyn Hood," and a hundred years later Wynkyn de Worde published a long narrative, fusing older ballads, and entitled "A Lytell Geste of Robyn Hoode." For many years this excellent knave continued to be the theme of ballads and plays substantially agreeing as to his personal traits, although they differed in their incidents, setting, and historical allusions. The "Lytell Geste" makes him a native of Barnsdale; later ballads transfer him to Sherwood Forest or to Plumpton Park in Cumberland; and Anthony Munday creates him Earl of Huntingdon. In most, however, Robin is the sworn enemy of the Sheriff of Nottingham; he delights in a fair fight with any who will dispute his authority; he hobnobs with the king come in disguise to see him, assists the unfortunate, gayly robs the rich, and ends by being treacherously bled to death by the prioress of Kirklees. Though a rogue beyond question, Robin is free from the sordid guile of the picaro. His love of the green wood, his fondness for sport, his defiance of oppressive forest laws, his generosity and gift for laughter, entitle him to admiration. Friar Tuck and Little John, with Much the Miller's son, William Scathlock or Scarlock, and Maid Marian keep him fit company, and have added not a little to the legend's charm. Other traditional outlaws shared the traits of Robin Hood, notably the famous trio, — Adam Bell, Clym of the Clough, and William of Cloudeslie, — as well as the more historical Murray and Johnnie Armstrong.

Legendary rascals of a different stripe contributed also to the making of the literature of roguery; and to this group belong Robin Goodfellow, Robert the Devil, and Friar Rush. As for Rush, he comes of Danish and German stock, and borders on the villain. In England the first version of his exploits that remains appeared as "The Historie of Frier Rvsh" (1620), but his sixteenth-century vogue is shown by frequent allusions.[1]

In English dress the legend relates how the prince of devils sent to a monastery fallen into spiritual decay this demoniacal emissary, commissioned to complete its ruin. Rush stood at the gate as if in sorrow, and so played upon the Prior's sympathies that he was given the office of under-cook. He procured the Prior a lady for whom the latter long had languished, and presently, having thrown the master-cook into a boiling pot, secured his place. After seven years' service Rush was promoted to be a friar, but he did not desist from roguery. He set the monks by the ears, and, putting out the lights in the midst of their quarrel, tumbled a great desk amongst them, and then bringing a taper deplored their conduct. When bidden to grease the wheels of a wagon, he grimed them with tar. When posted to report on the tardy at matins, he broke down the steps leading to the choir and caused them all to fall. The owner of a cow stolen by Rush reported to the Prior having beheld him by night surrounded by devils and announcing to Lucifer the success of his schemes. This news filled the Prior and his companions with horror, and Rush was dismissed from the monastery and was then transformed into a horse.

The story in its account of what followed this metamorphosis is inconsistent, for Rush is evidently quite human most of the time. He engages as servant to a husbandman whose wife is over familiar with her parish priest. Next he serves a gentleman whose daughter is possessed of an

---

[1] Cf. *Gammer Gurton's Needle* (1566): —

> Saw ye never Fryer Rushe
> Painted on a cloth, with a side long cow's tayle,
> And crooked cloven feet, and many a hooked nayle?

and the *Discoverie of Witchcraft* (1584), p. 521. An English prose *History of Friar Rush* was entered in the Stationers' Registers, 1567-68, and John Day had a play on the theme. Cf. F. G. Fleay, *Chronicle of the English Drama*, vol. i, p. 108.

evil spirit. The Prior relieves her, and receives in recognition lead roofing for a new church. Rush bears the lead and his Reverence to the church, and "then the Priour coniured Rush againe into his owne likenesse" and sent him to an old castle. "From which Deuill and all other Deuils, defend vs good Lord. Amen."

The original story was probably a monkish tale confined to incidents of the cloister. Icelandic manuscripts of the fourteenth century show a nameless devil becoming an abbot, but omit such pranks as are later ascribed to Rush. These, however, would be supplied by stories like those told of Hödekin of Hildesheim, "a house-cobold, serviceable in a monastery."[1]

The legend was early localized in Denmark, and a Low German version appeared toward 1486. The incident of the lady possessed of a devil seems to have been appropriated from the legend of Zeno, Bishop of Verona, but is not without other parallels. This episode in "Von Bruoder Rauschen vnd was Wunders er getrieben hat" (Strassburg, 1515) is referred to the king of England's daughter, into whom Rausch enters on leaving the cloister. Perhaps the English redactor of 1620 was so far influenced by the Spanish tales of rogue servants as to emphasize Rush's service of masters, which before had been merely incidental. At all events, he adds the episode of Rush's service with the husbandman, and, instead of sending Rush

[1] The suggestion of Professor G. L. Kittredge in his valuable paper, *The Friar's Lantern and Friar Rush* (*Publications of the Modern Language Association*, vol. xv, no. 4, p. 415, *et seq.*). Here in addition to the correspondence between Hödekin and Rush, first observed in Reginald Scot's *Discoverie of Witchcraft* (1584), are noted various analogues to parts of the English story. Professor Kittredge, after reëxamining Harsnett's *Declaration of Egregious Popish Impostures* (1603), concludes that there is no "reason for believing that Friar Rush was ever known in England as a frolicsome spirit to be equated with Puck or Robin Goodfellow." The *History* of 1620, however, makes him a rogue as well as villain, and in the process borrows from jest-books like *Eulenspiegel* and Valentin Schumann's *Nachtbüchlein*.

as a devil to possess the king's daughter, makes him serve a gentleman whose daughter proves already possessed by another and wholly unrelated spirit.

A legendary rogue resembling Rush figures in "Robert the Deuyll," the English version of a well-known French prose romance.[1] Robert is both rascal and jester, for a hermit commands him by way of penance for youthful devilries to go dumb and play the fool, thus affording opportunity for the perpetration of a string of practical jokes. On the whole, however, he is too much the villain at first and too genuinely convicted of sin at last to be more than a distant relative of the true picaro.

A closer cousin is Robin Goodfellow, the jester and rogue of the fairies, "famozed in every old wives' chronicle for his mad merrye prankes." Among the vulgar his popularity was great at an early period, but he attained literary celebrity chiefly during the reign of Elizabeth. Shakespeare was of course his principal patron, but Anthony Munday mentions him in his comedy "The Two Italian Gentlemen" (1584); an account of his exploits was printed before 1588; he appears in the epigrams of "Skialetheia, or a Shadowe of Truth" (1598); and he furnished Henry Chettle with the subject of a lost play (1602). The earliest extant edition of his jests is "Robin Good-Fellow; his Mad Prankes and Merry Jests. Full of Honest Mirth and is a Fit Medicine for Melancholy" (1628). Here the hostess of a Kentish alehouse tells the story of Robin's life.

Robin is the child of a country girl and of the king of the fairies, Obreon.[2] From the first he resembles Eulenspiegel, making faces before

---

[1] The French original was published in 1496 by P. Mareschall, Lyon. At Paris it was reissued in 1497 by Nic. de la Barre, and *c.* 1520 by Jehan Herouf. In English it was printed by Wynkyn de Worde (*c.* 1510).

[2] In an entertainment given before Elizabeth (1591) he is Auberon; in Greene's *James IV* (1598) he is Oboram; in *Midsummer Night's Dream* (pr. 1600) and in a seventeenth-century chap-book ballad he is Oberon, as

and gestures behind the companion who takes him to ride, running away to escape entering the service of a tailor, and doing over-literally all that his master commands. He appropriates the money confided to him for the purchase of wine, and his tricks are greatly facilitated by Obreon's gift of the power to transform himself at will into any animal. The interpolated magic weakens his affinity with the picaresque type, and in "The Second Part of Robin Good-Fellow," published at the same time, he is no longer the Eulenspiegel rascal, but rather the Puck of "Midsummer Night's Dream." Now he attends the fairies' frolics, and at night sings ballads in the guise of a beggar, a chimney sweep, or a bellman. He masquerades as a fiddler at a wedding, putting out the lights, and setting the good folk at farcical odds. He impersonates a brewer and receives payment from a nicking tapster who thus must pay twice, and he makes merry with such little people as Pinch, Patch, Gull, Grim, and Tom Thumb.

4. *Jest-Books*

The relation between legend and jest-book, illustrated in the case of such rogues as Robin, Robert, and Rush, is of earlier date and more intimate nature. Medieval *fabliaux* and the Eastern tales before them were the Renaissance jest-book's true progenitors. The jester, like the anti-hero of legend, emerged from folklore. His career, however, was both longer and merrier, and he contributed more directly to the development of picaresque fiction.

Such early jest collections as the "C. Mery Talys" (1525) and the "Tales, and quicke answeres, very mery and pleasant to rede" (1549) drew upon Continental sources, especially the German, and won attention; but only with William Copland's translation of "Eulenspiegel" (1548–60) as "Howleglass" did the jest-book fashion properly begin. The "Pfarrer von Kalenberg" was adapted to English manners as the "Parson of Kalenborow." The "Sack-Full of Newes" was licensed in 1557,

he is in *Huon of Bordeaux*. For the genealogy of Oberon, see S. L. Lee's Introduction to the English translation of *Huon* (1882).

"Scoggins Jests" in 1565 or 1566, Skelton's "Merie Tales Newly Imprinted" in 1567, and the first picaresque novel — itself a developed jest-book — was licensed as "The Marvelus Dedes and the Lyf of Lazaro de Tormes" in 1568. Richard Edwards's "Comic Stories" appeared in 1570, one of its tales, "The Waking Man's Dream," containing the trick that forms the basis of the "Induction" to the "Taming of the Shrew;" and in 1573 was issued the "XII. mery Jests of the wyddow Edyth." In 1590 appeared "Tarltons Newes Ovt of Pvrgatory" and "The Cobler of Caunterburie," and other collections soon followed, — "Pasquils Jests" in 1604, "Dobsons Drie Bobbes" in 1607, and "Tarltons Jests" in 1611. Of all these the most closely allied to the romance of roguery were such as fastened their anecdotes upon single celebrities like Scoggin, Skelton, and Peele.

Sixteenth-century editions of "Scoggins Jests" have perished, and although the Harleian Collection contained one of 1613, the earliest version remaining is "The First and Best Part of Scoggins Jests" of 1626.[1] Scoggin was a more learned Eulenspiegel, indebted for many of his tricks to German and French *facetiæ*. There is no rogue of the jest-books more prolific of cheats than he, and if most of his adventures are concluded with a moral, they are told solely for amusement.

At college Scoggin induces his room-mate to feign illness, and the two are enabled to live well during Lent, since the butler and the bursar yield up their keys in order to be spared possible infection. Scoggin deceives a skinner by promising to pay for a purchase of fur when next they meet; thereafter he will overtake or be overtaken by his creditor, but is careful never to meet him face to face. Having seen

[1] The original *Jests* are attributed to Andrew Boorde, physician to Henry VIII, and the original Merry Andrew. Other jests were fathered upon him, as well as a *Historie of the Mylner of Abyngton* and *Tales of the Wise Men of Gotham.*

a physician give his wife a silver cup, Scoggin brings her a pickerel as token from her husband that the cup be given him for engraving, — a trick that reappears in "Swalpo," "The English Rogue," Marston's "Dutch Courtezan," and in many plays and fictions beside. At one time he does up his leg and begs as a cripple; at another, he engages an accomplice to wager with a shepherd that his sheep are hogs, the decision being left to the next passerby, who, of course, is Scoggin himself. This fraud occurs in the Spanish "Conde Lucanor," in the "Sack-Full of Newes," and in many other collections. Scoggin pays for poultry by taking the poulterer's wife to a priest, who believes she has come for confession; and a draper is the victim of the same trick, which figures, indeed, in every jest-book from "Pfaffe Amis" and "Eulenspiegel" to the "C. Mery Talys" and the "Conceites of Old Hobson."

Here is the original of the man reported to have vomited three black crows, as also of the seller of a flea-powder to be applied with one hand while the flea is held with the other. One of the best stories, related also of Robin Hood, tells how a priest assures Scoggin and his man that all prayer shall be answered, whereupon the precious pair kneel in the road at frequent intervals to pray for money. At length Scoggin makes the priest kneel too and confess how much money he carries. But the priest, who is fearful, declares only five pounds of his fifty; and at the end of the prayer Scoggin, searching his scrip, pockets forty-five pounds as a miraculous answer from Heaven. The incidents of Scoggin's death resemble those of Eulenspiegel's. His last request is that he be buried beneath the waterspout at the east end of Westminster, since all his life he has loved drink.

The popularity of Scoggin is attested by the frequency of reference to him in literature. Harvey in deprecation said of Nash, "Sir Skelton and Master Scoggin are but innocents to Signor Capricio;" he with Skelton was a subject of a lost drama by Rankins and Hathway; and the two appear in Jonson's "Masque of the Fortunate Isles." In 1607 he gave birth to "Dobsons Drie Bobbes, Sonne and Heire to Scoggin," and Taylor the Water Poet and Martin Parker the balladist notice him.[1]

[1] *Scoggin* appeared as a chap-book *c.* 1680 and in 1796.

Skelton, who died in 1529, was the reputed author of the "Merie Tales Newly Imprinted & made by Master Skelton Poet Laureat." Among these tales, many of which are fragmentary, the thirteenth deserves especial notice. This is the story of "John Miller," referred to by Gabriel Harvey [1] as superior to "Lazarillo," "Scoggin," and "Howleglass." It is the longest of the fifteen, much the best, and its incidents are among the most ancient and widely diffused of roguish folklore.

Skelton has complained to Jack Miller of the theft of his corn, and, getting small satisfaction, sets a servant to watch the grinding; but the miller's wife throws one of her children into the mill-pond, and while the man and the miller aid in its rescue, the miller's boy has an opportunity to steal some of Skelton's corn. Skelton forces the miller to confess the cheat, and assures him he shall be hanged unless he can further attest his cleverness by stealing a cup from Skelton's own table. This is readily accomplished during the commotion caused by a fire set to a pigsty near by.

Then Skelton gives the miller the task of stealing the sheets from under him, and the miller hires a boy to hide beneath the bed and anoint them with yeast, obliging their removal. Skelton in wrath declares that the miller shall now be hanged of a surety unless he can steal the parson out of his bed. But, nothing daunted, the miller puts lighted tapers on snails crawling about the church, and, clad in the priest's robes, he tolls the bell. When the astonished priest has been summoned to church by the ghostly tolling, the disguised miller declares himself St. Peter come to take the parson to Paradise. So the parson obediently crawls into a sack, which the miller bears off and hangs aloft on his chimney.[2]

Skelton is now fully determined upon the miller's death, and warns

---

[1] In a MS. note in the copy of *Howleglass* preserved in the Bodleian, and professing to have been received by Harvey from Spenser along with *Scoggin*, *Skelton*, and *Lazarillo*.

[2] This device appears in the folklore of many peoples, and, like most of the incidents here related of John Miller, derives from the Master Thief Story. Cf. an interesting review of the latter's sources and variants by Francis Hindes Groome (*Gypsy Folk Tales*, 1899), as "The Two Thieves" and "The Gypsy and the Priest."

him that he must steal a gelding guarded by two men or lose his head at their hands. The miller procures a corpse from the gibbet, takes it to the roof under which the guards are keeping vigil, and breaking through the tiles lowers it cautiously. The guards, believing it to be the thieving miller who is entering, cut off its head, and when they are gone to inter their victim the miller walks away with the gelding.[1] Skelton thereupon gives up in despair, and, vowing that the miller excels all other thieves ever known, forgives him on condition that he will become an honest man and forsake his false dealing.

The "Merrie Conceited Jests of George Peele, Gentleman, sometimes Student in Oxford" (1607), went through several editions during the century.[2] If it did not add dignity to the reputation of its hero, the dramatist, who had died in 1598, at least, it was as popular as most of his plays. The George Peele of the jest-book is a thorough rogue, and his exploits are related with enough detail to constitute the separate parts of a picaresque fiction, although there is no unity among them, and they do not tell the story of Peele's life. Had they been combined to do this, the little book might have proved no mean romance of roguery.

Fourteen tricks are perpetrated, the choicest being at the expense of innkeepers. Thus George, pretending to be the master of several other rascals, engages rooms at an inn, sends off to London a nag hired from the host, borrows the hostess's mare through an accomplice who feigns a visit to a sweetheart, and himself secures the loan of a lute from a barber. Then he and his men joyously decamp. In the next jest when George has promised its owner the return of his lute, the barber is but the worse defrauded; for he gives George his coat that the latter may make a favorable appearance at the house where the lute is supposed to have been left, whereupon George slips away through the garden, assuring the people of the house that the barber is seeking to arrest him falsely. On one

---

[1] *Vide*, for later versions of this trick, *L'histoire générale des larrons*, pt. iii, ch. 10; and *The English Rogue*, pt. iv, ch. 20. Cf. also *La Garduña de Sevilla*, cap. v.

[2] There were editions in 1620, 1627, 1657, 1671, and one n. d. for Henry Bell. *Vide* especially that of 1809 by S. W. Singer.

occasion he plays the charlatan, brewing a miraculous herb tea; and on another, as actor, he speaks a prologue and then departs with the gate money, leaving some strollers to receive the audience's missiles, a trick which had figured in the "Mery Tales, and quick answeres" (1549), as well as in Rojas's "Viage Entretenido." Peele steals a gentleman's clothes, and leaves him to pay the reckoning after sending him to sleep by reading a play. Again at an inn when all the members of a party throw down their money on the table, he takes up the collected sum as if to discharge the bill, and vanishes. He practices the popular dodge of hiding a companion's dagger and professing to find it by magic; and from an awkward situation he makes his escape in a suit of armor.

For the most part, Peele is the traditional picaro, merry, careless, without deep malice; yet he lacks the saving grace of the Spaniards, — the satire upon current abuses concealed beneath mere surface rogueries. In "The Puritan" (pr. 1607), once attributed to Shakespeare, Peele furnishes the character of George Pyeboard, and many of these tricks reappear.[1]

An earlier roguish fiction was the "XII. mery Jests of the wyddow Edyth," by Walter Smith, printed in 1573, and no doubt of anterior origin.[2] Had this been composed in prose instead of doggerel verse, it might have ranked as perhaps the first in time of English picaresque tales. Its rhymed preface is really a part of the anti-heroine's story, describing her parentage and her early life in the city of Exeter.

Her mother, at her father's death, implores her to devote every effort to acquiring the gentle art of deception, and, warning her to meddle with nothing pertaining to "good huswyfry," concludes with what is ever the rogue's philosophy, thus epitomized, —

> Daughter, make mery, whiles thou may,
> For this world wyll not last alway.

---

[1] E. g., *The Puritan*, Act iii, sc. 5, 6, the trick on the barber somewhat altered; Act i, sc. 4, the magic trick; Act ii, sc. 2, the inn trick. This pretense of paying the reckoning with others' money reappears in Rowlands's *Knave of Clubbes* (1610).

[2] Ames, Dibdin, and Herbert suggest 1525. Cf. Collier, vol. ii, p. 357.

So Edyth sets forth upon her career, and her jests consist of frequent marriages under false pretenses, usually on the promise of "great aboundance of gooddes" to accrue to the new husband. She is also adroit in deluding innkeepers and shopmen, sending her creditors to one another for payment, and once at least being guilty of a piece of pure mischief in leading a poor man to unthatch his house, on the pledge that she would cover it again with lead.

The stories, however crude and poor in wit, claim to describe actual occurrences in contemporary England.

Other jest-books celebrating individuals, like the famous "Pleasant Conceites of Old Hobson the Merry Londoner" (1607), were scarcely roguish, or like "Richard Tarltons Jests" (1611), were roguish chiefly in repartee.[1] Of those subject to Italian influence two of the best were "Tarltons Newes Ovt of Pvrgatory" (1589) and "The Cobler of Caunterburie" (1590). Both employed a framework, and the second professed to be written as an invective against the first. The author of "Tarltons Newes" explains that, withdrawing from the crowded playhouse to sleep beneath a tree in the fields, he was visited by Tarlton's ghost. The spirit described Purgatory, and related eight stories of those he saw there to account for their punishments. These narratives are picaresque in flavor, as were their Italian originals. Most of the eight come from Boccaccio, and it is noteworthy that his Angel Gabriel *novella*, later used to good purpose by Grimmelshausen, should have been included.

In "The Cobler of Caunterburie" the six tales are supposed to be told in a barge between Billingsgate and Gravesend, "imitating herein old Father Chaucer." The author is modest, however, and declares, "As there must be admitted no compare between a cup of Darby ale and a dish of durty water; So sir Ieffrey Chaucer is so hie aboue my reach, that I take *Noli*

[1] Their hero was Richard Tarlton, the clown, whose death in 1589 suggested the use of his name both here and in the *Newes Ovt of Pvrgatory*.

altum sapere, for a warning, and onely looke at him with honour and reuerence." The cobbler's stories are better than Tarlton's, being told with considerable verve, but they deal chiefly with cuckoldry. The second tale somewhat resembles an incident in Aleman.[1] For a smith in love with a cobbler's wife persuades her to pretend setting out on a journey. Then from a window an accomplice throws bloody water upon her, as if by accident, at which she is invited to enter and rest until her mother-in-law can be sent home for fresh apparel. The amorous smith in the meantime entertains her. This book belongs to the same category as the more popular "Westward for Smelts" (1620). A single story of the sort had earlier appeared as a "Ryght Pleasaunt and Merye Historie of the Mylner of Abyngton," found also in Boccaccio and in Chaucer, of whose "Reves Tale" it is a poor *rifacimento*. There was occasionally issued with it, too, the "Mery Gest How a Sergeaunt Wolde Lerne to be a Frere" (*c.* 1520), an anecdote ascribed to Sir Thomas More, telling of a constable who, failing of all other means of apprehending a debtor, disguised himself as a friar, only to be discovered and beaten.

Allied with "Tarltons Newes" and the "Cobler," as deriving its framework from Boccaccio, was "The Meeting of Gallants at an Ordinarie, or the Walkes in Powles" (1604). During the plague gallants promenade and converse in Paul's and then take refuge, not in the garden of Fiesole, but in an adjacent ordinary, "where the fatte host telles tales at the upper ende of the table." He is "a madde round knaue and a merrie one too; and if you chaunce to talk of fatte Sir Iohn Old-castle he wil tell you, he was his great Grand-father." He delights in his own stories, crying, "I have them at my tongue's end, my gallant bullyes of five and twenty, my dainty liberall landlords, I have

[1] Cf. *Guzman de Alfarache*, pt. i, cap. 2.

them for you." But the tales are only four in number and slight enough. One tells of a drunken fellow's falling asleep on a stall and being taken up by the pest-cart for a corpse. Another describes the similar predicament of a citizen who tumbled drunk from his horse in the country, and was avoided as a plague-sick Londoner. At last, a fire being kindled about him, he came to himself.

Collections of separate unconnected specimens of wit like the "Cambridge Jests" or the rival Oxford series, "Iests from the Vniversity" (1628), were increasingly frequent, the most picaresque in this kind being "Pasquils Iests, mixed with Mother Bunches Merriments" (1604).[1] Here tricks of French and English origin mingle, and the old farce "Maître Patelin" is refurbished. A woman wraps the cat in baby clothes, and throwing it into a moat when her tipsy husband comes home, leads him to plunge in after it. A Parisian beggar secures from a credulous second wife the best suit of her living husband, in order to furnish out her dead spouse in Paradise, and when the pursuing owner has been defrauded of his horse by the rogue, he returns to his wife, saying that he has merely lent the steed to the beggar for his Paradise journey. One of three rogues poses in the pillory while his companions pick the bystanders' pockets; and a wise countryman at Bartholomew Fair captures light-fingered brethren by providing his pockets with fish-hooks. It is noteworthy that several of these tricks reappear in the "Histoire Générale des Larrons" and in "The English Rogue." Perhaps the best of such is the story of "The Conni-catcher and the Priest of Paris." The rogue induces the priest to try on a surplice, and complaining that the holy man's money pouch is in the way, secures its removal, and presently disappears with it.

[1] *Pasquil* was reprinted in 1608, 1609, 1612, 1625, 1629, 1635, 1637, 1650 (?), and 1669. Cf. also John Ashton, *Humour, Wit, and Satire of the Seventeenth Century*, London, 1883.

To be noticed among jest-books, although not altogether of them, is Robert Armin's "Foole Vpon Foole, or, Six sortes of Sottes" (1605), reprinted as "A Nest of Ninnies" (1608). Armin was a pupil of Tarlton and an actor of comedy parts in Shakespeare's plays. Nash refers to him in the "Strange Newes." He wrote a drama, "The Two Maids of More-clacke," and a versified story called "The Italian Taylor and his Boy,"[1] both of which were published in 1609. His "Foole Vpon Foole" is chiefly interesting as indicating the position of the jester under Elizabeth, the tolerance and commendation he received in the hall and at court. A work of the Eulenspiegel type, its jests are not carried so far, and its anti-heroes remain less roguish than Till.

Six fools are here presented, and most of them are beguiled rather than beguiling. Jacke Oates, the flat fool, is a rascal, however, feigning himself ill in order to be allowed to stand by the kitchen fire, and stealing there a quince pie preparing for his master. He puts it under his doublet and runs away, but it burns him, and to cool it he springs into the castle moat. Here he eats his prize while up to the arm-pits in water. Jemy Camber, the fat fool, wagers a footman to run a race. The king orders fat Jemy to be given a sleeping potion, and to be laid close to the goal. On awaking, he rises and runs on as though nothing had happened, while the footman posted in the rear pretends to strain up the hill. Jemy for the rest of his life brags of his victory, and wishes all the footmen turned away that he may serve in their stead. "Foole Vpon Foole" may have been patterned upon a somewhat similar work printed the year before, entitled "Iacke of Dover, His Quest of Inquirie, or his Priuy Search for the Veriest Foole in England."

Later jest-books include the satirical "Merry Jests Concern-

[1] From Straparola, night xvii, *novella* 5.

ing Popes, Monkes, and Friers" (1617), by Rowland Willet, derived from the Italian through the French; Taylor the Water Poet's one hundred and thirteen jests in his "Wit and Mirth, Chargeably Collected Ovt of Tavernes and Ordinaries" (1629); with "A Banquet of Jeasts or Change of Cheare," which contains a reference to Shakespeare, and the somewhat allied "Tincker of Turvey" (1630).

In significance, however, the jest-books declined after the first quarter of the seventeenth century. Although their numbers knew no decrease, they grew more fragmentary, and failing to associate separate tricks with single personalities, departed from fiction. Moreover they lost originality, vapidly drawing either upon their predecessors or upon more ambitious picaresque literature, instead of contributing to it. Thus the "Tales and Jests of Hugh Peters" (1660), like the later "Universal Jester," and the "Nugæ Venales" of Richard Head, simply reproduced old tricks and witticisms. Humphrey Crouch's "England's Jests Refin'd" (1687) contains such venerable favorites as Boccaccio's story of the crane, and the trick of the Lazarillo-like test questions put by a nobleman to his chaplain concerning the compass of the world, the depth of the sea, and his thought at the moment, the chaplain having a cobbler disguised as himself answer the last by saying the nobleman thinks him the chaplain. The "Pleasant History of the Frolicksome Courtier and the Jovial Tincker" opens with the Christopher Sly trick of Shakespeare and of Edwards's "Comic Stories," and two episodes from the Spanish and one from the German emerge in the "History of Tom Long the Carrier." [1]

The "Merry Frolics, or the Comical Cheats of Swalpo, a

[1] In chapters iii and iv Guzman de Alfarache's bad omelette reappears, and his cooked ass becomes a colt; in chapter xii the shoe cheat derives from *Eulenspiegel* and *The English Rogue*.

Notorious Pickpocket," is a tissue of practical jokes culled from English sources.

At Bartholomew Fair Swalpo contrives to steal a broad-piece that he knows another is holding for safety in his mouth, by getting a small boy to fall and then accuse the other of having appropriated the piece he had dropped, — a trick from "The English Rogue" and the "Histoire Générale des Larrons." The former supplies still other cheats, as for example, Swalpo's stealing a gentleman's watch on a wager as he brushes from the victim's coat a quillful of lice he has hired a boy to blow there, and his depredations at an inn while pretending to the host to be the servant of a guest and to the guest to be the waiter.[1] Like Scoggin he steals a tankard by presenting a wife with a professed token from her husband; and his confederate, Roger the Clown, regains the token of pheasants by the same trick in turn.

Chap-books galore kept life in the old jests and circulated them among the barely literate who found delight in such masterpieces as "The Birth, Life, and Death of John Frank," being an account of "the pranks and jests he played though a meer fool;" the "Comical Transactions of Lothian Tom," "a collection of roguish exploits done by him both in Scotland and England;" and "The Witty and Entertaining Exploits of George Buchanan." One of the best known of the more extensive collections appeared in 1739 as "Joe Miller's Jests, or the Wit's Vade-Mecum." Miller was a comedian notoriously devoid of humor. After his death, a hack writer, Motley, and a cheap publisher, Read, appropriated his name for their facetious anthology as a crowning joke. Ever since, the name has been synonymous with all that its original possessor lacked. Chap-book editions of jests endured well into the nineteenth century, and "Joe Miller's Jests" is still reprinted; but the influential affiliation of such collections with the literature of roguery is wholly a thing of the past.

[1] This was in the *Histoire générale des larrons*, pt. i, ch. 24.

5. *Popular Tales*

At the close of the sixteenth century appeared a series of fictions distinct from the jest-books and legends, although somewhat allied to Robin Hood literature in celebrating heroes of the people. Thomas Deloney, "the balleting silke weaver," as Nash called him, deserves the credit of launching this genre, which differs from such a hero tale in low-life as Croce's "Vita di Bertoldo" in its larger use of realism. For Deloney gives his reader pictures of actual weavers and cobblers and their merry or heroic doings where the Italian had been content with rehabilitating *fabliaux*. Before attempting prose fiction, Deloney had written and collected ballads,[1] making an enemy among others of Kemp, the morris dancer, who called him "a jig monger." His novels, however, won him more friends than the ballads lost, and he became the tradesman's laureate. His "Gentle Craft" (licensed 1597) accounted itself "a most merry and pleasant history, not altogether unprofitable nor anyway hurtfull, very fitte to passe away the tediousness of the long winters evenings." It sang the praises of cobbling, and should be associated with Dekker's comedy of "The Shoemaker's Holiday" (1600). Deloney's "Pleasant History of Thomas of Reading," often reprinted as "The Six Worthy Yeomen of the West," hailed the achievements of half a dozen clothiers, without whose friendly aid it would seem King Henry I could scarcely have ruled; and "The Pleasant Historie of Iohn Winchcomb, in His yovnger yeares called Iack of Newbery" (licensed 1596), made famous a jolly broadcloth weaver of Berkshire. The latter is by far the most interesting of Deloney's creations, and his story is crisp and almost a fictional unit.

[1] His first was written in 1586 upon an execution in Lincoln's Inn Fields. A collection was issued at the same time, and another in 1607.

John Winchcomb rises in the world from common 'prentice to be master merchant, received at court with "Welcome to me, Jacke of Newberie, said the Queene, though a Clothier by trade, yet a Gentleman by condition, and a faithful subiect in heart." He duels in wit with the king's jester, Will Sommers, who is rudely tricked by Jacke's weaving maids. He dispenses justice in his own household like an Eastern cadi, and is ever ready to enjoy a jest whether at his own expense or another's. As a young fellow his fortune is made when the widow of his master casts favorable eyes upon him, despite the attentions to her of the tanner, the tailor, and the parson. Jacke is too honest to understand her hints, so she takes him to church, tells the priest she awaits the bridegroom, and after some tarrying declares that since the bridegroom delays she will marry Jacke instead. One quarrel they have, for, when he has objected in vain to his wife's staying abroad at night, and locks her out, she pretends to have lost her wedding ring, and then as he comes forth to aid in the search for it, she shuts the door on him. More amusing, however, is the revenge inflicted by Jacke's maids upon a certain "dame tittle, tattle, Gossip pintpot," whom in their lady's absence they get roaring drunk in a cellar. The prose here approximates the low-life dialogue of Shakespeare. Her "braines wext as mellow as a Pippin at Michaelmas, and so light, that sitting in the Cellar, she thought the world ran round." "I knew your Master a boy," she tells a fellow servant, "when he was cald Jacke of Newbery. I, Jacke, I knew him cald plaine Jacke: and your Mistris, now she is rich and I am poore, but its no matter, I knew her a draggle tayle girle, mark yee. . . . But heare you, my masters, though mistresse Winchcombe goe in her Hood, I am as good as she, I care not who tell it her: I spend not my husbands money in Cherries and Codlings, go too, go too, I know what I say well enough: I thanke God I am not drunke." The servant so apostrophized hires a clown to carry the sleeping gossip in a basket through the town and cry loudly, "Who knowes this woman, who?" all the way to her door, where her husband comes out saying, "Marry that doe I too well, God helpe me!"

"Iack of Newbery" was deservedly popular, and enjoyed no less than fifteen editions during the seventeenth century.

In Deloney's "Thomas of Reading" one of the six yeomen was Sir John Hawkwood, of whose life of adventure several separate versions appeared in the seventeenth century. His exploits are recorded in Holinshed; his birthplace was Hedingham, Essex; and he died an old man in 1394. From a tailor he became knight, transforming his needle to a sword, and his thimble to a shield, hence the title of the popular book devoted to him in 1615, "The Honourable Prentice, or this Taylor is a Man."[1] Hawkwood is accompanied on his travels by William an apprentice and Ralph a journeyman, and their prowess is exhibited against every enemy from wild boars to the Emperor of Fez.

No less valiant and more characteristic as a plebeian hero was George a Green, celebrated in a prose fiction, "The Pinder of Wakefield" (1632), and in many chap-books thereafter, but much earlier a figure in the ballads and on the stage.[2]

In Wakefield where George was keeper of the pound there was no pastime "worth a fiddlestick if George a Greene had not a hand in it, especially when any poore man was wronged, still honest George was ready for to right his cause." For all his altruism, George was a merry soul, boon comrade of Tom the Taberer, Cuthbert the Cobler, Stitch the Taylor, Tobit the Thresher, Miles the Miller, and Smug the Smith, in which alliterative company cudgels were sure to swing at the expense of the Kendall or Halifax men. Then they would all repair to "my host Bankes his house" to exchange jests and repartee over the nut-brown ale.

George was fond of bringing about amendment in his fellow townsmen by tricks, correcting a jealous husband by rigging up as the devil, assisting a youth to fight a duel by providing him a cat for a buckler against an adversary known to have a mortal antipathy to cats. The hero's greatest achievement, however, was his battle with Robin Hood through "almost a long summer's day," after which with Scarlet and Little

---

[1] Used in an edition of 1616 also; the book in 1668 became *The Honour of the Merchant-Taylors*, and was attributed to William Winstanley; the same title reappeared in an edition of 1687.

[2] A play, *George a Greene*, acted December, 1593; another, or the same, *The Pinner of Wakefield*, acted January, 1593–94, licensed 1595, surviving in an edition of 1599, "as it was sundry times acted by the seruants of the right Honourable the Earle of Sussex."

John they feasted together at my host Bankes's and then lived merrily in the woods.

A similar story was the "Life and Death of the Merry Divell of Edmunton" (1631), containing "the pleasant pranks of Smug the Smith, Sir John, and Mine Host about the stealing of venison," reprinted in 1657 and 1819, and accompanied by such chap-books as "King Edward Fourth and the Miller of Tamworth," the "History of the King and the Cobbler," or "The Pleasant History of the Miller of Mansfield," describing in verse the miller's meeting the king in Sherwood Forest. "I ghesse thee to be but some gentleman Thiefe," says he, and yet entertains his guest, who in requital invites the miller, his wife Ginny, and their son Dick to court.

Ballads of this popular stamp were common, but the genre in prose declined, and the rude popular hero became either despicable in license, or the dullest of jesters. Of the latter type was Witty William of Wiltshire, an account of whose "birth, life, education, and strange adventures, with his unmatchable cheats" was issued by Laurence Price (1674), or Phillips, "the famous Merry Andrew," who figures in "A Fairing for the Merrily Disposed" (1688). Here belong such worthies as Tom Tram of the West, son-in-law to Mother Winter, and the Unfortunate Hodge of the South, whose "New and Pleasant History" was penned by Humphrey Crouch, and Tom Ladle, who shows occasional gleams of wit, answering his catechism to the effect that now there are but nine commandments, since his mother and the barber have broken one. "The Pleasant History of Thomas Hickathrift" brings forward a hero of prodigious size, with double muscles like those of Daudet's Tartarin; Tom Long descends from the half-satirical "Bought Wit is Best, or Tom Long's Journey to London to Buy Wit" (1634); and such an old favorite as Deloney's "Gentle Craft" was abridged in chap-books like the "Pleasant and Princely History of the Gentle Craft," the "Princely History of Crispin and Crispianus," and the "Shoemaker's Glory." Most, however, became wretchedly coarse, as, for example, the "Merry Sadler of Walden," "Wanton Tom, or the Merry History of Tom Stitch the Taylor," and "Fun upon Fun, or the Comical Merry Tricks of Leper the Taylor."

Only the popular "Blind Beggar of Bethnal Green" remains fairly attractive. Here the hero, once a valiant soldier in France, turns beggar, learns canting, and at the mendicants' rendezvous in Whitechapel finds, "instead of a ragged Regiment of lame, blind, and dumb, a rout of jovial Dancers as gay as the Spring and as merry as the maids." Thereafter with dog and bell he goes singing, —

A beggar lives a merry life,
  And has both wealth and ease;
His days are free from care and strife,
  He does whate'er he please.

When his pretty daughter Betty is beloved by a knight, the blind beggar is able to count him out gold piece for gold piece as dowry.

6. *Satires and Characters*

Of slighter service to picaresque fiction in England than the jest-books and popular tales were the satires and characters. The former, indeed, contributed so little to the English romance of roguery that it remains differentiated in this respect from the entire Continental development. In the reign of King John, Wireker's "Speculum Stultorum" had presented the ass Brunellus founding a new religious order to combine all the easy-going features of the others. Lydgate's "Order of Fools" had described sixty-three vicious persons associated in a fraternity; but it was Alexander Barclay's "Shyp of Folys" (1508), translated from the German of Brandt, that established fool-literature in England.

The most roguish exemplar of this type was "Cocke Lorelles Bote" (*c.* 1510), which, adopting the idea of a company of anti-heroes embarked together upon a voyage, emphasized the knavishness of the crew, mingled cheating tradesmen with ecclesiastical rogues, and depicted them with a zest for detail and a sympathy with the whimsical and the outlawed that gave new meaning to the scheme. The voyage itself lost the severely moral character intended by Brandt, seeming to be conducted by merry Cock for sheer joy, and apparently being threatened by no reproof of disaster.

Brandt and the "Bote" inspired Skelton's "Bowge of Court," which included among the seven "subtyll persons" of its allegorical crew Harvy Hafter, the cunning thief. They influenced also Tarlton's "Horseload of Fools," Armin's "Nest of Ninnies," and more remotely such works as will here be noticed among the beggar-books, — Copland's "Hye Way to the Spyttel Hous," and Awdeley's "Fraternitye of Vacabondes." The fool-satires of Erasmus and Garzoni found English translators also, the "Praise of Folie" coming from the Latin in 1549, and the "Hospitall of Incvrable Fooles" coming from the Italian in 1600. Dedekind's "Grobianus" appeared in 1605 as "The Schoole of Slovenrie," and four years later it was paraphrased as "The Gvls Horne-booke," by Thomas Dekker, who already had rendered the "Quinze Joyes de Mariage" as "The Batchelars Banquet" (1603).

Native satirists, too, at the close of the sixteenth century, in verse of Latin inspiration chastised abuses, which were handled with even greater freedom upon the Cambridge stage in the Parnassus Plays; but such works contained slight picaresque matter. Richard West, in "The Court of Conscience, or Dick

Whippers Sessions" (1607), might bring before the bar cheats, thieves, bawds, and witches; W. Parkes might offer an over-moralized "Diable Boiteux" in his "Curtaine-Drawer of the World" (1612); and Thomas Brewer's "Knot of Fooles" (1624) might present

> Fools or knaves, or both I care not,
> Here they are; come laugh and spare not;

but English roguery refused, as a rule, to run in the channels of satire. If Richard Johnson exposed the dangers and deceits of the town in "Look on me London" (1613), and if the "Birth, Life, Death, Wil and Epitaph of Iack Pvffe Gentleman" (1642) pictured a man of fashion skipping his debts to France and returning to die in the Counter, such sketches tended in the main to affiliate with the character-books. The satires on religion, from John Phillips's "Don Juan Lamberto" to Butler's "Hudibras," and the satires upon women, from Joseph Swetnam's "Arraignment of Lewd, Idle, Froward and Inconstant Women," to the anonymous "Look Ere You Leap," were little concerned with roguery. In the attacks upon usurers, however, especially in such a pamphlet as Thomas Lodge's "Alarum against Vsurers" (1584), there was matter that could contribute to full-fledged fiction in Chettle's "Piers Plainnes." Literary satires like Samuel Holland's "Don Zara del Fogo" (1656) [1] and "The Essex Champion, or the Famous History of Sir Billy of Billerecay and his Squire Ricardo" (*c.* 1683), both inspired by "Don Quixote," were of small consequence, although the latter is notable for the picaresque books it mentions as composing the library of the Essex knight. The curate who burns them remarks disapprovingly the absence of those of the more refined sort, "the Illustrious Bassa, Grand Cyrus, Astrea,

[1] Reprinted as *Romancio-Mastix, or a Romance of Romances* (1660) and as *The Spaniard* (1719).

Polexander, . . . Clelia, Cassandra, Cleopatra, Pharamond, Iphigenis and some others." Precisely such heroic fictions, however, were satirized in the burlesque "Zelinda" (1678), while Buckingham, Carey, and Fielding more memorably assailed stage heroism.

It was through Fielding, indeed, that satire entered the English romance of roguery, which before his day had been peculiarly devoid of it. Swift, though he possessed the gift of picaresque realism, never adopted the picaresque form, but preferred for his masterpiece the slightly allied imaginary journey of Lucian, Rabelais, and Cyrano de Bergerac. Yet Swift suggested to Gay the theme of his roguish "Beggar's Opera," and Fielding's "Jonathan Wild" owes a debt to "Gulliver's Travels" for something of its ironic spirit. If Fielding drew away presently from sheer satire to the novel proper and allowed humor to replace irony, Charles Johnstone continued in his romances of roguery the satiric tradition which Thackeray was to carry to perfection in "Barry Lyndon."

A more immediate and valuable contribution to fiction was made by the characters. Those of Theophrastus were done into Latin by Casaubon in 1592, and into English by Healey in 1616. Eight years before the latter date, Joseph Hall had issued the first considerable English collection as "Characters of Virtues and Vices." A host of such essays followed. At first they dealt chiefly with types of the ethical, setting the moral over against the immoral as in Nicholas Breton's "The Good and the Badde" (1616). Then they proceeded to anatomize things or places such as taverns, prisons, coffee-houses, or a whole city. Presently accounts applying more widely to nations became popular, while professional types were set forth either in collections like the "Micrologia" (1629), and "A True Character of Sundry Trades and Callings" (1670), or in single essays.

In characters of political and religious types satire was frequent, although hypocrisy was the worst vice railed at. It was the ethical, local, and professional characters that most nearly approached the literature of roguery. The ethical afforded a rare list of vices and the vicious to be vitalized by the novel. The characters of place gave scope to picturesque realism in describing the haunts of rogues. Thus, Geoffrey Mynshul's "Essayes and Characters of a Prison and Prisoners" (1618) dissected a jail and its government in the spirit of the beggar-books; and Bridewell, the Counters, Newgate, and Smithfield were drawn to the life in Donald Lupton's "London and the Countrey Carbonadoed" (1632). Prisons were also celebrated in the collection that bore the name of Sir Thomas Overbury (1614), by Gayton in characters contained in his "Wil Bagnal's Ghost" (1655), and by the "Twelve Ingenious Characters" of 1686. Taverns were portrayed in the latter work and separately in 1675, while coffee-houses were described in 1668 and in 1673.

It was the professional character, however, that contributed most to picaresque literature. This was perhaps natural, since the romance of roguery in Spain had emerged from satire upon professions and estates. Such beggar-books as Awdeley's "Fraternitye of Vacabondes" (1561) and Harman's "Caueat" (1567), which have been regarded as precursors of character-writing in England, dealt with the rascals they described according to professional distinctions, and a century later a whole group of such characters were separately issued. In the single year, 1675, for example, appeared the "Holborn Hector," describing "a profane, debauched gentleman;" the "Character of a Solicitor," noticing "the tricks and quillets of a pettifogger, with his manifold cheats and knaveries, extortions and other villanies;" and characters of "An Informer," "A Tally Man,"

"A Pawn Broker," "An Ape Gentlewoman," "An Exchange Wench," "A Pilfering Tailor," "A Town Gallant," and "A Town Miss." The last was replied to that year also in "The Town Miss's Declaration and Apology;" while in "News from Covent Garden" the gallant whose life had been declared to be a farce acted in three scenes — the ordinary, the playhouse, and the tavern — received satiric vindication. As early as 1615, in John Stephens's "Essayes and Characters, Ironicall and Instructive," gamesters, players, and tapsters were sketched along with a begging scholar, merely "an artificiall vagabond whose helpe extends farre and neere to fugitive Raga-muffins, under the signe of impotent soldiers or wandring Abraham-men." The Overbury "Characters" described a tinker who in mending one hole had rather make three than want work, and whose companion is "some foule sunne-burnt Queane, that since the terrible statute recanted gypsisme, and is termed pedleresse." Here too is the canting rogue, begot under a hedge, refusing to beg out of his appointed limit, and paying custom faithfully to the grand rogue. The professional characters, after exposing bailiffs, fops, horse-coursers, and what not, reached the eighteenth century in the "True Characters," describing "a deceitful pettifogger, vulgarly called attorney, a know-all astrological quack, or feigned physician, and a female hypocrite, or devil in disguise."

In order to develop realistic fiction from such essays, it was only necessary to render their general statements specific and to set their personages in action. The link between the characters and the novel was supplied by Addison, but the bearing of characters upon the romance of roguery is especially apparent in the case of direct borrowings by the latter from the former. Francis Kirkman in the Second Part of "The English Rogue" took over the "Character of a Pilfering Tailor" to describe one of the masters served by a picaro;[1] Richard Head in his First Part had given the "Character of a Bottle of Canary" and the "Character of an Hector or Trepan,"[2] and in his "Proteus Redivivus" he included many characters dependent upon previous essays. Here were described the wheedles of a town-shift in a coffee-house, ordinary, theatre, inn, on the road, with the watch, and in his lodgings; the wheedles of a quackling, astrological doctor, those of a self-edifying non-conformist, a country-attorney, a pettifogger, a catchpole or tenter-hook, and the miseries and wheedles of a prison.

An early character-book, "The Man in the Moone telling Strange Fortunes" (1609), gave characters through the ingenious device of a satirical philosopher setting up as a fortune-teller, and presenting to his patrons lively portraits of themselves. This scheme was later adopted in "The Wandering Jew telling Fortunes to Englishmen" (1649), where among others the serving man, the roaring boy, the thief, and the hangman received their due. More than a century afterwards Smollett in "Peregrine Pickle" had his anti-hero and a picaresque misanthrope engage in a similar fortune-telling venture in order to present a list of such characters as the clergyman, the usurer, the old man, and the poet.[3] So late as 1830, ten picaresque characters are given in the lucubrations of Tomlinson, the philosophic rogue of Bulwer's "Paul Clifford."

Since other volumes of this series are to deal with character-books and satire, it is enough to have indicated here the nature of their influence upon the spirit and technique of realistic writing. It is evident that, with the fairly honest plebeian hero established in fiction by the popular tales, and with a wide

[1] *The English Rogue*, pt. ii, ch. 12.
[2] *Ibid.*, pt. i, chs. 11, 12.
[3] *Peregrine Pickle*, chs. lxxxii, lxxxiii.

variety of cheats and a roguish anti-hero provided by the jest-books and legends, sufficient materials were at hand for the evolution of an English romance of roguery. But in the mean-time two other types had rendered peculiarly rich the native elements of picaresque literature in England. Both were de-voted to the study of low-life. One was the anatomy of roguery, which recorded its observations of vagabond manners statically like the characters. The other was the criminal biography, which recorded its observations dynamically in recounting the lives of rogues of reality.

BIBLIOGRAPHY

CHAPTER II

1

The legal and historical aspects of early English roguery are best presented in C. J. Ribton-Turner's *A History of Vagrants and Vagrancy and Beggars and Begging* (London, 1887) and Sir George Nicholls's *History of the English Poor Law* (new ed., N. Y., 1898, 2 vols.); the literary aspects are noticed in J. J. Jusserand's *English Wayfaring Life in the Middle Ages* (trans. by L. T. Smith, London, 1892, 4th ed.), his *Literary History of the English People* (N. Y., 1895, vol. i), B. ten Brink's *History of English Literature* (trans. by H. M. Kennedy, W. C. Robinson, Dora Schmitz, London, 1895–96), and Henry Morley's *English Writers* (London, 1887–95, 11 vols.). Volume iii of *Chaucer's Complete Works*, edited by W. W. Skeat (Oxford, 1894, 6 vols.), and the *Originals and Analogues of the . . . Canterbury Tales*, edited by F. J. Furnivall, Edmund Brock, and W. A. Clouston (London, 1872–87, *Chaucer Soc. Publ.*, 2d series, vii, x, xv, xx, xxii), point out the foreign sources and analogues of Chaucer's tales. Further sources and analogues of the *Milleres Tale* are considered in *Anglia*, by R. Köhler (i, 38 ff., 186 ff.; ii, 135 ff.); by H. Varnhagen (*Anzeiger*, vii, 81 ff.); by L. Proescholdt (vii, 117 ff.); by L. Fränkel (xvi, 261 ff.); and in the *Zeitschr. f. vergl. litteraturgeschichte*, by E. Kölbing (xii, 448 ff.; xiii, 112). A Swiss analogue of the *Freres Tale* is noted in *Anglia*, by F. Vetter (*Beiblatt*, xiii, 180 ff.). The *Reves Tale* is especially studied by Hermann Varnhagen in *Die Erzählung von der Wiege* (*Englische Studien*, 1885–86, ix). The *Tale of Beryn*, written by a Canterbury monk shortly after Chaucer's death, was first printed in 1721 in Urry's edition of Chaucer. Its Prologue, recounting the doings of the pilgrims during their stay at Canterbury, is rather roguish, and the tale itself in the wit of the cripple, Geffrey, resembles incidents in the *Gesta romanorum* and in *Eulenspiegel*. It is drawn from *L'histoire du Chevalier Berinus*, an outline of which, and of Persian, Indian, and Arabian variants, is given by W. A. Clouston (*Chaucer Soc. Publ.*, 2d series, xxiv, 1887). *Beryn* is edited by F. J. Furnivall and Walter G. Stone (*Chaucer Soc. Publ.*, 2d series, xvii, 1876). Cf. also Dunlop (*op. cit.*, vol. i, pp. 346 ff.). H. S. Ward's *Canterbury Pilgrimages* (London, 1904) and *Chaucer's England*, by Matthew Browne [W. B. Rands], (London, 1862, 2 vols.), consider social conditions of the time, and these are further exhibited in K. E. Günther's *Englisches Leben im vierzehnten Jahrhundert dargestellt nach The Vision of William Concerning Piers the Plowman* (Leipzig, 1889) and in J. J. Jusserand's *Piers Plowman* (N. Y., 1894). Skeat has supplemented his edition of Langland (London, 1867–85, 5 vols.) with a modern English version of the *Vision* (London, 1905).

2

The drama before Shakespeare receives attention in A. W. Ward's *History of English Dramatic Literature* (London, 1899, vol. i), J. P. Collier's *History of English Dramatic Poetry* (London, 1831, vol. i), J. A. Symonds's *Shakspere's Predecessors in the English Drama* (London, 1884), E. K. Chambers's *Mediaeval Stage* (Oxford, 1903, 2 vols.), A. W. Pollard's *English Miracle Plays, Moralities, and Interludes* (Oxford, 1904, 4th ed.), and Thomas Wright's *Early Mysteries and Latin Poems of the Twelfth and Thirteenth Centuries* (London, 1838). Texts are presented in J. S. Stevenson's *Towneley Mysteries* (*Surtees Soc.*, 1836), A. W. Pollard's *Towneley Plays* (*Early English Text Soc.*, 1897), Lucy Toulmin Smith's *York Plays* (Oxford, 1885), Thomas Wright's *Chester Mysteries* (*Shakespeare Soc.*, 1843–47), Hermann Deimling's *Chester Plays* (*Early English Text Soc.*, 1892), and J. O. Halliwell's *Ludus Coventriae* (*Shakespeare Soc.*, 1841). A further bibliography of this subject will be found in K. L. Bates's *English Religious Drama* (N. Y., 1893). Dodsley's *Old Plays* (4th ed. by W. C. Hazlitt, London, 1874) contains the later pieces. The best special studies bearing on roguery in the early drama are L. W. Cushman's *The Devil and the Vice in English Dramatic Literature before Shakespeare* (Morsbach's *Studien zur Engl. Philol.*, vi, Halle, 1900) and A. S. W. Rosenbach's *Influence of the Celestina in the Early English Drama* (*Jahrbuch d. deut. Shakespeare Gesellsch.*, Jahr. 39, pp. 43–61, Berlin, 1903).

3

On Robin Hood, see the Introduction to Hales and Furnivall's edition of the *Percy Folio MS.* (London, 1867), Thomas Wright's *Essays on Subjects Connected with the Literature, Popular Superstitions, and History of England in the Middle Ages* (London, 1846, 2 vols.), the Rev. Joseph Hunter's *Critical and Historical Tracts* (London, 1852, iv), and especially Francis J. Child's discussion in his *English and Scottish Popular Ballads* (Boston, 1888). The best summary of the subject is Sidney Lee's article in the *Dict. of Nat. Biography* (vol. xxvii). W. W. Campbell's *Historical Sketch of Robin Hood and Captain Kidd* (N. Y., 1853) is fanciful. The ballads are considered in Lorenz Hahner's *Kulturhistorisches im Englischen Volkslied* (Freiburg, 1892).

Friar Rush and *Robin Goodfellow* are discussed in C. H. Herford's invaluable *Literary Relations between England and Germany in the Sixteenth Century* (Cambridge, 1886). The Danish *Broder Russes Historie* (1555) is edited by Brunn (Copenhagen, 1868), and the Low German *Von Bruoder Rauschen* appears in editions by Ferdinand Wolf and Stephan Endlicher (Wien, 1835), and in Bobertag's *Narrenbuch* (1885). An Icelandic analogue was published by H. Gering (*Islendzk Æventýri*, 1882, xxvi, i, 104 ff.). The legend is studied by O. Schade (*Weimarisches Jahrbuch*, 1856, v, 357 ff.), by H. Anz (*Euphorion*, 1897, iv, 756 ff.), and by G. L. Kittredge with reference to Milton's use of "the Friar's lantern" (*Publ. of Mod. Lang. Ass. of America*, 1900, xv, 4, 415 ff.). The last article is especially rich in bibliographical notes. *The Historie of Frier Rvsh* was reprinted by Harding and Wright (London, 1810), and appears in William J. Thoms's *Early English Prose Romances* (London, 1858), along with *Robert the Deuyll*, *Thomas of Reading*, a *Robin Hood* romance of 1678, and the *Pinner of Wakefield.* With these it figures also in Henry Morley's *Early Prose Romances* (Carisbrooke Library, 1889). *Robin Goodfellow* was reprinted by J. P. Collier from the edition of 1628 (*Percy Soc. Publ.*, ii, 1840).

4

For jesters and jest-books, consult Dr. J. Doran's *History of Court Fools* (London, 1858), W. C. Hazlitt's standard *Shakespeare Jest Books* (London, 1864, 3 vols.), J. P. Collier's *Fools and Jesters, with a Reprint of Robert Armin's Nest of Ninnies* (*Shakespeare Soc.*, 1842), *Tarlton's Jests*, reprinted by J. O. Halliwell (London, 1844), John Ashton's *Humour, Wit, and Satire of the Seventeenth Century* (London, 1883), A. B. Grosart's reprint of Armin's *Foole vpon Foole* (London, 1880), Thomas Wright's reprint of *Jack of Dover* (*Percy Soc.*

Publ., vii), J. O. Halliwell's reprint of the *Meeting of Gallants at an Ordinarie* (*Percy Soc. Publ.*, v), and F. W. D. Brie's *Eulenspiegel in England* (Berlin, 1903, *Palaestra*, xxvii).

5

The popular literature is discussed in Richard Sievers's *Thomas Deloney, eine Studie über Balladen-litteratur der Shakspere-Zeit, nebst Neudruck von Deloney's Roman Jack of Newbury* (Berlin, 1904, *Palaestra*, xxxvi), Alexis F. Lange's *Deloney's Gentle Craft* (Berlin, 1903, *Palaestra*, xviii), J. O. Halliwell's *Catalogue of Chap-Books, Garlands, and Popular Histories* (London, 1849), John Ashton's *Chap-Books of the Eighteenth Century* (London, 1882), Edwin Pearson's *Banbury Chap-Books* (London, 1890), Charles A. Federer's *Yorkshire Chap-Books* (London, 1889), and *John Cheap the Chapman's Library: the Scottish Chap Literature of the Last Century Classified* (Glasgow, 1877–78, 3 vols.). J. O. Halliwell reprinted *The History of John Winchcomb* in 1859.

6

The development of English satire is studied by C. H. Herford (*op. cit.*) in R. M. Alden's *Rise of Formal Satire in England under Classical Influence* (Philadelphia, 1899), and in Ernst Rühl's *Grobianus in England, nebst Neudruck der ersten Uebersetzung* (Berlin, 1904, *Palaestra*, xxxviii).

Character-books are treated in J. O. Halliwell's *Books of Characters* (London, 1857), Earle's *Microcosmography* (edited by Dr. Bliss, London, 1811), and Henry Morley's *Character Writing of the Seventeenth Century* (London, 1891). Edward Chauncey Baldwin has surveyed aspects of the subject in several articles: *The Relation of the English Character to its Greek Prototype* and *The Relation of the Seventeenth Century Character to the Periodical Essay* (*Publ. of the Mod. Lang. Ass. of America*, 1903, xviii, and 1904, xix), and *Character Books of the Seventeenth Century in Relation to the Development of the Novel* (*Western Reserve Bulletin*, Oct., 1900). The whole subject will be exhaustively discussed by Dr. C. N. Greenough in his forthcoming volume on character-writing in the present series.

CHAPTER III

THE ANATOMIES OF ROGUERY

1. *Beggar-Books*

S the rogue stands low in the social scale, so much of the literature devoted to him ranks low as art. This is notably true of two types,—the criminal biography and the anatomy of roguery; yet both deserve attention because of their intrinsic significance, and because they have hitherto been so little understood. The anatomy of roguery may be defined as an essay descriptive of the grades, cheats, or manners of professional criminals. It embraces such works as the beggar-books of Awdeley and Harman; the conny-catching pamphlets of Greene, Dekker, and Rowlands; the prison tracts of Hutton, Fennor, and Mynshul; the later discoveries of criminal mysteries by the repentant; canting lexicons and scoundrel verse; and modern sociological studies of crime.

The English anatomies of roguery transcend in number, interest, and importance those of the Continent. Germany may claim the earliest in the "Liber Vagatorum," France the most artistic in "La Vie Genereuse," Spain the most extensive in the "Desordenada Codicia," and Italy the most succinct in "Il Vagabondo;" but the English precede any save the German, and surpass all others in graphic detail.

The first attempt to chronicle picaresque manners and speech in England was due to the printer, Robert Copland. His "Hye Way to the Spyttel Hous" (pr. after 1535) described in more than a thousand lines of verse the vagrants and impostors whose manner of life leads them to St. Bartholomew's Hospital. The porter of this institution, within whose porch Copland has taken refuge during a shower, vouchsafes much curious information regarding the losels, mighty beggars and vagabonds, the mychers, hedge creepers, fylloks, and luskes that besiege the gate for alms. He repeats their canting phrases, notes the tricks of pretended soldiers, idle scholars, and wandering quacks, relates the cheat practiced by a feigned oriental physician upon a hostess, and devotes the latter half of the poem to an elaborate classification of the types of folly that result in beggary. This portion of the "Hye Way" is directly descended from the German fool-satires.

Of similar descent, but more accurate in its knowledge of the orders actually established among rogues, was the "Fraternitye of Vacabondes, as wel of ruflying Vacabondes, as of beggerly, of women as of men, of Gyrles as of Boyes, with their proper names and qualities" (1561). This was a full-fledged beggar-book, issued by a printer of Little Britain, John Awdeley, known also as Sampson Awdeley, or Awdelay. In doggerel stanzas he explained that a vagabond had revealed these secrets when assured that his name should be withheld.

> But if my fellowes do know (sayd he)
> That thus I dyd, they would kyll me.

The pamphlet falls into three parts: the first describing nineteen varieties of rogues from the Abraham Man to the Patriarke Co; the second treating of "The Company of Cousoners and Shifters;" the third, more especially suggested by the fool-satires and "Cocke Lorelles Bote," naming twenty-five orders of knaves whose titles are self-explanatory, as Rince Pytcher, a servant who will take his master's drink, and Commitour of Tidinges, a tale-bearer.

The first part of the "Fraternitye" is of value as reflecting actual low-life. It employs the cant and sets forth the hierarchy of vagabonds as it reappears persistently through the anatomies, fiction, and the drama. Here the Abraham Man feigns madness, calling himself Tom of Bedlam and poor Tom, like Edgar in "Lear." [1] The Ruffeler pretends to be a decayed soldier; the Whipiacke begs as a shipwrecked sailor; the Prygman steals horses; the Frater begs for hospitals; the Quire Bird rejoices in release from jail; and the Vpright Man rules the crew. Curtalls are short-cloaked rogues; Palliards raise blisters on their legs; Irish Toyles carry laces and pins to peddle while stealing; Jarkmen forge seals; Swygmen bear packs on their backs; Washmen are Palliards with genuine sores; and Tinkards feign tinkering to steal. Wylde Roges are those born to roguery; Kitchin Coes are little boys employed to creep in at windows and cellar doors; Kitchin Mortes carry infants to be stuck with pins that their cries may excite pity; Doxies are girls who consort with any of the rabble; and the Patriarke Co is their hedge priest.

The "Fraternitye's" second part, however, transcends in interest the mere catalogue of the first and third parts, for here three cheats are described in detail; the first that of the Curtesy Man, a genteel beggar who threatens and then robs if refused; the second that of the Fingerer, who posing as a rustic loses at cards to associates, and suddenly changes his game in order to fleece the young gallant persuaded to play; and the third that of the Ring-faller, who dropping a gilded copper ring pretends to spy it at the same moment as his victim, but consents to sell or to game for it.

Awdeley's beggar-book suggested to Thomas Harman the plan of his more elaborate "Caueat or Warening, For commen Cvrsetors Vvlgarely Called Vagabones," first printed in 1566.[2] Harman was a country gentleman of Crayford in Kent. Being detained at home through illness, he amused himself by con-

[1] Cf. *Mad Tom a Bedlam's Desires of Peace* (1648) and contemporary ballads like *Bess of Bedlam's Garland* and *Mad Tom's Garland*.

[2] Or early in 1567; see below, p. 136. Harman's usage of the term "Caveat" was generally adopted. Cf. a *Caveat for all men to Beware of False Coseners* (1579); *Beware of Pick-Purses, or a Caveat for Sicke Folkes to take Heed of Unlearned Philistines* (1605); a *Caveat for Knaves* (1648); and a *Caveat for Cutpurses*, a broadside, n. d.

versing with the rogues who besought him for charity, until by "fayre flatteringe words, money, and good chere" he got them to unbosom their secrets. Though he promised never to discover what they showed him, he appears to have had no scruple in breaking faith, and is even curious to know how they will regard his work. "Now, methinketh, I se how these peuysh, peruerse, and pestilent people begyn to freat, fume, and sweare, and stare at this my booke." He hopes, however, to "do them more good than they could haue deuised for themselues." [1]

Harman's "Caueat" is a collection of anecdotes based upon hearsay or experience and clustered about a list of twenty-three criminal orders. These repeat most of Awdeley's and add several others; the Hoker or Angglear who carries a hooked staff with which he fishes for booty; the Counterfet-Cranke who with soap in his mouth feigns fits; the Dummerar who doubling back his tongue pretends to be dumb; and the Demaunder for Glymmer who tells a tale of having been burnt out of house and home. Among women are added Bawdy Baskets who peddle; Autem Morts, or married mothers, "autem" signifying church; Walking Morts, or mothers not married; and Dells, or virgins.

Most are treated at length and with excellent picaresque spirit. Thus in the account of two "Roges" of East Kent who, meeting at an alehouse, profess to the hostess to be twin nephews and godsons of the parson, there is evinced a good deal of merriment. Leaving the inn at night on the pretext of going to lodge with their godfather, they make a pitiful noise beneath his window, and, when the old gentleman stretches his

---

[1] In his dedicatory epistle to the Lady Elizabeth, Countess of Shrewsbury, Harman explains that by "Cursetors" he means runners or rangers about the country. He apologizes for his plain style, saying, "Eloquence haue I none. I neuer was acquainted with the Muses; I neuer tasted of Helycon."

hand through the mullion to give them alms, they clap upon it a horse-lock that holds him fast. Then they assure him they will smite off his arm if he will not give them all, and they release him only on the further condition that next day he drink twelve pence worth at the alehouse and thank the hostess for her kindness to them. The scene next day, when the hostess inquires after the parson's nephews, may be imagined. "'My neuewes,' quoth this parson; 'I trowe thou art mad.'" But he soon understands and cries resignedly, "'Fill in and geue me some meat; for they made me sweare and promise them faithfully that I should drinke xii. pence with you this day.' 'What! did they?' quoth she; 'now, by the mary masse, they be mery knaues,'" and she advises the parson to be ruled by her. "'By my troth, neuer speake more of it: when they shal vnderstand of it in the parish, they wyll but laugh you to skorne.'"

Another amusing story is told of a Glimmering Mort beloved by the unthrifty son of an innkeeping widow. He steals a silver whistle from his mother as a present for this woman, and the mother sends a hostler to recover it. The hostler, however, is assaulted by an Upright Man and his own purse is nabbed. When he comes home he can only moan "Your whystell, your whistel;" at which, "'Why, fole,' quoth his mystrisse, 'take no care for that, for I doe not greatly waye it; it was worth but three shyllinges foure pens.'"

Still another victim, an old man who had been up to London to sell farm produce, falls in with a Ruffler, who robs him of his gains and also of an angel-piece that his wife had forgotten to take from his purse. He has confessed to having only the other sum, and when the Ruffler comes upon the angel he exclaims, "What an old knaue and a false knaue haue we here! . . . oure Lorde haue mercy on us, wyll this worlde neuer be better?"

These are the only instances of humor in the tract, and when Harman describes the one good deed of a Walking Mort in warning a wife of her unfaithful husband, or pictures Nycholas Genings and his begging wiles, it is with the gravity of a sociologist. To Genings is given much space, and in the 1573 edition of the "Caueat" his adventures are extended to the point of his being pilloried, and whipped through London at the cart's tail.

The last section of Harman's "bolde Beggars booke" presents "The Names of the Vpright Men, Roges, and Pallyards . . . lyuinge nowe at this present," in an array of two hundred and fifty, the owners of some of them being slightly described, as "Thomas Graye, his toes be gonne," and "Wylliam Gynkes, with a whyte bearde, a lusty and stronge man; he runneth about the countrey to seeke worke, with a byg boy, his sonne, carying his toles as a dawber or playsterer, but lytle worke serueth him." Then follows "the leud, lousey language of these lewtering Luskes and lasy Lorrels," and a dialogue in cant between an Vpright Man and a Roge. This language "began but within these XXX yeeres, lytle above," says Harman, "and . . . the first inuentor therof was hanged." [1]

There can be no doubt that Awdeley and Harman were influenced by the German "Liber Vagatorum." The aim and scope of their beggar-books and the threefold arrangement of material are similar, and although the catalogued orders do not correspond so precisely with the German as do those of "Il Vagabondo," yet the number of classes remains about the same and many tricks are identical.

Harman's work furnished an account of the vagabond hierarchy to the Rev. William Harrison, whose contribution to Holinshed's "Chronicles," entitled a "Description of England," suggests measures of social reform.[2] Harman's experiments in the canting speech inspired many imitators, and picaresque drama and fiction long felt his influence. This was exerted most directly, however, upon Robert Greene, who was destined to modify and perpetuate the beggar-book type in his conny-catching pamphlets.

[1] Harrison, in 1577, makes the same statement; Head, in 1665 (*The English Rogue*, pt. i, ch. 5), declares that the inventor was hanged "fourscore years since."

[2] Harrison, bk. iii, ch. 5 (1577); bk. ii, ch. 10 (1586).

2. *Conny-Catching Pamphlets*

Greene the Bohemian is one of the few Englishmen of standing in letters who furthered the development of the romance of roguery prior to the eighteenth century. Yet until within two years of his death he had won fame in fiction only as a love-romancer in the tradition of Lyly. From such romantic stories as "Mamillia," "Arbasto," "Euphues, his Censure to Philautus," and the delicate "Pandosto," — source of Shakespeare's "Winter's Tale," — Greene turned to realistic conny-catching pamphlets and repentances. The change came in 1590, when he began to show signs of contrition for the wild life he had led; and this frame of mind continuing until his death in September, 1592, he filled the interval by composing a numerous series of picaresque writings. These were often brief and careless, but the knowledge of low-life they conveyed was a fund upon which pamphleteers, dramatists, and story-tellers were for long to draw. Their moral purpose is unquestionable, although Greene took delight in portraying the underworld he had come to know so well. His earnestness, increasing toward the end, culminated in the appalling "Repentance of Robert Greene, Maister of Artes" (1592), which has been thought a forgery or the work of Luke Hutton, but is certainly genuine, and explains and vouches for many facts detailed in Greene's other rogue writings.

The first of the repentant tracts was the "Mourning Garment" (1590), in which Greene speaks of himself as resembling Nineveh suddenly awakened to consciousness of sin by Jonah. The tract pictures the younger son of a rabbi going forth to see the world, and, despite the warnings of shepherds, despoiled by three women, companions in beauty and vice. He is pitied by the shepherds, and finally returns, like the Prodigal

Son, to be better welcomed by the rabbi than he could have hoped. The scene on the banks of the Euphrates strangely mixes the pastoral with the picaresque.

Greene's "Neuer too late" (1590) comes closer to the literature of roguery. Francisco, an Italian adventurer, relates his wanderings, his marriage, his desertion of his wife for a courtesan who robbed him, his life with actors and as a dramatic poet, and his reconciliation with his wife. Except for this last incident, most of the account was autobiographic, and it fairly parallels the later "Groatsworth of Wit." The "Farewell to Follie" (1591), whose title has been construed to mean a farewell to love tales, is patterned on Italian *novelle*, stories being told by a party of disputants to illustrate passions and vices; but as the moral obtrudes in all, the title seems as likely to indicate a valedictory to Greene's old way of life.[1]

The "Groatsworth of Wit, bought with a Million of Repentance" (1592), was edited by Chettle, and enjoyed several reprintings. Its interest is lessened by the lack of humor, and a tendency to verge upon villainy.

A usurer has two sons, Lucanio and Roberto. To the first he leaves all his property, to the second only a groat, and instructions to buy with it wit. The incensed Roberto secures the aid of Lamilia, a cunning courtesan, to fleece his brother; but, disagreeing with Roberto as to her share of the profits, she reveals the plot to Lucanio, and the discomfited rogue is turned out of doors. He frequents ill company, becomes apt for every rascality, and learns the current tricks at cards and dice, — "the legerdemaine of nips, foysters, conni-catchers, crosbyters, lifts, high lawyers, and all the rabble of that uncleane generation of vipers." His brother in the interval has met a bad end, and Roberto now seems about to follow suit, when he comes upon his one groat and cries out, "O now it is too late, too late to buy witte with thee." Ill unto death, he

[1] Henry Morley (*English Writers*, vol. x, p. 95) points out that Greene evidently intended each of the seven personages here to illustrate one of the seven deadly sins. He got no further than Pride, Lust, and Gluttony.

determines to sell to careless youth what he himself forgot to buy. At this point Greene emerges in his own person, speaking of Roberto's life as in most parts agreeing with his own, urging Marlowe to turn from his atheism, and Nash, that young Juvenal and sweet boy, to "get not many enemies by bitter words." Then after the classic reference to Shakespeare with his "Tygers heart wrapt in a Players hide," and "in his owne conceit the onely Shake-scene in a countrie," Greene concludes with a salvo of proverbs and the fable of the grasshopper and the ant.

In the meantime the first of Greene's conny-catching pamphlets proper had appeared, published as "A Notable Discouery of Coosnage," in 1591, with a second edition the subsequent year. Conny, cony, conie, or coney was the cant term applied to the silly victim of London rogues. Greene, if he had not assisted in the catching of connies, must have witnessed the sport a hundred times, and in his early days he may himself have suffered from conny-catchers. Now he undertook to describe the wiles employed against the innocent, that forewarned might make forearmed.

He begins by explaining the forerunner of the modern confidence game, dignified under the name of Barnard's Law. Five are required to put it into execution, including the victim, who is found by the Taker, and then met by the Verser. The Taker pretends to know the rustic, and, learning his name, tells it to the Verser, who calls him by it and invites him to an inn. The Barnard is the chief card player, who, pretending to be drunk, leads the victim into the game. The Rutter is a blusterer who fights with the others, so that when the booty is won all can get away.

Greene further describes the familiar trick of crosbiting. Here a gallant is lured to a safe place, and his innamorata's pretended husband enters to demand financial reparation. A vocabulary of "words of art vsed in effecting these base villanies" and the terms descriptive of seven laws or cheats are added, together with the so-called "cheating law." Then follows "A Pleasant Discovery Of the coosenage of Colliars," devoted to exposing the London colliers, who go out of town early in the mornings to buy sacks of coal from country members of the fraternity, and return to empty these into short-weight sacks of their own with choice coals on top.

The reception of this tract was favorable, and Greene in the "Second part of Conny-catching" (1591) is proud of his achievement. The rogues have vowed to cut off his right hand, but he laughs at them. "I liue still, and I liue to display their villanies." When a merchant in the author's room picks up the "Discouery of Coosnage," we hear that "he smiled at it for the strangenesse of the title, . . . fetcht a great sigh and sayd: 'Sir, if I had seene this booke but two dayes since, it had saued me nine pound in my purse.'" For his style in the former pamphlet Greene has suffered rebuke, so now he is at pains to explain that "fine figuratiue conueiance" would have been amiss, since he must write basely of a base subject.

First is noticed the Prigging Law, or horse-stealing, the Prigger being the thief, the Prancer the horse, and the Marter the seller of the animal; and the description of this form of the art is illustrated, as with most other Laws, by a story. Vincent's Law pertains to bowls; the Lifting Law to thievery by sleight of hand; the Black Art is that of the picklock, and the Curbing Law is Harman's old trick of the angler.

The stories are frequently amusing. Thus a miller in Newgate Market is robbed by a clever device. Two rogues pretend a quarrel; one flings flour over the other and runs away; he who remains begs the laughing miller to brush the flour from him, and as the miller complies cuts his victim's purse. Another rogue in Paul's feigns a swoon, and, being helped by a countryman, signals confederates to pick the charitable fellow's pockets. Still another buys an odd knife he has ordered of a cutler, and when the cutler begs to know its use, the nip slits the other's pocket as he explains it. A tinker suspected of being a picklock is paid to deliver a message to a jailer, and finds himself clapped into jail, the message having been his *mittimus*.[1]

[1] This reappears in the *Life and Death of Gamaliel Ratsey*, 1605.

In the "Thirde and last Part of Conny-catching" (1592), a distinct advance was made toward pure fiction, and the beggar-book features dropped away. Greene relates that once at dinner the conversation turned on conny-catchers and the two books that had appeared about them, whereupon an ex-magistrate volunteered to add to those works several fresh examples. The result is a collection of ten excellent stories. Some are slight, as that describing the ballad singers who gather a crowd, and then by warning the audience of pick-pockets enable confederates to perceive where the purses are kept as the victims feel for them; or that in which a rogue, inviting young men to drink, pretends his wine needs rose water and sugar and steps out as if to get it, so running off with the tankard and leaving them the bill.[1] Others are told at length, and had they possessed more humor might have compared favorably with the exploits of any Spanish picaro.

In one story a serving-maid discovers a cousin, who, on the strength of his pretended relationship, gains admittance to her master's house and robs it. In another a rogue secures satin and lace from a tailor by trickery, getting himself measured for a suit, and picking the tailor's pocket of a purse and a signet ring during the operation. The ring he sends to the apprentices as a token from the tailor that the silk and lace be delivered to him, and the booty he disposes of to a broker. The latter will pay but little for it, so to be revenged the rogue visits the tailor, assures him that for five pounds he can tell him by magic where his silk and lace have gone, and, receiving that sum, informs on the broker. "Thus one craftie knaue beguiled another; let each take heede of dealing with any such kinde of people."

Perhaps the best tales are the second and the eighth, the scene of both being laid in Paul's Church, which for Elizabethan

[1] This reappears verbally in Dekker's *Belman of London* (1608) as "The Third Jump at Leap Frog;" it figures less literally in *The Groundworke of Conny-catching* (1592).

rogues was "a vsuall place of their assembly, both to determine on their driftes, as also to speede of manie a bootie." In the former tale the "fair purple velvet purse" of a lawyer is picked by a lady who pretends to consult him on business, while her accomplice comes behind and blindfolds him, bidding him guess who it is, and then, as if having made a mistake, bows off. In the latter a rogue warns a gentleman in Paul's against wearing his gold chain so openly. The gentleman ties his chain in a kerchief and hides it in his sleeve. Then the rogue, having dropped a key, stoops to pick it up, and is set upon by accomplices. The gentleman takes his part, is bowled over in the *mêlée*, and his purse, as well as his chain, disappears with the quarrelers, who make off as if to settle their dispute by a duel.

Obviously in these pamphlets Greene was progressing from an account of rogues' tricks to the more interesting business of using rogues as anti-heroes in fiction. The first pamphlet contains direct information merely; the second amplifies such information with anecdotes; while the third consists wholly of stories. Greene's two other pamphlets of 1592 were even more frankly fictional.

"A Dispvtation Betweene a Hee Conny-catcher and a Shee Conny-catcher" showed "Laurence a Foist and faire Nan a Traffique" disputing on the comparative merits of their sexes and professions. Both tell tales in support of their claims, and Laurence at last confesses himself worsted by Nan and all women. "You are Crocodiles when you weepe, Basilisks when you smile, Serpents when you deuise, and diuels chiefest broakers to bring the world to distruction. And so Nan lets sit downe to our meate and be merry."

Some of the tales are Spanish in flavor, as that describing a gallant, roused at night by a false cry of police, who hides in a closet only to be robbed of his clothes and forced to give up his last ring as pledge for a blanket to slink home in.[1] Nan herself is an adept at the crosbiting trick, for, when she has lured a foolish gentleman into her toils, up will come her pretended husband, who "with a few terrible oathes and countenance set, as if he were the proudest Souldado that euer bare armes against Don Iohn of Austria, will face him quite out of his money." The disputation is followed by a narrative in the first person describing "The conuersion of an English Courtizan," strongly moralized, and no mean prototype of the story of Miss Williams in "Roderick Random." The pamphlet concludes with an anecdote of slight merit, entitled "A merry Tale taken not far from Fetter Lane end, of a new found Conny-catcher, that was conny-catcht himselfe." Greene's method of advertising his own wares is revealed when Laurence refrains from describing the laws of rogues "because R. G. hath so amply pend them downe in the first part of Conny-catching, that though I be one of the facultie, yet I can not discouer more than hee hath layde open."

Finally, the tireless Greene issued "The Blacke Bookes Messenger, laying open the Life and Death of Ned Browne," and achieved what of all his writings most nearly approaches picaresque fiction. Here he promises in the preface that a "Conny-catchers Repentance" and his "Blacke Booke" will constitute a compendious revelation of rogues' iniquity.[2] He gives a canting vocabulary devised by Ned Browne and his associates, to be later adopted along with much else pilfered from Greene by Dekker in the "Belman of London."

[1] Borrowed by Samuel Rowlands in *Greenes Ghost Havnting Coniecatchers* (1602).

[2] He did not live to fulfill the pledge, although in the Registers this is entered Aug. 21, 1592, as the *Repentance of a Conny-catcher*. Thomas Middleton's *Blacke Book* (1604) is a satirical review of the London slums by Lucifer, who concludes with ironical bequests to sundry rogues.

Ned Browne is supposed to tell his story before execution at Arx in France, and it is meant to be merry as well as moral, for the world is bidden to call him base knave after his death, and forget him if his rogueries can be heard without laughing. His parents were honest, but he was early given to filching. At eighteen, purse-cutting, horse-stealing, lifting, and lock-picking were toys to him. He particularly practiced bullying. Once he had a pretended constable threaten a maltster, and so secure his signet ring as bail. This ring was then taken to a friend of the maltster's as a token accompanying a request for the loan of ten pounds, which, with the ring itself, was naturally never returned. Ned, believing that wiving and hanging come by destiny, married a woman as bad as himself, and then fell in love with another rogue's wife, and effected an exchange for five pounds.

Ned had many disguises, and even used an artificial tail for his horse. Once he fooled a priest who was riding with a well-filled cap-case on his saddle's pommel. For the priest exchanged horses with Ned and gave him twenty nobles to boot, but at an inn Ned tied a hair about his former nag's fetlock over a vein, which presently made him limp. The priest complained, and Ned offered to try him, so the priest got down and Ned got up, first cutting the hair on the sly. Then away he sped with the priest's new purchase, his saddle, his cap-case, and the twenty nobles.[1]

"I liued wantonly," he says, "and therefore let me end merrily, and tel you two or three of my mad pranks and so bid you farewell." Seeing a fine lady in Smithfield, he went up to her and, kissing her effusively, cut her purse, and then pretending to have been in error, departed begging pardon. By dropping a key and stooping to pick it up he would suddenly halt his victim when a crowd was entering the doorway of Paul's, thus being enabled to pick the jostled conny's pocket unobserved. As for Ned's wife, she would arrange with accomplices armed with hooks to snatch gentlemen's garments through the window as they slept, although sometimes these anglers got more than they bargained for.[2]

Having done villainies in England, Ned passed over into the Low Countries to gain credit as a soldier, and it was then that in robbing a church he was apprehended and, because the people had no gallows, condemned to be hanged at a window. Having given this breezy con-

[1] This trick is appropriated by Fidge in his criminal pamphlet, *The English Gusman, or the History of that Unparallel'd Thief James Hind*, 1652.

[2] Rowlands steals this trick in *Greenes Ghost Havnting Conie-catchers.*

fession of his achievements, beginning with bold defiance and ending with abject repentance, "he himselfe sprung out at the window and died." Greene declares that wolves dug him up after he was buried, and concludes, "If any be profited, I haue the desired ende of my labour."

In the year of Greene's "Thirde and last Part of Conny-catching," Harman's "Caueat" was reprinted as "The Groundworke of Conny-catching," intimating that this was the source of such pamphlets, or using that name to make salable an old article. The "Groundworke" omits Harman's list of actual vagabonds and their "pelting speche," but adds three anecdotes: the first of rogues who at inns claim cloaks and swords not their own; the second, of a knave who sends a victim to look for his gold in a magic oak; the third, of a shifter who orders a feast and leaves it to be paid for by others, pretending he is going out to hasten the hostess.[1]

More important was "Cuthbert Cunny-catcher's" "Defence of Conny catching" (1592). Cuthbert, just come from Newgate, has found himself everywhere detected by such as have perused Greene's pamphlets. He tells six tales accordingly to prove roguery no exclusive possession of professional criminals. A cheating usurer is paid back by the wife of his victim who entices him to a window, shuts it down on his neck, and nails his ears to the ledge. A miller is discovered keeping a false hole in his hopper from which his own sacks are filled. Two lawyers are deceived by Will Sommers, who decides their rival claims by means of a walnut, awarding to each half the shell, and to their client the meat. A suitor wins the love of a citizen's daughter by talk of his Cheshire estate, only to be exposed at a feast; and a bigamist and a tailor who secretes his remnants are both brought to grief. "Was not this a conny-

[1] A version of the inn-trick in the *Thirde and last Part of Conny-catching.*

catcher, maister R. G.?" cries the author,[1] after the recital of each knavery. You "would straine a gnat, and lette passe an elephant;" for "we conny-catchers are like little flies in the grasse which live on little leaves and doe no more harme; whereas there bee in Englande other professions that bee great conny-catchers and caterpillers, that make barraine the field wherein they baite."

Strewn through the tract are allusions to other trades, and the public is warned that the alewife nicks her pots, hostlers have shifts, the vintner waters his wine, the draper darkens his shop, lawyers lengthen their pleas, the butcher "hath pollicies to puffe vp his meate," and Greene himself is a conny-catcher, to prove which he is bidden "aske the Queens Players if you sold them not Orlando Furioso for twenty nobles, and when they were in the country sold the same play to the Lord Admiral's men for much more."

The significance of the "Defence" lies in its aim to extend the discoveries of roguery from criminals to tradesmen. The Spanish fictions did this from the first by exposing the vices of the masters served by the picaros, and Greene, in the "Discouery of Coosnage" and the "Qvippe for an Vpstart Courtier" (1592), had noted the tricks of colliers and jailers. The cue was fully taken, however, only in the anonymous "Greenes Newes both from Heauen and Hell" (1593), describing the hard fate of Greene's ghost.

St. Peter turned him back from Heaven's gate saying, "I haue heard of you, you haue beene a busie fellowe with your penne, it was you that writ the Bookes of cony-catching, but sirra, could you finde out the base abuses of a company of petty varlets that liued by pilfering cosonages,

[1] Grosart thinks he may have been Valentine Bird, to whom Nash refers in *Haue with you to Saffron-walden* as a friend of Gabriel Harvey, and as writing against Greene.

and could you not as well haue descryed the subtill and fraudulent practises of great conny-catchers, such as rides upon footeclothes, and sometime in coatches, and walkes the streetes in long gownes and veluet coates?" In Hell the afflicted ghost fares no better, for there the conny-catchers themselves inveigh against him with horrible threats; and Lucifer thrusts him forth, to remain a restless soul wandering through the world.

Another pamphlet that bore Greene's name in the title and conjured up his ghost was "Greene in Conceipt, new raised from his graue to write the Tragique Historie of faire Valeria of London" (1598). This was composed by John Dickenson, a disciple of Lyly. The story of Valeria describes a well-born wanton who forsakes her husband for a rake, and deserted by the latter dies repentant, after her children have come to bad ends, and her paramour, tired of "scouring the westerne plaines for pursses," has been hanged. Extravagant euphuism marks the style, and the imitation of Greene is rather that of his early romantic works, although Dickenson makes him refer to these slightingly: "I am hee whose pen was first emploied in the aduancement of vanitie, and afterward in the discouering of villanie . . . in the former of which I confesse I haue offended . . . yet dare I boldly affirme, that my later labours haue made a large part of amends for those former vanities." The ghost of Valeria is supposed to have been met by that of Greene, and her story is told by Greene to Dickenson to show that there is one woman of ill repute who has died reformed, and who being dead does not wish to return to life.

Samuel Rowlands in "Greenes Ghost Havnting Conie-catchers" (1602) pretended to edit what is really a theft from previous conny-catching pamphlets, those of Greene especially. Rowlands declares that "the name of Conicatchers is so odious, that now a dayes it is had vp, and vsed for an opprobrious name for euerie one that sheweth the least occasion of deceit."

Among his fifteen stories appear the tricks of colliers, as detailed in the "Blacke Bookes Messenger;" the trick of reclaiming others' property at inns and fairs, from the "Groundworke of Conny-catching;" the story of a false cry of justice, from the "Dispvtation Betweene a Hee Conny-catcher and a Shee Conny-catcher;" the fraud of blindfolding a victim in Paul's as if by mistake, from the "Thirde Part of Conny-catching;" and an abridgment of the bigamist story, from the "Defence of Conny catching." Tricks as old as the securing of a loan on a chest filled with stones, harking back to the "Cid," are in evidence, and "the notable, slie, and deceitfull pranks of Doctor Pinchbacke" are based on the old cheat of discovering by magic an object really stolen.

In "The Art of Iugling or Legerdemaine" (1612), probably by Rowlands, the magic cheat reappears in illustration of the "foppery of foolish cosoning charmes." Here Cuthbert Conycatcher and Swart Rutter, having stolen certain horses, reveal their whereabouts through a charm. A number of juggling tricks, too, are explained, and the possibilities of cheating at cards and dice are dwelt upon in the spirit of another and earlier gaming tract. This was "Mihil Mumchance, his Discouerie of the Art of Cheating in false Dyce play, and other vnlawful games" (1597).[1] Like other unsigned works of the kind, it was attributed to Greene, although inferior to his recognized writing.[2] After treating of dicing and card tricks, it sets forth cheats practiced at fairs and markets. Here Awdeley's ringfaller dodge reappears with a gilt sword for the ring, and a lady substitutes a copper for a gold chain as she hangs caressingly

[1] Cf. Gilbert Walker's *Detection of Detestable Use of Dyce Play* (1552), and the Puritanic *Treatises Touchyng Dyce Play and Prophane Gaming*, by Thomas Newton, and a *Treatise of Dicing* (1577), by J. Northbrooke, "wherein dicing, dauncing, vaine playes, or enterluds" are reproved.

[2] Cf. *Questions concerning Coniehood and the nature of the Conie* (n. d.).

upon her gallant's neck. The dedication reads, "To all the chiefe cheators[1] in the gamning [*sic*] houses, as Bedlam, Coleman-street, Morefields, Northhouse, Charterhouse, Shoolane, Westminster, & all others, Mihil Mumchance sendeth greeting, and with all wisheth confusion to your damnable profession." Three years later in "The Letting of Hvmovrs Blood in the Head-Vaine," a satire marked by picaresque touches,[2] we hear, —

> But come to Dice; why thats his onely trade,
> Michell Mum-chaunce, his owne invention made.

A far echo of the tract sounds in "Hocus Pocus Iunior, the Anatomy of Legerdemain" (1634), in "The Nicker Nicked" (1669), and in "Leather-More, or Advice Concerning Gaming" (2d ed., 1668).[3]

The most eminent pilferer from "Mumchance," and from Greene and Harman also, was Thomas Dekker, the dramatist, who in much that he wrote gave rein to realism and satire. His "Wonderfull Yeare 1603" approaches Defoe's "Journal of the Plague Year;" his dependence upon Nash is significant,[4] and his adaptation of "Grobianus" proves him a master of irony. But he deserves especial notice as the first after Greene to unify in a fiction separate accounts of rogues.[5] If he showed little originality in matter, his treatment of it justified his thefts.

[1] The term "cheat" is here explained as derived from "our Lawyers, with whom all such casualls as fall to the Lord at the holding of his leetes, as waifs, straies, and such like be called Chetes, and are accustomably said to be escheted to the Lordes use."

[2] Cf. Epigram 7 and Satyre 3.

[3] Reflections on allied amusements may be found in George Wilson's *Commendation of Cockes and Cock-Fighting* (1607) and in Taylor the Water Poet's *Bull and Bear Baiting* (1638).

[4] Jusserand, *English Novel*, p. 332, *et seq.*

[5] Dekker and George Wilkins issued *Iests to make you Merie; With the Coniuring vp of Cock Watt* (*the walking Spirit of Newgate*), in which, however, the low-life scenes are inferior to those in the *Belman*.

Dekker's "Belman of London" (1608) [1] provides "a discourse of all the idle vagabonds of England, their conditions, their lawes amongst themselues, their decrees and orders, their meetings, and their maners of liuing." The author chances upon a cottage in the country where the "ragged regiment" is about to attend its quarter dinner.

"An olde, nimble tongd beldame" having hid him, he observes the initiation of a candidate upon whom the leader pours a pot of ale, declaring: "I doe stall thee to the Rogue, by vertue of this Soueraigne English liquor, so that henceforth it shall be lawful for thee to Cant (that is to say) to be a Vagabond and Beg, and to speake that Pedlers French, or that Canting language which is to be found among none but beggars." Then all the rogues hang on their new brother for joy, and he is instructed by the master that he must walk only in an allotted quarter, and give way to those in office on the holding up of a finger. The names of the rogue orders are told him exactly as enumerated by Harman in the "Caueat," whereupon all the company draw knives, rap out round oaths, and instead of a grace fall to.

When an orator rises to speak in praise of beggary, he begins, "My noble hearts, old weather-beaten fellowes, and braue English spirits . . . shall wee not walke up and downe in the world like Beggars, with olde blankets pind about us? Yes, yes, we will, roared all the Kennell as though it had beene the dogs of Palace Garden." The beggar's walk is a kingdom, says the orator, a whole city is his parish, in every man's kitchen his meat is dressed, in every man's cellar lies his beer, and the best men's purses keep a penny for him.

After the rout has broken up and the old woman has vouchsafed further information, derived from Harman and to be repeated in "The English Rogue," Dekker returns to town and from the "Belman of London" learns of city tricks called "Laws." "Mihil Mumchance" provides the Cheating Law; Greene's "Discouery of Coosnage" furnishes Barnard's Law, which also echoes the terminology of the "Blacke Bookes

[1] Robert Daborne had a play, *The Bellman of London* (1613). Cf. Fleay, vol. i, p. 83.

Messenger." Vincent's Law, the Black Art, the Curbing Law, the Prigging Law, the Lifting Law, all come from the "Second part of Conny-catching," as does Dekker's Figging Law, a mere compression of Greene's Discovery of the Nip and Foist. What Greene had called crosbiting, Dekker terms the Sacking Law; and of the Five Jumps at Leap Frog, so named because one man in each leaps over another, Greene's "Thirde and last Part of Conny-catching" provides two jumps[1] and Rowlands's "Greenes Ghost" three. The conclusion of the "Belman" offers a "short discourse of canting," which turns out to be the very dialogue between an Upright Man and a Rogue given by Harman in the "Caueat."[2] Thus Dekker's work is an unblushing plagiarism from several sources, prefaced by an original and interesting narrative. The latter resembles Cervantes's "Rinconete y Cortadillo" in presenting a session of rogues, but it differs from that *novela* in offering the first such account in its own literature, Cervantes having profited by the example of Mateo Aleman.

In Dekker's "Lanthorne and Candle-light" of the same year,[3] a council sits in Hell to consider retaliating upon the "Belman of London" for his revelations, but the infernal mes-

[1] The third is Greene's fourth story, here called Fawning; the fourth is Greene's third story, here called Foole-taking.

[2] Burton, author of *The Anatomy of Melancholy*, in his copy of Dekker's *Belman* of 1608, now in the Bodleian, noted passages taken from Harman; but, so far as I know, the dependence of Dekker upon Rowlands and Greene has never before been indicated.

[3] Hazlitt and others speak only of a 1609 edition; but that of 1608 is in the British Museum. In Dekker's *Seuen deadlie Sinnes of London* (1606) the terms candle-light and Bell-man are juxtaposed. "O candle-light, candle-light! to howe manie costly Sacke-possets and reare Banquets hast thou beene inuited by Prentices and Kitchen-maidens? When the Bell-man for anger . . . hath bounced at the doore like a madde man," p. 22. A ballad "Lantron and Candle-lyghte" was licensed to W. Griffith in 1569–70.

senger who is sent to the metropolis merely presents the Belman with a map of his own observations of cheats, "which map he hath set out in such collors as you see, tho not with such cunning as he could wish." This account includes a chapter on canting, with a glossary and rhymes drawn out of Harman. New names are given to the actors in several old frauds, and among fresh ones appear the dedicating of patched-up books to the rich, the stealing of jewels from goldsmiths by the use of duplicate boxes, and the waxing of horses' teeth to prevent their eating.[1]

The knavery of horse coursers is exhibited in devices by which cheap jades bought at Smithfield are furbished up for profitable sale. If the horse suffers from the glanders, the courser tickles his nose with feathers and the juice of garlic, or puts ale and mustard in the nostrils to keep them clean until the sale be over. A foundered horse he heats with running before exposing him for sale. If the horse halts, he removes a shoe and suggests that this is the cause; if the joints be bad he fouls and conceals them. An old nag he will make afraid of him with beatings so that it shall seem skittish. He will either burn its teeth to proper shape, or else prick its mouth so that none will venture to look at them. The description of Moon-men recalls Falstaff's characterization of his brethren,[2] yet here the term applies to Gypsies; "they call themselues Egiptians, others in mockery call them Moone-men."

This tract appears to have won even greater success than the original "Belman," and in 1612 it was reissued with an addition as "O per se O, or A new Cryer of Lanthorne and Candle-light." The author rejoices that he can supplement the Belman's nocturnal researches with such as pertain to the day,

[1] This hostler's ruse figures in *The Three Ladies of London;* cf. *ante*, p. 53.

[2] "We that take purses go by the moon and the seven stars, and not by Phœbus; . . . let us be Diana's foresters, gentlemen of the shade, minions of the moon; and let men say we be men of good government, being governed, as the sea is, by our noble and chaste mistress the moon, under whose countenance we steal." *1 Henry IV*, Act i, sc. 2.

for having taken into service a rogue, he has secured new information from this "diuellish schoolemaister whom I call by the name of O per se O." The name [1] serves also for the refrain of a song which the vagabonds sing. The addition is made up by expanding old tricks. The Abraham Man and the Counterfeit Soldier are again described, and the sores worn by Palliards and other rogues are especially noticed. These are made by applications of unslaked lime, soap, and iron-rust, the spot being bound with a garter and pieces of leather. Then a linen cloth which has adhered to the blister is torn off, causing the place to bleed, and, in the case of the Great Cleyme, ratsbane is rubbed in, after further doses of "crowe-foote, sperewort, and salt." A sore on the forearm is called a soldier's maund, on the back of the hand a footman's maund, and above the elbow a mason's maund.

Dekker describes the congregation of the rogues at "Durrest-Fayre, kept on two Holy-Roode dayes, neere Tiwksbury," and assigns seven reasons for their gathering, chief of which is the hope of each to be chosen lord of the Fair. The work closes with a canting song later appropriated by "The English Rogue," and handed down even to Mark Twain's "Prince and the Pauper." Editions of the pamphlet after 1612 were entitled "Villanies Discovered," until in 1638 it appeared as "English Villanies." [2]

Dekker in the original "Lanthorne and Candle-light" had

[1] In *Greenes Newes both from Heauen and Hell*, the ghostly paper delivered to the author begins, "It is I, *I per se I*, Robert Greene, in Artibus Magister," to which Dekker's *O per se O* may be an allusion.

[2] The full title was *English Villanies Seven Severall Times Prest to Death by the Printers; But (still reviving againe) are now the eighth time, (as at the first) discovered by Lanthorne and Candle-Light; by the helpe of a New Cryer, called O-Per-Se-O.* The ninth edition of 1648 substituted "eight" for "seven," and, like the former, added Harman's canting dictionary and four canting songs.

attacked Samuel Rowlands, from whose "Greenes Ghost," nevertheless, he did not scruple to borrow. He spoke of Rowlands as "an Vsurper that of late hath taken upon him the name of the Bel-man, but not beeing able to maintaine that Title, he doth now call himselfe the Bel-man's brother." Rowlands retorted in "Martin Mark-All, Beadle of Bridewell" (1610), by exposing Dekker as a purloiner from Harman.

This tract falls into two parts, the first giving an allegory of roguery and a map of its country, not unlike the famous "Carte du Tendre" of the *précieuses*, and the second and more important presenting a history of vagabonds from Jack Cade to Cock Lorrell. When Cade was slain, Hugh Roberts kept the rogues together with four laws providing that he himself was to have first pick of all booty, that those who were unfortunate in stealing might share with the successful, that no robbery was to be done within four miles of their haunt, and that no one should seek refuge there if pursued. Jenkin Cowdiddle followed and ordered that all rogues should spend their gains by Saturday night; Spysing, who succeeded him, attempted to capture London, but was hanged; and Puffing Dicke, who became ruler, invented the terminology for robbing on the highway, but discountenanced murders and the hoarding of treasure. Laurence Crosbiter, an old serving-man, held sway from 1491 to 1497, giving his name to the famous bullying trick. Then in the days of Perkin Warbeck, Richard Skelton, a tailor, came to the fore, and among other acts ordained fines for such as threw away their crutches. Cock Lorrell, "the most notorious knaue that euer liued," reigned from 1501 to 1533.[1] He it was who first devised the twenty-five orders of vagabonds, "but because it is extant and in euery mans shop, I passe them over."[2]

A brief account of the Gypsies and their king and queen is followed by the statement that their language is devised from

[1] Cock Lorrell was frequently referred to. Cf. such ballads as *A Strange Banquet, or the Devil's Entertainment by Cock Laurel at the Peak in Derbyshire* and *The Treatyse Answerynge the Boke of Beardes*. For the reference to him in Jonson's *Gipsies Metamorphosed*, see *infra*, ch. vi, sect. 1, p. 241.

[2] An allusion to *Cocke Lorelles Bote* and to the *Fraternitye of Vacabondes*, whose twenty-five orders were "confirmed foreuer by Cocke Lorell."

Latin, English, and Dutch, with some admixture of Spanish and French. A promised sequel to this picaresque chronicle never appeared.

Of Samuel Rowlands himself little is known. Like Lodge and Greene, he began as a euphuist and later turned to satire and crude realism. His versified knave series included the "Knave of Clubbes" (1609), the "Knave of Hearts" (1612), and the "Knaues of Spades and Diamonds" (1613). These were influenced by English anatomies of roguery, and slightly by Italian *novelle*. One story in the "Knave of Hearts" describes the tricks of two conny-catchers upon a third. They get him drunk, put out the light, and then as though it were still lit bid him judge of their throws at dice. He believes himself struck suddenly blind, so they leave him groping and with the score to pay. Similar elements are to be found in Rowlands's "A Paire of Spy-Knaves" and "Good Newes and Bad Newes" (1622), a rhymed jest-book. It is to be noted that Rowlands when he exposed Dekker's "Belman" as largely a rewriting of Harman's "Caueat" had no word to say concerning Dekker's more abundant thefts from Greene, though his own work shows perfect familiarity with Greene's conny-catching pamphlets, and he must have recognized the piracies. No doubt he realized that by calling attention to his rival's excerpts he would inevitably expose his own.

3. *Prison Tracts and Repentances*

A curious set of books dealing with prisons was inaugurated by "The Blacke Dogge of Newgate" (*c.* 1600), composed by Luke Hutton, whose father was either Matthew Hutton, the Archbishop of York, or Robert Hutton, the Prebendary of Durham. It is certain that Luke was well reared, that he entered Cambridge in 1582, and that in 1598 he was executed at York for a robbery. His versified "Repentance" was dedicated to Henry, Earl of Huntingdon, and seems to have preceded "The Blacke Dogge,"[1] which is addressed to the Lord Chief Justice, Sir John Popham, and describes the customs of Newgate through the medium of a vision. Only the latter portion of the pamphlet is in prose, and this sets forth in a dialogue with a prisoner "the knauerie, villanie, robberie, and cunnicatching, committed daily by diuers, who in the name of seruice and office were, as it were, attendants at Newgate." Here are pilloried such prototypes of Jonathan Wild as make a practice of ascertaining those who have been robbed, and from them securing sums to apprehend the thieves. They then proceed with a warrant to any thieves whatever, and frighten them into paying to keep out of jail. A new edition called "The Discovery of a London Monster" (1638) altered several features, particularly those relating to the legend of the "Blacke Dogge" itself. This in the early work had been referred to the jailer's person. But here it is lugubriously described as either the ghost of one eaten in prison by his associates in the days of Henry III, or a black stone against which a desperate prisoner once dashed out his brains. Various cheating tricks are added, notably that of Awdeley's ring-faller.

In the "Compters Common-Wealth" (1617), by William Fennor, the rogue pamphlets of the preceding generation were imitated, and in ten autobiographic chapters the writer described his arrest for debt, his incarceration in the Wood Street Counter, and his experiences there.

[1] Hazlitt suggests 1597 for the *editio princeps*, and notes editions of 1612 and 1638. *Luke Huttons Lamentation* (1598) is a folio sheet of twenty-two stanzas. Cf. also *Old Ballads* (*Percy Soc.*, p. 117). A lost play, by Hathway, Wentworth Smith, and Day, was entitled *The Black Dog of Newgate* (pl. 1602). Middleton's *Blacke Booke* (1604) pities a gentleman seized in Fleet Street by catchpoles, "some six of your black dogs of Newgate."

Like Pablos in prison[1] he was on every hand bled to pay for "a garnish," but finally in the lower depths of the jail, being invited to drink and smoke, the leader of the roguish crew offered to reveal to him the secrets of the jail. "Why sir, sayd I, there is a booke called Greenes Ghost haunts Cony-catchers; another called Legerdemaine, and The Blacke Dog of New-gate, but the most wittiest, elegantest and eloquentest Peece (Master Dekkers, the true heire of Apollo composed) called The Bell-man of London, have already set foorth the vices of the time so viuely, that it is vnpossible the Anchor of any other mans braine can sound the sea of a more deepe and dreadfull mischeefe." He was persuaded to listen, however, and so learned the tricks of sergeants and of rogues, some of which, like that of the prisoner escaping while treating his captor to a shave, hark back to jest-books.

In the new edition of Fennor's tract, published in 1619, the title read "The Miseries of a Iaile," and in that of 1629 it was "A True Description of the Lawes, Ivstice, and Eqvity of a Compter." In 1653 the same prison was sung in verse in "The Counter-Scuffle, Whereunto is added the Counter-Rat," whose author, R. S., referred to Fennor with defiance but patterned on him closely.[2]

The "Essayes and Characters of a Prison and Prisoners" (1618), by Geffray Mynshul, was in part a character-book in which everything connected with a prison from the keepers to the entertainment was described without humor, but in aphoristic style. A more interesting performance was "Wil Bagnal's Ghost, or the Merry Devill of Gadmvnton in his perambulation of the Prisons of London" (1655), by Edmund Gayton, author

[1] *Buscon*, lib. ii, cap. 4.

[2] Cf. also a four-leaved tract — *Wonderful Newes from Wood-Street Counter* (1642) — and Nathan Wickins's slightly earlier *Wood-Street Compter's Plea for its Prisoner*. Taylor the Water Poet in 1623 issued a satirical *Praise and Vertue of a Jayle and Jaylers* after having attacked Fennor himself eight years before in *A Cast Over the Water*, "given gratis to William Fennor the Rimer; . . . persuading the said Fennor to penitence that he may hang with the clearer conscience at Saint Thomas of Waterings."

of the better known "Pleasant Notes upon Don Quixot" (1654). The gossiping humor of that commentary was repeated in this prison pamphlet, a compilation of prose and verse, the latter resembling in matter and metre the "Counter-Scuffle." After recounting in rhyme the escapes and pranks of one Hanon, as well as his own adventures in prison, Gayton presents in prose a series of opposite characters, and concludes with a discussion of such momentous queries as to whether one Christian may arrest another as is common in New and Old England, and whether it is more proper or convenient to a prisoner to sing psalms or drink sack. Canting and low-life wittily portrayed played a further rôle in "Hell upon Earth" (1703), which professed to relate "the most pleasant and delectable history of Whittington Colledge, otherwise vulgarly called Newgate."

After the death of Greene, Dekker, and Rowlands, the anatomies of roguery declined. Dekker's "O per se O" saw nine editions before the middle of the seventeenth century, and Greene's "Dispvtation Betweene a Hee Conny-catcher and a Shee Conny-catcher" was reissued in 1615 and 1637 as "Thieves Falling Out, True Men Come by Their Goods;" [1] yet new beggar-books were rare. Those that appeared added little fresh material and succumbed to inane reiteration.

A case in point is John Clavell's "Recantation Of an ill led Life" (1628) and the use made of it by others. This "discouerie of the High-way Law" professed to be printed at the king's command.[2] It is a versified account of road-knights

[1] Here the names of the rogues were altered to Stephen and Kate, and the subtitle of the 1637 edition sought to benefit by the popularity of Dekker's work. It ran "The Bel-man wanted a clapper. A Peale of new Villanies rung out."

[2] Clavell was nephew and heir of Sir William Clavell, knight banneret. His first robbery was done at Gadshill. Condemned to death for highway robbery, he was pardoned in 1625 as a result of his rhymed apology to the king. He did not die till 1642.

and their ways, and contains "Instructions for the honest traveller that he may pass in safety."

Under the former head are described the oath of the young thief on being admitted to the brotherhood of highwaymen, the charge delivered to him by the leader, and the manner of the robber's assault upon the road. The directions for the traveler include hints for recognizing rogues and for tracking them. Those with money are urged to journey by night, to select byways, and ride in straggling order. A stout heart must be shown in the encounter. In pursuing thieves the next road is to be taken, and spies must be set at inns, while if the band be large they are to be sought forthwith in London. If robbed in the eastern quarter, know they will be in the west; if in the north, look in Southwark, Bankside, or Lambeth. To so much of the elaborately commonplace were appended instructions to innkeepers how to know thieves from honest guests, and Clavell, reverting to his own precarious situation, concluded with the pertinent query:—

> Yet must I die? and is there no relief?
> The king of kings had mercy on a thief.

Dull as this pamphlet was, it saw reissues, and even enlargment in a third edition of 1634. Moreover, transformed from verse to prose, it contributed to "The Catterpillers of this Nation Anatomized" (1659).[1] Here the chief additions concerned the Hector, a crosbiter under another name, the Bung-Nibber or Cutpurse; the Ken-Miller, who gains entrance to houses by means of his Hobgoblin, a boy in a cask; and the Filer or Cloyer, who steals from shops as the merchant is reaching down wares, or blows out candles and grabs what he can, and snatches cloaks and caps in dark places. Richard Head may have written this plagiarizing tract. At all events, his "English Rogue" (1665) takes over most of it literally.[2]

[1] Cf. for this usage of the term "catterpiller" the brief versified *Frogges of Egypt, or the Catterpillers of the Commonwealth Truly Dissected and Laid Open* (1641). Rowlands in *Martin Mark-All* (1610) refers to vagabonds as "The congregation of catterpillers gathered together."

[2] Cf. *The English Rogue*, pt. i, chs. 59–64. Here even the chapter head-

The information first formulated by Clavell would not down. In 1674 it crops up again in "Jackson's Recantation," which has also been ascribed to Head.[1] Jackson, "the notorious High-way-man now hanging in chains at Hampstead," is represented as composing this confession in Newgate, but he gives no circumstantial account of himself beyond relating how first he found and kept a wallet, and then joined a crew "incomparable in the art of wheedling."[2] His chief endeavor is confined to repeating Clavell's indestructible directions to travelers and innkeepers. In 1679 and again about 1700 appeared an abridged version of "The English Rogue," consisting of this matter together with a canting dictionary and Harman's classification of vagabonds. Many years later in a fiction attributed to Defoe — "Street-Robberies Consider'd" (1728) — the whole thing revives as "A Warning for Travellers" to celebrate the centenary of its birth in Clavell's tract, while even an echo of Greene is still audible.

Other rogue pamphlets in the meantime strove with little success to be informing or entertaining. One of the latter type was the "History of the Famous and Renowned Knights of the Blade, Commonly called Hectors" (1652).[3] Tricks and laws of the order are given, the laws providing that none shall be admitted to the brotherhood without spending his all upon its members; that there shall be no dueling without consent; that Hectors shall willingly cheat even their parents; that they shall keep an account of all booty, and set aside part for the gang in common; that they shall never reveal their

ings are identical. The "Observations of the Hector and his Rum-Mort" is not used, although it seems the basis of an incident, pt. i, ch. 12.

[1] In a MS. note in the Bodleian copy.

[2] Cf. Head's exposition of this art in *Proteus Redivivus, or the Art of Wheedling or Insinuation* (1675).

[3] Cf. also a comedy, *The Hectors, or the False Challenge* (1656).

rendezvous; that if taken, they shall not discover their friends, or in ranting disclose their manner of life.

The still briefer tract, " A Warning for House-Keepers" (1676), described old rogues under new names, the pick-lock becoming a Gilter, the pick-pocket a File, the confidence-man a Tongue Padder. Here the Glazier is one who removes window-panes to steal; the Budg and Snudg enter open doors and thieve if unobserved, but ask for some one when encountered;[1] and the Private Thief takes service with the rich to inform on the whereabouts of his treasures.

By "The Discoveries of John Poulter"[2] similar information is more freely afforded in "A Full Discovery of Thieving and Defrauding in all Shapes" appended to the rogue's account of himself.

Ancient tricks come up smiling in fresh terminology. Awdeley's ring-faller device is known as Old Nobb, Harman's Dummerar and Bawdy Basket are called Gaggers, those who pretend to have been burnt out are now Sky Farmers. Here are the Scamp, a highwayman in league with an innkeeper; the Petter Lay, who cuts portmanteaux from behind coaches; and the Ringing Tagg, who at fairs and inns calls for others' coats, having changed the checks pinned upon them.[3] Turners and Pinchers make false change; Dudders pretend to be smugglers, and offer goods for sale at low prices; and Gibbers are false horse-dealers. A dictionary of cant terms and a list of actual thieves informed against by Poulter and of those prematurely returned from transportation are given.

Few separate essays of this kind followed, but occasionally in longer works of fiction or autobiography, beggar-book passages played a part. Thus in eccentric George Parker's "View of Society and Manners in High and Low Life" (1781) there

[1] A trick advised in *The English Rogue*, pt. i, ch. 6.

[2] Ninth edition, 1754.

[3] A version of the first addition to Harman in the *Groundworke;* and the fourth story, or " Wil St. Lift," in Rowlands's *Greenes Ghost.*

figured an account of seventy-four orders of thieves, beggars, and rogues. Many are new in their functions, and practically all are novel as to name.

Daisy Kickers are cheating hostlers, the Blue Pigeon Flyer is a thieving plumber, Traps are thief-takers, Maces steal watches as a speciality, and Queer Roosters feign sleep. Body-snatching is known as the Resurrection Rig, deception by quackery is the Crocussing Rig, and Jibber the Kibber is the Cornwall wrecker's trick of fixing a lantern to the head of a horse, one of whose legs is bound up that its irregular motion may suggest a vessel's. Harman's Kitchen Co, the small boy, who, wriggling into a house, opens the door to the gang, is the Little Snakes Man; the soldier, sailor, Gypsy, or tinker, with an artificial sore upon his leg is a Low Gagger; and Academy Buz-Nappers are acolytes in the faith who, like those of Hugo's "Notre-Dame de Paris," practice stealing from lay-figures dressed in bells.

Parker in 1789 supplemented this account by his "Life's Painter of Variegated Characters."[1] Here, before explaining cant terms, he declared his aim to be the exposure of the frauds of "these invaders of our property, our safety, and our lives, who have a language quite unintelligible to any but themselves, and an established code of laws productive of their common safety at the same time, and live in splendour without the exertion of industry, labour, or care." Most of the cheats and very little of the splendor were obvious. Fawny, "an old stale trick called ring-dropping," goes back to Awdeley; the Flash-man is merely Greene's Crosbiter; Tollibon Nan is a woman Dummerar; and Gentlemen of the Drop are players of the confidence game. Only the wiles of the Queer Plungers can boast originality. These rogues practice their conny-catching upon the Humane Society. One falls into the water, another effects his rescue, and a third as a physician restores both to life. Then with becoming reluctance they accept the collection taken up

[1] Cf. chapters xiv and xv, "Low life dramatically introduced in the neighbourhood of St. Giles."

on the spot, and profit later by the medals bestowed and the glory achieved.[1] In the "Memoirs of James Hardy Vaux" (1819) are described such devices as spanking, or breaking shop-windows at night; the snuff-racket, or the flinging of snuff in the eyes of tradesmen; and the kid-rig, or the defrauding of errand-boys and porters.

A few briefer anatomies contained similar information. Such, for example, were "The London Spy, or the Frauds of London Described" (1809), by the celebrated George Barrington, superintendent of the convicts at Botany Bay; William Perry's "London Guide and Strangers' Safeguard" (1818), by a convict signing himself euphemistically "a gentleman who has made the police of the metropolis an object of enquiry for two and twenty years;" and John Badock's "Strangers' Guide Through the Streets of the Metropolis" (1828), "shewing the frauds, the arts, snares, and wiles of all descriptions of rogues that everywhere abound."

4. *Canting Lexicons and Scoundrel Verse*

Since the first celebration of canting by Copland, Awdeley, and Harman, this gentle art has never lacked professors. For more than a century Harman's words and phrases were repeated from glossary to glossary with little variation. Then the speech of rogues began to alter, until, by the nineteenth century, flash had wholly elbowed out of court Elizabethan cant.[2] In addition to the many volumes concerning rogues and their language already noted, "a compleat canting dictionary"

[1] Maxime du Camp's *L'assistance par travail* (*Revue des deux mondes*, vol. lxxxv, p. 306) describes a recent Parisian performance of this trick.

[2] The latter has kept its hold in fiction alone. It appears with some historical justification in Scott's *Fortunes of Nigel*, in Mark Twain's *Prince and the Pauper*, and in I. Hooper's *His Grace o' the Gunne;* but its use in Scott's *Guy Mannering* and in Ainsworth's *Rookwood* is anachronistic.

drawn from "The English Rogue" was part of Richard Head's "Canting Academy, or Villainies Discovered" (1674), where were shown "the mysterious and villainous practices of that wicked crew, hectors, trappaners and gilts." A "Dictionary of the Canting Crew" appeared before 1700, and was followed in 1710 by "A New Dictionary of the Terms Ancient and Modern of the Canting Crew," reprinted in 1754 as "The Scoundrel's Dictionary." It contributed also to a "Canting Dictionary" in 1725, and formed part of the extensive "Bacchus and Venus" (1737, 1738), a select collection of "near two hundred of the most witty diverting songs and catches in love and gallantry, with songs in the canting dialect." In "The Amorous Gallant's Tongue Tipp'd with Golden Expressions" (*c.* 1740) there figured "A canting academy or the pedlar's French dictionary" derived from Head. Captain Smith's rather burlesque "Thieves' Grammar" and his formal "Thieves' Dictionary" (1719) explained cant terms, which were also briefly arranged in glossaries appended to criminal pamphlets, one such of 1750 dealing with Jonathan Wild, Joseph Blake, and Jack Sheppard. In 1786 an "explanation of most of the cant terms in the thieving language" was added to "The Whole Art of Thieving and Defrauding Discovered." Editions of the Life of Bampfylde-Moore Carew after the second contained a dictionary of the cant language, and beggar-book passages. The latter detailed the laws of the Gypsies, described a Gypsy election, classified offices in the rogue hierarchy, — the Dummerar, Abraham Man, and Whipjacke, — and explained the making of artificial sores in the very words of Dekker's "O per se O" (1612).

There were canting passages also in witty sketches like "The Two Convicted Thieves" (1641), describing the accidental meeting of Peter Pycklock and Matthew Make-Them-Stand, in satirical pieces like the "Total Rout, or a Discovery of a Pack of Knaves and Drabs" (1653), in brief exposures of rogues and their haunts like "The Devil's Cabinet Broken Open" (1658) and "A Second Part of the Discovery of Thieves" (1676), or in longer essays such as the Rev. Robert Dixon's "Canidia, or the Witches; a Rhapsody" (1683), which Hazlitt characterized as "a perfect cyclopedia of slang and all the vices of the age."

But the first authoritative study of the subject was made by the antiquary, Captain Francis Grose, whose "Classical Dictionary of the Vulgar Tongue" (1785) superseded all that had gone before. Grose was charged with immorality in setting forth obscenities, but his work was well done. It reached a third edition by 1796, and was incorporated in James Caulfield's swindling volume, "Blackguardiana," of the previous year. It was levied on, too, by a "Dictionary of all the Cant and Flash Languages," twice issued at the end of the century, and was reprinted in 1811 as "The Lexicon Balatronicum." "The Bang-up Dictionary" of the next year pilfered from it, and Pierce Egan edited and supplemented Grose in 1823.

Aside from incidental cant in criminal pamphlets and descriptions of London life, only a few inferior dictionaries intervened between Grose's work and that of John Camden Hotten, in 1859. There were small glossaries like those of Andrews (1809) and Duncombe (1820), John Badock's "Dictionary of the Turf, the Ring, the Chase, the Pit, the Bon Ton," with editions in 1823 and 1825,[1] two "Modern Flash"

[1] In 1823 Professor John Wilson (Christopher North) reviewed this work in *Blackwood's Magazine*, and there tried his own hand in slang pieces. He had earlier issued a sentimental dramatic poem in blank verse, — *The Convict* (1816), — setting forth in two parts and five scenes the woes of one wrongly convicted of robbery and murder. His hero is rescued at the scaffold by the discovery and capture of the real offender.

lexicons in the latter year, Ducange Anglicus's "The Vulgar Tongue" (1857), and G. W. Matsell's "American Vocabulum, or the Rogue's Lexicon" (1859). But Hotten's "Dictionary of Modern Slang, Cant, and Vulgar Words," which was largely augmented in its second edition (1860), remains the foundation of every later book of the kind. Its essays concerning the language and the hieroglyphics used by vagabonds were also valuable.

Since Hotten's day there have appeared a number of minor treatises, such as Fox's "Slang Dictionary of New York, London, and Paris" (1880) and Maitland's "American Slang Dictionary," as well as two extensive works, the "Dictionary of Slang, Jargon, and Cant" (1887), of Barrère and Leland, and the four-volume "Slang and its Analogues Past and Present" (1890–96), compiled by J. S. Farmer and W. E. Henley. The last professes to give an historical and comparative account "of the heterodox speech of all classes of society for more than three hundred years, with synonyms in English, French, German, and Italian."

Mere word-books of roguery must yield in interest, however, to the literature in cant. Much of this has already been noticed; some will be discussed elsewhere, but one department remains to be considered here. This is the body of scoundrel verse eulogizing, as a rule, the free life of vagabonds and thieves. To it belong such songs as "Jack Begger under the Bush" (1594) and the somewhat later "Brave English Gypsy" in the Roxburgh Collection, the "Song of the Beggar" in "The Description of Love" (1620), and "The Cunning Northerne Begger," who "all the by-standers doth earnestly pray to bestow a penny upon him to-day," a piece designed to be sung "to the tune of Tom of Bedlam." This fellow has his tricks as well as any of Harman's or Greene's rascals. He is a wandering sailor or a cripple; he feigns the falling sickness, concocts sores, daubs his face with blood, carries a child at his back as having been burned out, or, like the blind master of Lazarillo de Tormes, is led about by a boy.

> I have my shifts about me,
> Like Proteus often changing,
> My shape when I will
> I alter still,
> About the country ranging.

A friend of his in "The Joviall Crew, or Beggars-Bush" of the Bagford Collection pleasantly sings:—

> A Craver my father,
> A Maunder my mother,
> A Filer my sister, a Filcher my brother,
> A Canter my Unckle,
> That cared not for Pelfe,
> A Lifter my aunt, a Beggar myselfe.

Taylor the Water Poet in the same rollicking spirit wrote "The Praise, Antiquity, and Commodity of Beggery, Beggers, and Begging" (1621), where chiefly in pentameter he lauded the beggar's life.[1] Homer was a blind beggar, and Ovid a beggar in his exile. Virgil was born in a ditch. The beggar's garden is the whole earth, and

> His musicke waytes on him in every bush,
> The mavis, bulfinch, blackbird and the thrush;
> The mounting larke sings in the lofty sky,
> And robin redbreast makes him melody.

A prose interlude shows further "some part of their formes, carriage, manners, and behaviour, their severall garbs, tones,

[1] Taylor had some acquaintance with picaresque fiction. In 1644 he speaks in *Crop-eare Curried, or Tom Nash his Ghost* of such popular novels as "Lazarillo, Don Quixote, Gusman of Alfarache, Bevis of Hampton, the Mirror of Knighthood, and John Dory."

and salutations that they accost their clyents or benefactors withall," according as these chance to be knights, lawyers, or russet, home-spun plow-joggers.

Fletcher in his merry comedy, "The Beggars' Bush," presented among others a canting song sung by the "Gypsies" on electing a new king:—

> I crown thy nab with a gage of ben bouse,
> And stall thee by the salmon into clowes,
> To maund on the pad, and strike all the cheats,
> To mill from the Ruffmans, Commission, and Slates,
> Twang dells i' the stiromel, and let the Quire Cuffin
> And Harman Beck strine and trine to the ruffin.

To Fletcher, also, is ascribed "The High Pad's Boast," a fourteen-stanza song, later included in "The New Canting Dictionary."

Better than these were the incidental ditties of Brome's popular comedy, "A Joviall Crew, or The Merry Beggars" (1641), wherein the rogues carol in chorus:—

> Here safe in our Skipper, let's cly off our Peck,
> And bowse in defiance o' th' Harman-Beck.
> Here's Pannum and Lap, and good Poplars of Yarrum,
> To fill up the Crib and comfort the Quarron.
> Now bowse a round health to the Go-well and Com-well
> Of Cisley Bumtrincket that lies in the Strummel.

The "Warning for House-Keepers" (1676), already noticed, contains an amusing "Budg and Snudg" song, which reappears with many other cant lyrics in Shirley's "Triumph of Wit" (1712). Here are to be found such choice specimens as "The Maunder's Praise of his Strowling Mort" and a companion piece, "The Rum-Mort's Praise of her Faithless Maunder," together with "The Black Procession," portraying "twenty black tradesmen who were brought up in hell." The tradesmen are none other than our old friends, the coiner, the voucher (to put off the counterfeit), the padder, the mill-ken, the glazier, the file-cly, the budge, the bulk, the angler, the shop-lift, the bubber (an ale-house thief), the bean-trap (a confidence-man), the famble (who deals in false rings), the gamester, the prancer, the sheep-napper, the dunaker (a cattle-lifter), the kid-napper, the prigger of cacklers, and the thief-catcher. "The Triumph of Wit" further offers an account of "the mystery and art of canting with the original and present management thereof, and the ends to which it serves and is employed."

The best songs of this collection were drawn upon in the "New Canting Dictionary" (1725) and in "Bacchus and Venus" (1737). The former's "Canter's Serenade" is typical: —

> Ye morts and ye dells
> Come out of your cells,
> And charm all the palliards about ye;
> Here birds of all feathers,
> Through deep roads and all weathers,
> Are gathered together to toute ye.

"Frisky Moll's Song," by John Harper, sung in Thurmond's "Harlequin Sheppard" at Drury Lane (1725), and the lyrics of Gay's "Beggar's Opera" and its sequel "Polly" caught the popular fancy early in the eighteenth century, to be later replaced by such pieces as George Parker's cantata, "The Sandman's Wedding" (1789), describing the mating of the Sandman and Bess the bunter in a booze-ken of St. Giles, or "Ye Scamps, ye Pads, ye Divers" from Messink's "Choice of Harlequin" (1781). The latter extends an invitation from the keeper of Bridewell difficult to decline: —

> Ye scamps, ye pads, ye divers, and all upon the lay,
> In Tothill-fields' gay sheep-walk, like lambs ye sport and play;
> Rattling up your darbies, come hither at my call;
> I 'm jigger dubber [1] here, and you are welcome to mill doll.[2]

---

[1] Warder. [2] Pick oakum.

A similar invitation, "Come all you Buffers Gay," had appeared in "The Humourist" (1760). In "The Busy Bee" (1790) "The Flash Man of St. Giles" recounts the course of his true love for Nelly Stiles. They drink together and are arrested, but when released live joyously.

> She pick'd up the flats as they pass'd by,
> And I mill'd their wipes from their side clye.

Only one minor note sounds in these songs, and that is when Tomlinson in "A Slang Pastoral" (1780), parodying Dr. Byrom's "My time, O ye Muses, was happily spent," laments the doxy who has been jailed and leaves her rogue despairing.

A fitting climax to the picaresque verse of the eighteenth century was Burns's "Jolly Beggars" (1785). This cantata, although containing little beggar-book lore, sings ragged freedom so light-heartedly that it is better worth remembering than most of the serious anatomies of roguery. Its characters are the true picaresque gentry, from the valiant ex-soldier in his red tatters, his naughty doxy once a regimental darling, and the poor Merry Andrew, to the amorous pigmy fiddler, the swaggering tinker, the itinerant ballad-singer, and the widow of a Highlander who to his cost held Lowland laws in scorn. As for the widow she knows the sound of silver: —

> For monie a pursie she had hookit,
> And had in monie a well been doukit.

The tinker, however, prefers gold: —

> I've ta'en the gold, I've been enroll'd
>   In many a noble squadron:
> But vain they search'd when off I march'd
>   To go and clout the caudron.

The song these rogues chant together is occasionally couched in language too lofty; but it returns to the right beggar's strain, and concludes with an uproarious: —

Here's to budgets, bags, and wallets!
Here 's to all the wandering train!
Here's our ragged brats and callets!
One and all cry out — Amen.

Later scoundrel verse includes contributions from the nameless and the famous. "Life in St. George's Fields" (1821), devoted to the rambles and adventures of Disconsolate William and his Surrey friend, Flash Dick, included songs and a flash dictionary. Byron tuned his lyre to this key in "Don Juan,"[1] referring his readers to Jackson, the pugilist, for an explanation of the terms. Tom Moore, the poet, gave a burlesque translation of the fifth book of the "Æneid" by "One of the Fancy" in "Tom Crib's Memorial to Congress" (1819), together with an essay on the classic origin of slang.[2] Pierce Egan issued "Sonnets for the Fancy" in his "Boxiana" and a series of picaresque songs in "Captain Macheath" (1842). About the same time Sir Theodore Martin and W. E. Aytoun contributed to their "Bon Gaultier Ballads" four "Flowers of Hemp, or the Newgate Garland," and Leman Rede adorned "Sixteen String Jack" with similar songs. In the thirties Harrison Ainsworth, the novelist, cultivated the picaresque lyric in "Rookwood" and "Jack Sheppard," and plumed himself unwarrantably upon having invented the genre. More recently vagabond verse has been written by G. R. Sims and W. E. Henley.

[1] Canto xi, stanzas 17–19.

[2] To Moore has also been attributed *Randall's Diary of Proceedings at the House of Call for Genius* (1820), "edited by Mr. Breakwindow, to which are added several of Mr. B.'s minor pieces." Moore probably had to do with *Jack Randall, a few Selections from his Scrap Book* (1822), which contains flash verse "on the late fight for the championship."

Accessions from the less known or the unknown, however, have not lacked merit. Thus the translation of Vidocq's "Mémoires" in 1829 by H. T. R. included several lively cant songs; Maginn did Vidocq's "En Roulant de Vergne en Vergne" into canting English as "The Pickpocket's Chaunt;" W. H. Smith penned "The Thieves' Chaunt" in "The Individual" (1836), and two years later W. M. Reynolds sang a "House Breaker's Song" in "Pickwick Abroad." Collections, too, like the "Universal Songster" (1826) and Labern's "Popular Comic Song Book" (1852) catered to that picaresque taste, which is still fed in Wallace Irwin's "Love Sonnets of a Hoodlum" (1902), a sonnet cycle, emulating George Ade's slang essays in prose and Villon's ballades in *argot*, and devoted to the lament of Willie the Hoodlum that his Mame should have preferred Kid Murphy. But it is in such anonymous pieces as "The Night Before Larry was Stretched" (*c.* 1816), "The Song of the Young Prig" (*c.* 1819), "The Leary Man" (1857), and "A Hundred Stretches Hence" (1859) that most power is shown. The last appeared in Matsell's "Vocabulum," and is not unworthy of Villon: —

Oh! where will be the culls of the bing
  A hundred stretches hence?
The bene morts who sweetly sing,
  A hundred stretches hence?
The autum-cacklers, autum-coves,
  The jolly blade who wildly roves;
And where the bluffer, bruiser, blowen,
And all the cops and beaks so knowin,
  A hundred stretches hence?

Permanently to establish the status of canting verse only one thing was needful, — an anthology; and this J. S. Farmer has supplied in his admirable "Musa Pedestris" (1896), "three centuries of canting songs and slang rhymes."

5. *Sociological Studies of Roguery*

In all these scoundrel verses, records of canting, discoveries by the repentant, prison tracts, conny-catching pamphlets, and beggar-books, the dominant spirit was literary or linguistic curiosity. Of humanitarian motives few could boast with justice, and not until the second half of the nineteenth century did the scientific and philanthropic view of criminal life prevail. J. T. Smith's "Vagabondiana" (1817), with its etchings of London rogues and its appeal to such painters of beggars as Michael Angelo, Murillo, Callot, Reynolds, and West, was typical. But by 1848, when George Cruikshank lent his pencil to "The Sinks of London Laid Open," the picturesque and sociological elements had combined, and thereafter many sociological studies of crime appeared.[1]

Chief of these was Henry Mayhew's "London Labour and the London Poor." Three volumes dealing with the industrious or incapacitated poor (1851) were followed by a fourth devoted to rogues (1861). Here the section upon beggars was provided by Andrew Halliday, that on thieves by John Binny, that on prostitutes by Mayhew and Bracebridge Hemyng, while the chaplain to the Society for the Rescue of Young Women and Children furnished a description of agencies for the suppression of crime. Statistics, maps, and tables were accompanied by graphic studies of the types of rascals, by narratives of adventure among the slums, and by rogue autobiographies.

In this picaresque *comédie humaine* what humors are displayed in the five main groups of vagrants, professional beg-

[1] E. g., J. C. Symons, *Tactics for the Times* (1849); T. Plint, *Crime in England* (1851); F. Hill, *Crime, its Amount, Causes, and Remedies* (1853); J. Holmes, *Thieves, Beggars, and Prostitutes* (1853); M. D. Hill, *Suggestions for the Suppression of Crime* (1857); and Mary Carpenter, *Our Convicts* (1864).

gars, swindlers, thieves and their dependents, and prostitutes! Among the mendicants are naval and military beggars, distressed operative beggars, and the disaster beggars in all their subdivisions. The bodily afflicted count seven kinds, from those with sores who work the scaldrum dodge to shallow coves who go half naked in winter to excite compassion. The famished chalk on the pavement "I am starving," and hang their heads; the foreigners feign ignorance of the language; the petty traders offer trinkets for sale as a blind to the police; while screevers indite begging letters, and referees give forged characters.

Not less complete is the classification of thieves. Those who plunder with violence are the cracksmen, the footpads or rampsmen, and the bludgers or bullies who rob with the assistance of low women. Those who plunder the stupefied are either bug-hunters preying on the drunken, or drummers who hocus liquor or use chloroform. The mobsmen rely upon manual dexterity, and comprise pick-pockets, prop-nailers, thimble-screwers, and shop-lifters. The sneaksmen include drag-sneaks who steal from coaches, snoozers who prey on luggage at railway hotels, star-glazers who cut the glass from shop-windows, area-sneaks and till-friskers, dead-lurkers who haunt hallways in quest of coats and umbrellas, snow-gatherers who like Autolycus steal linen from hedges, noisy-racketmen addicted to china and glass, sawney-hunters with a passion for bacon, bluey-hunters who rip the lead from roofs, cat-and-kitten-hunters who purloin pewter pots, and skinners who strip victims for their clothes. Here too are such water-side sneaks as the toshers who hunt copper, and the mud-larks who dally with coal and rope, as well as stealers of animals, kidnappers, and resurrection men.

Still another group, coördinate with the mobsmen and the sneakers, is composed of plunderers by breach of trust, to which class belong rascally servants, stealers of letters, pawners of bedding taken from lodgings and of work confided by employers, and every stripe of embezzler. Finally, the republic of thieves includes its skilled artisans, the coiners and forgers; and its financiers, the receivers of stolen goods.

But the mendicants and the thieves are not more potent in evil than the regiment of swindlers and the tawdry army of harpies. The former embraces gamblers, sharpers, and bonnets, horse-chaunters, bouncers and besters, flat-catchers, smugglers, jiggers, and bubble-men. The harpies include many varieties from the prima donna seclusives living in private apartments, to the convives dwelling together and differentiated as board and dress lodgers, and from the sailors' and soldiers' doxies, park ladies, and thieves' women, to such nefarious male followers as fancymen, bullies, bawds, panders, and pimps.

It is not alone the types and professional duties of rogues that are portrayed; their tricks, methods, motives, and rewards, all receive careful attention. No one can come from the reading of Mayhew's remarkable work without an oppressive sense of the multiplicity of baneful forces arrayed to prey upon society. The photographic realism of this anatomy of roguery provides the best antidote to the allurements of romantic roguery as presented by an Ainsworth or a Hornung.

"London Labour and the London Poor" appeared originally in the "Morning Chronicle," and a continuation in serial monthly parts, entitled "The Great World of London," was completed in collaboration with John Binny, and published as "The Criminal Prisons of London" (1862). Mayhew in 1864 and 1865 gave his *magnum opus* its final form. In the latter year he issued "The Shops and Companies of London," and in 1874 he published "London Characters."

Since Mayhew's day scientific studies of criminal manners have greatly multiplied, and the prisons and the police have shared in the anatomizing. To give more than a few titles would exceed the scope of this chapter, which cannot pretend to invade the field of criminology. But such volumes as "State Prison Life," "by one who has been there" (1871), Sutton's "New York Tombs; its Secrets and Mysteries" (1874), Toulmin's "Rogues and Vagabonds of the Race Course" (1872), "The Tramp; his Tricks, Tallies, and Tell-Tales" (1878), Brace's "Dangerous Classes of New York" (1880), Major Griffiths's "Memorials of Millbank" (1884), "Chronicles of Newgate" (1884), "Secrets of the Prison House" (1894), and "Mysteries of Police and Crime" (1899), the anonymous "Defenders and Offenders" (1888) and "Life in Sing Sing" (1904), Walling's "Recollections of a New York Chief of Police" (1887), Fitzgerald's "Chronicles of Bow Street" (1888), Campbell's "Insurance and Crime" (1902), and Byrnes's "Professional Criminals of America" (1895) and "Darkness and Daylight" (1891) illustrate the sociological anatomy of roguery in whole or in part.

"Darkness and Daylight," for example, seeks to do for New York what Mayhew did for London, exhibiting the criminal poor as seen by a missionary, Mrs. Helen Campbell, a journalist, Colonel Thomas W. Knox, and the Chief of Detectives, Thomas Byrnes. Life in the slums, tenements, lodging houses, dispensaries, and prisons is minutely described. Newsboys, shop-girls, dock-rats, hoodlums, land-sharks, pawn-brokers, street-venders, beggars, and gamblers are studied in their haunts. The cheats of the shyster, the mock-auctioneer, the confidence-man, and the whole crew of petty swindlers are exposed, together with the professional methods of delinquents more daring.

Records of social experiments like Wyckoff's "Day with a Tramp, and Other Days" (1901) and Meriwether's "Tramp Trip" (1887) and "Tramp at Home" (1889) have pictured conditions among the laboring poor and incidentally among the criminal classes. But the most entertaining of recent anatomies have been those by Josiah Flynt [Willard]. His "Tramping with Tramps" (1899) is of especial value as a study of vagabonds by one who for years shared their life. It differs therefore from Mayhew's more elaborate anatomy in two respects, — it observes only the milder rascals, and regards them from their own level. Flynt delights to run atilt at Lombroso and the criminal anthropologists who have attended chiefly to the delinquent's physical and psychological peculiarities. His initial essay, "The Criminal in the Open," denies most of the orthodox school's contentions.

Flynt believes that the average criminal is above his environment; that he is happy; that he rarely exhibits physical degeneracy at the outset; that the prison rather than his business breeds his diseases; and that he has misled observers because they have examined him under the abnormal conditions of confinement. The reader learns that the criminal is not in his own class the revolutionary he seems to those above it; that his intelligence does not differ from that of the honest man; that his good fellowship is the result of spontaneous emotion, not self-interest; and that to study his *milieu* is a surer way to understand him than to study his skull.

"The Children of the Road" considers those born to low-life, those driven there, those enticed there, and those who enter vagabondage voluntarily. The two last categories are most numerous, and the tramp "jocker" who can lure the imaginative youngster to become his "prushun" is the envied Pied Piper of Hoboland. "Club Life Among Outcasts" divides rogue societies into those of the Kids, the Natives, and the Old Bucks. The Kids may be animated by mischief, by love of thieving, or by love of fighting, but the Natives, or adults, stick closely to business, and the Old Bucks descant upon past glories and pick up small charities from their juniors. Tramps on the road congregate at hang-outs, and in prison their Kangaroo Court searches each recruit and asks half his property for the general good, — a survival of the Elizabethan garnish.

The urban tramp's order embraces the "tomato can vag," picking his meals from refuse and sleeping in boxes and cellars, the "two-cent dosser" scrambling at night for spots on restaurant benches and floors, all grades of the lodging-house gang, and the exclusive room-beggar. There are house and office, street and old clothes specialists, too, with tricks three centuries old.

Tramp life on the railways and in Germany, Russia, and England; sketches of rogues of reality from Old Boston Mary to Jamie the Kid; and narratives of such episodes as a Mexican spree and a fatal tramp duel with razors, round out the picture of roguery.

Like its sixteenth-century prototypes, "Tramping with Tramps" concludes with notes on the jargon of nomads and a glossary. But not a word here derives from the lexicons of Harman and Dekker, and few if any are even so old as Hotten's "Slang Dictionary." Metaphorical terms like "baldy" for an old man, "leather" for a pocket-book, "lighthouse" for one whose acquaintance with detectives enables him to "tip off" his comrades, predominate; and if less obvious expressions intrude, such as "gay-cat" for the tramp unweaned from work, and "monikey" for the roadster's *nom de guerre*, they are less distinctive than Elizabethan and Restoration cant.

In the "Notes of an Itinerant Policeman" (1900) Flynt no

longer rubs elbows with the vagabond as a brother, but studies him as the special detective of a railroad company. He distinguishes here six classes of rogues. The professional criminal, the instinctive criminal, and the tramp are supplemented by less obvious types, — the petty rogue, the backwoods criminal, and the unknown thief who uses a legitimate position to screen his own or another's stealing. Chapters dealing with pocket-picking, the corrupt protection of towns, prisons, and reformatories, the politics and reading of the tramp, and his tricks in begging, mingle with those concerning special types or gangs like the "gay-cats" and the "Lake Shore push."

The rogue's standpoint is reassumed in the "World of Graft" (1901) in order to criticise the shortcomings of American municipal government, and to discuss police corruption in Chicago, New York, and Boston. The rogue who has "squared it," or reformed, is allowed to hand down his verdict upon the joys and sorrows of criminal life and the sins of the thief-catchers. Much curious information is also afforded concerning such matters as the thief's expenditures, his cost to society, and the "mouth-piece system" whereby he is forced by the police to inform on his professional brethren.

It is evident that such essays as these represent a reaction from the ultra-scientific and unpicturesque treatment of rogues accorded by the criminal anthropologists. Although the contemporary anatomies of roguery will scarcely revert to the unmethodical fashion of the early beggar-books, conny-catching pamphlets, and prison and repentance tracts, nevertheless if they are to survive as literature they must retain much of the vividness, virility, and personal charm of their Elizabethan predecessors.

BIBLIOGRAPHY

CHAPTER III

1

The *Liber vagatorum* is translated by J. C. Hotten as *The Book of Vagabonds and Beggars* (London, 1860). H. R. Plomer discusses Robert Copland in the *Bibliographical Soc. Trans.* (London, 1896, vol. iii, p. 211). His *Hye Way to the Spyttel Hous* is reprinted in E. V. Utterson's *Select Pieces of Early Popular Poetry* (1817, vol. ii, p. 1) and in W. C. Hazlitt's *Remains of the Early Popular Poetry of England* (vol. iv, p. 17). The best edition of *Cocke Lorelles Bote* is that by E. F. Rimbault (*Percy Soc. Publ.*, vol. vi). The *Rogues and Vagabonds of Shakespeare's Youth* (edited by Edward Viles and F. J. Furnivall, *Early English Text Soc.*, 1869, and reprinted for the *New Shakspere Soc.*, 1880) contains an interesting preface together with Awdeley's *Fraternitye* and Harman's *Caueat.* The first edition of the *Caueat* has disappeared. Viles and Furnivall collate two copies of the second edition, the earlier in the Bodleian, dated 8 Jan., 1567–68, the other in the library of Henry Huth. The *Caueat* was earlier reprinted from the edition of 1573 (London, T. Bensley, 1814). The *Fraternitye of Vacabondes* was licensed c. July, 1561, and was reprinted in 1565 and 1575. Strype's *Annals* (Edinburgh, 1824) includes an amusing letter of complaint against the police, rogues, and Gypsies, written in 1596 by Hext, a justice of the peace for Somersetshire.

2

Greene's *Plays and Poems*, edited by Alex. Dyce (London, 1831, revised 1861), is now supplemented by J. Churton Collins's new edition of the *Plays and Poems* (Oxford, 1905, 2 vols.). This is especially valuable for its General Introduction. Greene's work is noticed in W. Bernhardi's *Robert Greenes Leben und Schriften* (Leipzig, 1874) and Nikolai Storojenko's somewhat inaccurate *Life* (Moscow, 1878), translated from the Russian by E. A. B. Hodgetts, and included in vol. i of Alex. B. Grosart's edition of Greene's *Complete Works* (*Huth Library*, 1881–

86, 15 vols.). The *Notable Discouery of Coosnage* was reprinted by J. O. Halliwell (London, 1859), *The Defence of Conny catching*, by J. E. Adlard (London, 1859), The *Groatsworth of Wit*, by Sir Egerton Brydges (London, 1889), and *Greenes Ghost Havnting Conie-catchers*, by J. O. Halliwell (London, 1860). The *Complete Works of Samuel Rowlands* was issued for the Hunterian Club (Glasgow, 1880, 3 vols.). Dekker's *Non-Dramatic Works* are edited by Dr. Grosart (*Huth Library*, 1884–86, 5 vols.). The *Gvls Horne-booke* is separately reprinted in Dr. Nott's annotated edition (1812), in G. E. B. Saintsbury's *Elizabethan and Jacobean Pamphlets* (1892), by R. B. McKerrow in the *King's Library* (London, 1902, vol. ii), and together with the *Belman of London* and *Lanthorne and Candle-light* in the *Temple Classics* (London, 1904).

3

Luke Hutton is briefly noticed in the *Dict. of Nat. Biog.* (vol. xxviii). Clavell has received more attention; cf. Stephen Collet's *Relics of Literature* (1823, p. 230), James Granger's *Biographical History of Great Britain* (5th ed., vol. iii, p. 251), James Caulfield's *Portraits and Memoirs* (1813, vol. i, p. 97), and W. C. Hazlitt's *Handbook to the Popular Poetical and Dramatic Literature of Great Britain* (London, 1867). The influence of Clavell's *Recantation* has not before been remarked. Mynshul's *Essayes and Characters of a Prison* is reprinted (London, 1821). George Parker, who died in the Coventry Poor House (Apr. 1800), is noticed by Gordon Goodwin (*Dict. of Nat. Biog.*, vol. xliii). His *Life's Painter* saw a second edition (Dublin, *c.* 1800), and was later issued as a London chap-book.

4

Ribton-Turner's *History of Vagrants and Vagrancy* (1887, ch. xx) discusses the secret jargon of the vagrant. A descriptive bibliography of slang, cant, and the vulgar language is given in the third edition of Hotten's *Slang Dictionary* (1874, p. 371, *et seq.*), and bibliographies figure also in the dictionaries of Barrère and Leland, and Farmer and Henley. Henley and Henderson review the canting literature that precedes *The Jolly Beggars* in *The Poetry of Robert Burns* (Edinburgh, 1896, vol. ii, pp. 291 ff.). I am especially indebted to Farmer's *Musa Pedestris* (1896) for its anthology of scoundrel verse.

5

The sociological studies of roguery are sufficiently noted in the text. Most treatises upon criminology include such matter; cf. the bibliography appended to chapter i. Henry Morley's *Memoirs of Bartholomew Fair* (London, 1859), Cornelius Walford's *Fairs Past and Present* (London, 1883), and Jacob A. Riis's *How the Other Half Lives* (1890), incidentally take account of rogueries; and such books as H. Dixon's *London Prisons* (1850), E. Alboize and A. Maquet's *Les prisons de l'Europe* (1845, 8 vols. in 4), J. Greenwood's *Seven Curses of London* (1869) and *Unsentimental Journeys, or Byways of the Modern Babylon* (1867), and J. W. Horsley's *Prisons and Prisoners* (1898) more closely illustrate the type.

The periodicals, too, frequently contain miniature anatomies of roguery. Among these may be noted: *Curiosities in Roguery* (*Chambers's Journal*, 13: 180), *The World of Rogues* (*Dublin Univ. Mag.*, 67: 363), *Some Old Rogueries* (*All the Year*, 29: 420), *Amongst Beggars* (*Once a Week*, 30: 720), *Beggars and Beggary* (*Western*, 3: 511), *Beggars and Begging in America* (*Penny Mag.*, 6: 322), *Mendicancy and Vagabondage in England* (*Temple Bar*, 17: 178), *Mendicant Orders* (*Baptist Quarterly*, 11: 233), *The Tramp* (*Macmillan's*, 90: 28), *Ethics of the Tramp* (*Cornhill*, 4: 682), *Tramps and Hoboes* (*Forum*, 26: 217), *The Real Hobo* (*Forum*, 33: 438), *Thieves and Thieving* (*Cornhill*, 2: 326, and 6: 640). Josiah Flynt's autobiography, *My Life — So Far*, began its serial appearance in the *Success Magazine*, N. Y., Dec., 1906. The author died, Jan., 1907.

The *Bulletin of the New York Public Library* (May, 1906) includes a *List of Works Relating to Beggars, Mendicants, Tramps, Vagrants*, etc.

CHAPTER IV

THE CRIMINAL BIOGRAPHIES

1. *Early Pirates and Picaros*

NGLISH rogues of reality can boast a literature as ample as those of the imagination. At first the anatomies were both character sketches and brief chronicles of individual rascals. Ere long, however, the two types diverged, and anti-heroes of actual life secured posthumous glory in plays and ballads, or more often through criminal pamphlets.

Of a multitude of such tracts that flourished during the seventeenth and eighteenth centuries, few fall within the pale of art. They were written by the unliterary who, thinking to take advantage of public attention bestowed for nine days of wonder upon some luckless thief or murderer, issued an account of his life and latest exploit, to be hawked at his execution or immediately thereafter. Corresponding to the criminal columns of the modern newspaper, and feeding the same tastes, these productions aimed and claimed to be veracious; but where fact failed, fancy stepped into the breach, and many a jest-book anecdote or pleasing invention of the author's own came to be fathered upon hanged reprobates.

Sometimes by exception humor crept into these narratives, and the sordidness of a bald, grim story of villainy was relieved by gleams of mirth, until rogues who thumbed such accounts, instead of finding there a morbid pleasure merely, were amused and sought to make their own exploits laughable as well. In such facetious criminal pamphlets, inspired as they often were by fiction, the romance of roguery found a close parallel. Ratsey and Sadler, Hind and Hainam, Ramsay and Morrell were true picaros in print and out of it. As the vogue of the single criminal pamphlet showed signs of decline at the end of the seventeenth century, compilations of the best in this kind began to be made, more and more leavened with the picaresque spirit and with episodes taken direct from picaresque literature. Thus arose a popular series embracing the "Memoirs of Gamesters," the "Lives of Highwaymen," the "History of Pirates," and the "Newgate Calendars," all more or less allied with the "Histoire Générale des Larrons."

Pirates were among the earliest rogues of reality to be sung in the criminal pamphlets, and the versified laments of Arnold, Clinton, and Walton, *alias* Purser, date from the year of their hanging, 1583. Walton and Clinton stepped on the stage in Heywood and Rowley's "Fortune by Land and Sea," printed only in 1655, but written at the end of Elizabeth's reign; and in 1639 both figured in a curious tract, — "The Lives and Deaths of the Two Most Famous English Pyrats." Classical pirates and medieval were celebrated in Thomas Lodge's "Of Manie Famous Pirats" (1593), where Dionides offers to Alexander the Great a bit of picaresque philosophy, "O Alexander, both thou and I are of one nature, and the selfsame office: the onlie difference is that I am called a Pyrat for that I assault other men with a little armie, and thou art called a prince, because thou subduest and signiorest with a mightie hoast."

Somewhat later the deeds of a brace of jolly sea thieves, Ward and Dansiker, were made the basis of Robert Daborn's mediocre tragedy "A Christian Turn'd Turke" (1612). Captain Ward had previously been honored by a ballad, as had

"Daneker the Dutchman"[1] and Sir Andrew Barton "a pyrate and rover on the seas." Another rover, Captain George Cusack, who with six companions swung at Execution Dock, played leading rôle in "The Grand Pyrate" (1674, 1676), where, after an amusing narrative of the rogues' lives, they are heard to sing in unison a ditty beginning bravely, "Hang sorrow," but ending mournfully enough, —

> The bell shall ring, the clerk shall sing,
> The good old wife shall wind us,
> The sexton shall lay our bodies in clay,
> Where the Devil in Hell shall find us.

In the meantime, land rogues had proved even more popular, many of them mere bloody villains, others gentlemen of wit.[2] Of the former type were the rascals noticed by John Awdeley, author of the "Fraternitye of Vacabondes," in a folio sheet "Of the Endes and Deathes of Two Prisoners" (1569). To the same class belongs Arnold Cosby, slayer of "the vertuous and valerous" John Lord Bourgh, the account of whose "horrible and tragicall murther" (1591) presents perhaps the oldest specimen of non-dramatic blank-verse dealing with a popular theme. In the same year appeared the "Sundry Strange and Inhumane Murders lately Committed," the basis of a lost tragedy by Dekker and Jonson, together with "The Lamentable and True Tragedy of Arden of Feversham in Kent," rehearsing a noteworthy crime of 1551. Here too belongs the sensational account in 1592 of the "murthering of John Brewen, goldsmith

[1] Percy Society; *Early English Poetry*, vol. ii, pp. 55, 58. Daborn probably refers to this ballad and to *Newes from the Sea of 2 Notorious Pyrats*, 1609, when he says, —

> What heretofore set others pennes aworke,
> Was Ward turn'd Pyrate, ours is Ward turn'd Turke.

[2] Consult the bibliography appended to this chapter for a list of early criminal pamphlets, *infra*, pp. 188, 189.

of London, committed by his own wife," from the pen of Thomas Kyd, author of the much bemocked "Spanish Tragedy." The "Two Most Unnatural and Bloodie Murthers" (1605) affords the foundation of "A Yorkshire Tragedy," which, like "Arden of Feversham," has been attributed to Shakespeare; and many other plays [1] of the type have similar sources. Even in the eighteenth century George Lillo went back to a criminal pamphlet, "Newes from Perin," and a ballad of 1618 on the "Murder at Bohelland Farm near Penryn in Cornwall," for the matter of his "Fatal Curiosity" (1736), while his more famous bourgeois drama, "George Barnwell, or the London Merchant" (1731), revived a ballad in Percy's "Reliques" based upon another actual crime.

Less tragic, and touched even with humor, was Thomas Lodge's "Life and Death of William Longbeard" (1593), where this "craftie citizen" is no hero of the people, but a subtle rogue, "held for a second God among the poore." A courtier, who vowed any hair in his own beard was a better gentleman than William, found repayment by being shaved close, head and face, with witty William "pleasantlie gibing at him." The rogue persuaded a merchant's daughter, "the louelie Mawdelin," to be his "lemmon," and wooed her poetically; but, on discovering her infidelity, he slew by stealth his rival, making it appear that the latter had killed himself. William's mind was planted on ambition. "At a beck, coblers, tinkers, tailors, and all sortes of the hare brainde multitude attended him." After his last great battle with the bailiffs in Bow Church he made confession of his rogueries, and Lodge concludes: "Let this example serue to withdraw the bad-minded from Bedlem

[1] Ward, *English Dramatic Literature*, vol. ii, pp. 218, 219, notes several: *The Warning for Fair Women* (pr. 1599), Robert Yarrington's *Two Tragedies in One* (pr. 1601), Houghton and Day's *Thomas Merry* (pl. 1594), and *The Fair Maid of Bristol* (pr. 1605).

insolence, and incorage the good to followe godlinesse." What renders the pamphlet of note is its realistic detail and perfect fictional style.

Best of all the early criminal biographies was "The Life and Death of Gamaliel Ratsey, a Famous Theefe of England" (1605).[1] This heralded the achievements of a real rascal, most of whose tricks seem to have been derived from jest-books or conny-catching pamphlets. Although he fails to enter service, he is otherwise a thorough picaro.

He was early the pride of virtuous parents and went as soldier with the Earl of Essex into Ireland. Upon his return as a sergeant, however, he took to roguery, first practicing on the affections of a serving-maid at an inn in order the better to pilfer a bag of money from the hostelry.[2] On breaking jail after this affair, he tricked a groom who was leading his master's horse and riding another. For he persuaded the fellow to allow him to mount the free nag and so passed for the master himself, and presently sold one horse and ran away with the other. In his bolder highway expeditions, Ratsey on one occasion robbed a scholar of Cambridge whom he forced to preach a sermon in a wood, an echo of the old legend of Parson Haben's or Hyberdyne's sermon.[3] Next he robbed two woolmen and knighted them as Sir Walter Woolsack and Sir Samuel Sheepskin. Upon a poor man going to market he bestowed a bounty, but a rival in roguery he sent to a jailer to deliver a letter which proved a forged *mittimus*.[4] With two other rascals — Henry Shorthose and George Snell — he played pranks

[1] Two "ballets of Gamaliell Ratsey and Snell his companie" (*sic*) were licensed to Thomas Pavier, May 2, 1605.

[2] Of the hostess on this occasion it is said, ". . . but it stroke such a quandarie to her stomache as if shee had drunke a draught of small beere next her heart in a frostie morning." Cf. *The Defence of Conny catching* (1592) where the author, when discovered in roguery, declares, "Never went a cup of small beare so sorrowfully down an ale-knight's belly in a frosty morning, as that word stroke to my hart."

[3] Cf. Lansdowne MS., 98, leaf 210; and MS. Cott. Vesp., A. xxv, leaf 53.

[4] A trick derived *verbatim* from Greene's *Second part of Conny-catching*, 1591.

of more moment. One of these consisted in having Shorthose masquerade as his servant and steal a gentleman's money, whereupon Ratsey and Snell, as if horrified at the theft, would ride in pursuit, all three thus disappearing. At length Snell, being captured for theft, informed on the others, and all were condemned to be hanged at Bedford, March 27, 1605.

"Ratsey's repentance which he wrote with his owne hand when he was in New-gate" follows the prose story, and its six-line stanzas recall those of the "Lamentation" of Luke Hutton the highwayman. This anonymous account of Ratsey was followed in the same month of May by John Hodgett's "Ratseys Ghoaste, or the Second Part of his Life, with the Note of his Mad Prancks," a pamphlet chiefly remarkable for containing a reference to Shakespeare and Burbage.[1] Ratsey's fame remained green for some years, and Ben Jonson in "The Alchemist" paid him tribute.[2]

2. *Rogues of the Seventeenth Century*

As was fitting, the rogue pamphlet did not delay in taking cognizance of the fair sex. The "Life and Pranks of Long Meg of Westminster" was printed as early as 1582, and the Amazon there celebrated appears in the Stationers' Registers as the subject for ballads or books in 1590 and 1594.[3] Her name was well known during the second half of the seventeenth century and survived in chap-books even into the eighteenth. In 1635 appeared a biography from which most of these chap-books drew. Longa Margarita was a valiant Lancashire girl,

[1] Cf. Collier, *History of English Dramatic Poetry*, vol. i, p. 333.

[2] Act i, sc. 1, for his ugliness. Gabriel Harvey was similarly impressed, and referred to him as Gamaliel Hobgoblin, while an ill-faced woman in Thomas Randolph's *Hey for Honesty* is compared to him.

[3] A *Life* licensed August 10, 1590; a *Ballad*, August 27. She figured in a lost play acted at The Rose in 1594–95, and in Tyro's *Roaring Megge*, 1598.

who, coming up to London in Henry VIII's reign, beat the carrier out of his fare, and went into service at a taphouse. She loved good company, especially affecting that of Dr. Skelton, the jester Will Sommers, and the Spanish Knight, Sir James of Castille. She delighted to assume man's apparel, and at last went to the wars with King Henry and returned wedded to a soldier, and set up a public house at Islington.[1]

More roguish and scarcely less famous was Mary Frith, or Moll Cutpurse, of whose life and stratagems frequent accounts appeared during the seventeenth century.[2] As a girl "a sampler was as grievous as a winding-sheet" to her. She affected male attire, was one of the first of her sex to smoke, and rode astride in breeches from Charing Cross to Shoreditch. She told fortunes, played the procuress, and acted as a receiver of stolen goods. Most contemporary allusions refer to her roguishness, but Taylor the Water Poet defended her in "The Water Comorant," and Middleton and Dekker in their rollicking comedy "The Roaring Girle" (pl. 1611) depict her as coarse and rude, but not unchaste.

Here she consents to assignations only to turn up dressed as a man and defeat with the sword her too aspiring admirers. It is for her that Sebastian Wentgrave, the hero, feigns a passion in order to throw his father from the scent of his genuine love for the daughter of a hated house. The old gentleman is so horrified that he finally consents to the

[1] Contemporary allusions to Long Meg abound. She is referred to in Nash's *Strange Newes*, Harvey's *Pierce's Supererogation*, Vaughan's *Golden Grove*, in *Westward Hoe*, in Taylor's *Sir Gregory Nonsense*, in *The Hog Hath Lost his Pearl*, in *Pappe with a Hatchet*, in Middleton and Dekker's *Roaring Girle*, in *Vercingetorixa*, *Hollands Leagver*, *The Town Spy*, *The Scornful Lady*, Gayton's *Notes on Don Quixot*, and by Ben Jonson, *Works*, Gifford, vol. viii, p. 78.

[2] Cf. *The Madde Pranckes of Merry Mall of the Banckside*, licensed to Henry Gosson, Aug. 7, 1610, and *The Womans Champion;* or "the strange wonder, being a true relation of the mad pranks, merry conceits, politick figaries and most unheard of stratagems of Mrs. Mary Frith," 1662.

other match, after having engaged Ralph Trapdore, a roaring boy, to track Moll up and down and attempt to bring her to grief. Trapdore and Teare-Cat, his mentor in begging and canting, are greater rogues than Moll, who on the whole comes off lightly here.[1] Yet all three are adepts in low-life craft. Moll pronounces Teare-Cat to be "a meere Whip-Iacke, and that is in the Common-wealth of rogues a Slaue, that can talke of sea-fight, name all your chief Pirats, discouer more countries to you, then either the Dutch, Spanish, French, or English euer found out, yet indeed all his service is by land, and that is to rob a Faire, or some such venturous exploit." This fellow and she sing together a canting song, and Trapdore, in a jargon derived from Harman's "Caueat," avows, "I have by the Salomon a doxy, that carries a kitchin mort in her slat at her backe, besides my dell and my dainty wilde dell with all whom I'll tumble this next darkmans in the strommel, and drink ben-baufe, and eat a fat gruntling cheate, a cackling cheate, and a quacking cheate."

Moll plays chorus in characterizing different members of the rogues' fraternity quite in the beggar-book fashion. One is "a diver with two fingers, a picke-pocket; all his traine study the figging law, that's to say cutting of purses and foysting." Another "is a nip, I tooke him once in the two penny gallery at the Fortune; then there's a cloyer, or snap, that dogges any new brother in the trade, and snappes will have half in any booty." And she admits, —

> I know they haue their orders, offices,
> Circuits and circles, unto which they are bound,
> To raise their owne damnation in.

The play, then, proves merrily picaresque, and Goshawke's verdict upon Moll, "'T is the maddest, fantasticalst girle," is well borne out.[2]

Another woman of even more notorious life amused London

[1] Middleton's Preface says, "Worse things I must needs confesse the world has taxt her for, then has beene written of her; but 't is the excellency of a writer to leave things better then he finds 'em."

[2] Moll figured less agreeably in Nathaniel Field's play, *Amends for Ladies, with the Merry Prankes of Moll Cutpurse* (1618), and was referred to in Brome's *Court Beggar*, in *The Feigned Astrologer*, in Thomas Shipman's *Carolina*, and in Thomas Freeman's *Epigrams*. Captain Smith gave her an epitaph, which he absurdly attributed to Milton.

a generation later, and in 1632 became the anti-heroine of a pamphlet and a play. The latter was by Shackerley Marmion, who may have had a hand also in the former, although Nicholas Goodman professed to be its author. Dona Britanica Hollandia was an English Celestina, who had taken up her abode on the south shore of the Thames in an establishment impregnable except to her well-wishers, and furnishing for the moment the scandal of the town. In both pamphlet and play, however, the redoubtable lady is regarded with humor and picaresque appreciation. In the former her exploits are ironically referred to the Kingdom of Eutopia.

After a career of more folly than wisdom, she is instructed by a "Puritan Jesuit" in the fine rôle courtesans have played in history. She escapes arrest, and posts herself accordingly in a castle cut off from the mainland by moats, ditches, trenches, and bulwarks, yet close to the city, her source of custom. Here with her fair forces and a ruffian to mind the drawbridge she defies the world. When after a prosperous season the enemy come to take her, she drops the invaders from her drawbridge into the river. At the conclusion of the pamphlet "they dare no more assault her, but with a continuall Leaguer, meane to tyre her out." Those who survive deem her half immortal and able to encounter with Bradamant, Marphysa, and Clardana; though "for us here in Great Brittaine," says the author, "we neither either read, heard, or bred a creature of her temper, our clime is too cold, our instructions too seuere, and our punishments too sharpe and piercing; let Hollandia then live in Eutopia, and as it was worthy to give her breath so let it write her Epitaph."

In the play, "Hollands Leagver," Marmion begs that his Muse may be considered a reprover, not an interpreter of wickedness; wherefore perhaps the castle of the valiant bawd does not figure until the fourth act.

The main plot turns upon the winning of a young nobleman from evil courses by his sister, who plays the courtesan unrecognized and reads him a moral lecture. As for the description of Dona Britanica and her stronghold, it is here but a side issue. "Pray what newes from Holland?" asks one of the characters. "Holland 's beleaguer'd," is the reply, "and wil hold out as long as Busse or Bulloign. They haue their mote and drawbridge. I haue given them besides, a draft of a fortification will hold them play this twelve month." The queen of Holland is shown ruling supreme. At the sound of knocking she cries: —

> Go bid the watch looke out; and if their number
> Be not too plurall, then let them come in.
> But if they chance to be those ruffian soldiers,
> Let fall the purcullis.

She is particular naturally as to toll for entrance to her castle.

> Ile take no tickets, nor no future stipends.
> Tis not false titles, or denominations
> Of offices can do it. I must have money.
> Tell them so, draw the bridge.

Yet she shows no scruple at ejecting from the fortress gallants once stripped of their cloaks, swords, and purses.

Other women figured as anti-heroines in less literary tracts from the serious "Notorious Cosenages of Dorothie Phillips" (1595) or the "Practises of Elizabeth Caldwell" (1604), by Robert Armin, to the tragical "Unnatural Grandmother" (1654) and the merry "Cony-Catching Bride" (1643). In 1656 a single cheat that had been played by two women upon an old "Dyar in Southwark" received half-fictional treatment in "The Trepan." Here the story of Mr. Wessel Goodwin's gullibility was detailed with humor and no doubt to the victim's chagrin; for he had succumbed to being wooed with tender verses and locks of hair, and had made a will in the ladies' favor. "The Highwaywoman" (1665) was devoted to the exploits of Marcy Clay, who successfully performed the old trick of hiring an inn room as servant to a lady, placing there for security a trunk filled with stones, prevailing upon tradesmen to leave with her goods on approval, and then decamping. In man's attire she robbed her own husband on the road in order to test his mettle, and accomplished many other feats.

"The Lawyers Clarke Trappan'd" and "A True Account of the Tryal of Mrs. Mary Carlton," both published in 1663, celebrate a certain Mary Maunders whose father was a fiddler in Canterbury. She early got into Newgate for playing the fine lady and running up accounts with tradesmen, and before and after that event was adroit at picking pockets and securing husbands through her high pretensions. Her greatest exploit was playing the rôle of German princess and forging letters to herself from a supposed chamberlain. Her latest victim, John Carleton of the Middle Temple, whose name she had assumed, issued his "Replication" in 1663, confessing the manner of his being gulled. Two years later another woman, Mrs. Eleanor Chadwick, came in for part of the interest in "The Cheating Sollicitor Cheated," "a true and perfect relation of the life and death of Richard Farr." This fellow, son of a charwoman, took to forging deeds and soon commanded a company of night thieves, of whose booty he alone made disposition. He would borrow from innkeepers, feigning to be a grazier engaged in a lawsuit about to be decided in his favor, and he was apt at selling goods and then reclaiming them through an accomplice as stolen.

The accounts of such early highwaymen as Luke Hutton and John Clavell belong rather to the anatomies of roguery, as does "Jackson's Recantation," adapted from Clavell's "Recantation" in 1674. But before that date Spanish picaresque influence had begun to play upon the criminal pamphlets, especially in narratives dealing with Hind, Hainam, Sadler, and Morrell.

James Hind was a highwayman drawn, hanged, and quartered "on Friday, an unlucky day for him," September 24, 1652. Before his death, as well as after it, Hind was celebrated in an imposing array of pamphlets, entitling him to be considered as one of the most popular among English rogues of reality. It was the jaunty *nonchalance* of the picaro which rendered him a favorite, and that quality shines out in the titles of most of the pamphlets devoted to him. In 1651 alone appeared "An Excellent Comedy Called the Prince of Priggs Revels," dealing with "the practices of that grand thief, Captain James Hind;" another "most pleasant and historical narrative" entitled "We Have Brought our Hogs to a Fair Market;" a "description of his manner of life" as "Hinds Ramble;" a collection of his "pleasant jests, witty conceits, and excellent cozenages" labeled "A Pill to Purge Melancholy;" a "Last Will and Testament" "full of various conceits beyond expectation;" and a few serious sheets such as his "Declaration," his "Humble Petition," his "Trial and Confession," and a "True and Perfect Relation of the Taking of James Hind." In the next year the unwearying public welcomed "a fuller relation of his rambles, robberies and cheats in England, Ireland, Scotland, with his voyage to Holland," and another account of his "merry conceits and pretty pranks" entitled "Wit for Money," as well as "The English Gusman" written by George Fidge, author of the "Ramble" (1651).[1]

Of all this ephemeral literature "The English Gusman" was a fair specimen. "Thou wilt find it pleasant and witty," says Fidge, "and that our English Gusman is as famous in these times, as ever the Spanish in his time." Many of the rogue's exploits are mythical, as, for example, his being enchanted for

[1] Fidge was the author, too, of a popular satire upon John Marriot, *The Great Eater of Gray's Inn*, reissued in the same year (1652) as *The Mountebank.* It called out a spirited *Defense* of Marriot, and in 1657 a curious tract *The Trapper Trapt*, "or the true relation of a cunning, cogging, crafty, counterfeiting, cosening, and cheating knight alias knave, with his matchless mischiefs against a merchant named John Marriott."

three years into invulnerability and his telling a Dutch mountebank that his wife had a flux, in proof of which he shows a purse to be cured of its emptiness, a story in the "Histoire Générale des Larrons," to be reproduced in "The English Rogue."[1] Here, too, is the episode, derived from Greene's "Blacke Bookes Messenger" of sixty years before, of trading off a horse and stealing it back. One of Hind's pleasantest devices is an escape effected after he has committed a robbery. The enraged victims are in hot pursuit, but Hind, meeting a parson, and giving him a loaded pistol, declares he is chased by robbers, and advises the parson to hold them at bay while he gallops on to raise the countryside. Of course the parson shoots at the pursuers, who promptly apprehend him for the highwayman.

In 1657 the matter of "The English Gusman" was utilized again with less elaboration in "No Jest Like a True Jest," omitting such passages of merely passing interest as Hind's trial, confession, and last conversations. This was reprinted in 1674, 1817, and 1820. There were two editions of it as a chap-book in 1750, together with chap-book renderings of "The Merry Life and Mad Exploits" of the same arch-rogue in 1765, 1775, 1805, and 1820.

Richard Hainam, executed at Smithfield in 1656, enjoyed notoriety first in a tract entitled "The Witty Rogue Arraigned, Condemned, and Executed," and then in "The English Villain, or the Grand Thief." It is affirmed in the latter that he "far exceeds that arch villain, the Spanish Gusman, and the late famous robber of England, Captain James Hind, yea, and all

[1] A contemporary MS. note in the Bodleian copy of *The English Gusman* describes Hind as a "little, dapper, desperat fellow." It adds reminiscences of some of his companions, — Dewy, Haywood, and Rowe, — and says of this pamphlet, "Many things are true, but most are false, and many material things omitted."

the notorious thieves that ever yet were heard of," another indication of the British propensity for transcribing fiction into fact. In the former and more extended account, the author philosophically explains that in this world talents differ, for some are given wit and others virtue, Hainam possessing one, but not the other. He flies at high game, robbing the Portuguese ambassador, the Duke of Normandy, and the King of France, and his chronicler's familiarity with the Spanish type is shown by the use here of the word "picaro." [1]

A briefer pamphlet in the Spanish vein appeared in 1677 as "Sadler's Memoirs," describing the "most notorious pranks in city and country" of Thomas Sadler, who, although illiterate, seems to have been a wit. He told a gentleman whose purse he picked in the Temple Church that he should have watched as well as prayed; and by masquerading in a sheet like a ghost, he readily robbed the affrighted. Among other tricks he played the venerable one of taking a creditor to a physician to be paid, and telling the physician the creditor suffered from a delusion that everybody owed him money.

Of more manifest Spanish inspiration was "The Notorious Impostor," issued in two parts in 1692, and reprinted in 1694. "We hope the life of our English Guzman . . . will be no undiverting entertainment," says the author, who, eschewing the customary moralizing, relates a story of considerable wit and satire.

[1] The popularity of Hind and Hainam is apparent from contemporary pamphlets: cf. *Hind's Elder Brother, or the Master Thief Discovered* (1652), an account of "the life, exploits, escapes, and witty robberies of Thomas Knowls;" *Guzman Hind and Hannam Outstript* (1657) "being a discovery of the whole art, mystery, and antiquity of theeves and theeving, with their statutes, laws, customs, and practices, together with many new and unheard of cheats and trepannings;" the *Witty Jests and Mad Pranks of John Frith . . . with Captain James Hinde, the Famous Highwayman* (1673); and *The Yorkshire Rogue, or Captain Hind Improv'd* (1684).

William Morrell, this rogue of reality, was a surgeon in Banbury. After twenty years innocently passed in the bosom of his family he suddenly developed a taste for adventure which led him to exploits that foreshadow those of Ferdinand, Count Fathom. The resemblance, indeed, between the two anti-heroes and the terms in which the accounts of their cheating are couched is so strong as to suggest actual borrowing on the part of Smollett. Morrell would ingratiate himself with a family by dangling before the pretty daughter his aristocratic pretensions. He would pose as the cadet of a knight unwilling to consent to the alliance, and having secured a loan on the girl's portion, together with a vehicle in which to fetch his chattels from his estate, he would neatly decamp. Sometimes he seemed to be a great man incognito, forging letters to himself and leaving them where they could be read, like Quevedo's Don Pablos. Once accepted as a son-in-law, he would enjoy a week's honeymoon and then disappear.

When nothing else would avail, Morrell might fall ill and summon a lawyer to draw up a will bequeathing to the lady's family imaginary estates. Then on convalescing he would be given the heiress in a burst of gratitude.[1] Once, having just been wed, he galloped beside the coach bearing home his bride and her relatives, and, pretending that he saw a highwayman approaching, gathered all their jewels and money with which he promised to escape to safety; and this vow he fulfilled to the letter. He was expert at other rogueries as well, counterfeiting, substituting copper rings for gold, and exchanging tankards at inns. Even in adversity he never lost good nature, and when dying in a baker's house after having made a grandiose will in the proprietor's favor, his attendants observed him "to laugh to himself very pleasantly, which they suppose proceeded from the pleasure he took in defrauding the world he was then just upon leaving." Of course Morrell's story is heartless, like that of most picaros, but its harshness is softened by humor and it reads like fiction, despite the author's declaration that there is so much fact to be drawn upon in this life that "excepting a little garniture (that common pardonable liberty) the whole feast we treat you with has not one borrow'd dish." [2]

---

[1] This trick is practiced also by the Master Drugster in *The English Rogue*, pt. ii, ch. 30.

[2] One of Morrell's descendants was "David Huntley, the famous English Fortune Hunter," whose *Most Surprising Adventures and Wonderful Intrigues* found favor as an eighteenth-century chap-book. A less dis-

Better bred than Morrell, and unfailing in his chivalry to the ladies, Claude Du Vall, the gentleman highwayman, was their special darling. His "Memoirs" (1670) was eagerly devoured by his admirers, not a few of whom had suffered from his polished audacity. Indeed, the attention sentimental women lavished upon this anti-hero during his captivity gave rise to a "Pindaric Ode" (1671) professedly by the author of "Hudibras," and quite in the spirit of Fielding's "Jonathan Wild." It was a biting satire upon the distinguished Du Vall,

> That liv'd and dy'd, to leave behind
> A great example to mankind.

In the same vein, Nathaniel Tomkins, a criminal executed thirty years before, had been sung in a "Satyrick Elegie" (1643). And rogues of greater actual pretension were chronicled in such pamphlets as "The History of Mistris Jane Shore" or Thomas Gainsford's "True and Wonderfvll History of Perkin Warbeck" (1618), a theme introduced to literature proper by Ford and Mrs. Shelley.

Beside such entertaining scoundrels there continued to be ranked the grim or mediocre. Different counties were honored by collections of their own proper cheats and horrors; Cheshire, Berkshire, Shropshire, and the rest contending to contribute their quota of the harrowing or laughable. From the picaresque levity of "The Whole Life and Progresse of Henry Walker the Ironmonger" (1641), giving a "true relation of his severall escapes and rescues from the hands of justice," [1] to the moral

tinguished rogue of the same type was discussed in *The Comical Bargain, or Trick upon Trick* (1707), "being a pleasant and true relation of one Thomas Brocks, a baker's prentice near Milk Street, that went for a Hamburg merchant, and courted an eminent doctor's daughter near King Street in Bloomsbury."

[1] As usual, Walker found defenders. Cf. *An Answer to a Foolish Pamphlet* (1641), and *The Modest Vindication of Henry Walker* (1642).

edification of "The Penitent Murderer" (1657),[1] embalming the memory of Nathaniel Butler, or the "six horrid and bloody cruelties" of "Murther upon Murther" (1684), every shade of popular taste was appealed to. For the merrily disposed there was Colonel Turner, executed in 1663 for a burglary upon a friend. His deeds were discussed in at least four pamphlets, one with the high-sounding title, — "The Triumph of Truth."[2] Turner was a bully who delighted to pose as a great slayer of men. From his window he suspended naked swords and, although in war ready enough to cut and run, ordered a cart to follow him about to carry his dead. For the sentimental there was Robert Foulkes, "late minister of Stanton Lucy," a perfect "Scarlet Letter" hero, who made his confession in "An Alarme for Sinners" (1678); and for impressionable youth what more could be asked than the story of the boy, Thomas Savage, who in 1668 killed a maid-servant with a hammer, and then heartily repented of it?

3. *Jonathan Wild and His Circle*

England sank to the nadir of social misrule in the first third of the eighteenth century, and its prince of darkness was Jonathan Wild. He represents the acme of professionalism in crime. As a terror inspirer he has long been invoked by novelists and dramatists, and every criminal chronicle holds him its darling.

Jonathan Wild shaped the age, and the age shaped him. For while Augustan suavity distinguished the manners and letters of the favored few, vice was rampant and justice asleep or groping among the indigent many. Hangings at Tyburn proved

[1] Five editions in two years.

[2] The chief are the *Life and Death of James, Commonly called Collonel Turner*, and *The Speech and Deportment of Col. James Turner*, "who was condemned for felony and burglary in breaking up the house and robbing of Mr. Francis Tryon, merchant."

for the victims gala days of applauded heroism, and for pick-pockets who plied in the throng occasions of golden harvest. The newspapers, then in their youth, were already devoted to accounts of robberies, rogueries, and executions, as well as to advertisements of articles lost, but to be returned at a price and no questions asked. The roads converging on London were infested by highwaymen riding singly or in bands. In the town itself the City Marshal in 1718 declared, "It is the general complaint of the taverns, the coffee-houses, the shop-keepers, and others that many of their customers are afraid when it is dark to come to their houses and shops, for fear that their hats and wigs should be snatched from off their heads, or their swords taken from their sides, or that they may be blinded, knock'd down, cut or stabbed."[1] A contemporary said of the prisons, "They are known to be the sanctuaries of villains, from whence their emissaries are despatch'd, and a regular and settled correspondence is said to be fix'd and carried on, through the whole fraternity of rogues in England."[2] Transportation to America had few terrors, for the rascals returned with celerity, their health improved by the voyage. Officials everywhere were corrupt and no match, except in immorality, for the swarming picaros.

Defoe in his "Augusta Triumphans" (1728) bestowed attention upon practical suggestions for preventing street robberies, which he amplified in his pamphlets, "Second Thoughts are Best" and "Street-Robberies Consider'd" of the same year.

[1] Hitchin, *Discovery of the Conduct of Receivers and Thief-Takers*.

[2] *Hanging not Punishment enough for Murtherers, High-way Men, and House Breakers* (1701). This tract, "offered to the consideration of the two Houses of Parliament," advocates the resort to torture and death by burning, since hanging is awarded him who steals the value of five shillings and has proved no deterrent to crime. In 1652 *A Cry Against . . . Killing of Men Meerly for Theft* had urged leniency in vain.

Bernard de Mandeville in similar spirit issued an "Enquiry Into the Causes of the Frequent Executions at Tyburn; and a Proposal for Some Regulations Concerning Felons in Prison" (1725).[1] Somewhat later the "Newgate Calendar" described with serenity revolting horrors, — hangings upon mere suspicion, criminals killed by missiles flung at them as they stood in the pillory, political suspects beheaded, disemboweled, and burned to the hangman's cries of "God save King George!" In Dublin affairs were so bad that when Ebenezer Elliston was executed there for a street robbery (May 2, 1722), Jonathan Swift wrote a "Last Speech and Dying Confession" purporting to be his, expressly to frighten wrongdoers into virtue. Elliston in this hypothetical address with veiled humor declares the government justified in showing no mercy to rogues, sets forth the miseries of the life he has led, and announces that he has confided to a friend a list of criminals and their crimes, and a list of gentlemen who through cowardice have allowed themselves to be robbed. When any victim shall again yield without resistance, or when any rogue shall again offend, these lists he promises shall be published in full. That this jest for a while proved efficient testifies not alone to the Dean's knowledge of human nature, but equally to the eagerness with which criminal pamphlets must have been read by the public. In 1732 one pamphlet, indeed, frankly begins: "As the lives and infamous actions of the most profligate criminals have met with a reception from persons of all ranks and conditions, we

[1] Works of this type were by no means novel, as witness the following: *A Pollitique Platt . . . for the Reformation of Roges and Idle Persons* (1580); *Orders Appointed to be Executed in the City of London for Setting Roges and Idle Persons to Worke, and for Reliefe of the Poore* (n. d.); *Heavens Speedie Hue and Cry after Lust and Murder* — "a discoverie of those places where such kinde of lewde people haunt" (1635); and *Stanley's Remedy; or the Way how to Reform Wandering Beggars, Thieves, Highway Robbers, and Pickpockets* (1646).

hope that an account of John Waller's crimes will have the like success."

Such were the conditions to which Jonathan Wild adapted himself. Born at Wolverhampton in 1682 and executed at Tyburn in 1725, he occupied the intervening period in devising ingenious iniquities. By trade he was a buckle-maker, but the combined professions of thief, instructor of thieves, fence, and thief-catcher engaged all his efforts. For a time he dwelt as a debtor in the Wood Street Counter, and then, having deserted his first wife, set up a brothel. He was employed by Charles Hitchin, the City Marshal, as thief-taker, but entered into competition with his master and throve mightily, keeping three offices for the pawn and return of stolen property, apportioning his bands of thieves to their special duties and districts, and maintaining discipline by giving the refractory over to justice.

No doubt Wild had a softer side, for on the occasion of his second marriage he did not fail to treat the hangman and the prisoners of Newgate to a feast, and Captain Smith reports of him a remarkable mildness of disposition, avowing to have seen him "kikt, buffeted, and pull'd by the Nose, without resenting it in the least." But in the main Jonathan was not lovable. His speciality, the practice of informing on malefactors, had been celebrated long before in Luke Hutton's "Blacke Dogge of Newgate" and more fully in "The Life and Death of Griffin Flood" (1623). Flood was an informer sometimes worsted by his intended victims, and eventually pressed to death for having killed a vintner in a quarrel. Informing as a distinct art, dignified as thief-taking, is indissolubly associated with Wild, who was stimulated to it by the government policy inaugurated in 1692 of paying blood money for the apprehension of criminals. It is best exposed by Wild's disgruntled rival in the business, Charles Hitchin, whose "True Discovery of the Conduct of Receivers and Thief-Takers" appeared in 1718.

The body of this pamphlet is a dialogue between a thief and a countryman during the latter's introduction into the mysteries of thief-taking and the receipt of stolen goods.

"What are all that heap of boys at that table, that are playing dice, swearing, cursing, and grinning at each other like so many hell-cats?" asks the countryman, "and that man in the silver buttoned coat and knotted peruke, with a sword by his side, what does he do amongst them?"

"Sir," replies a thief, "those boys are all Clouters alias Pick-Pockets, and that man in the silver button'd Coat is their Thief-Taker, to help them to Money for the pocket books, shop books or writings, and other goods that they shall steal."

When the countryman inquires if there be no way to suppress this abomination, the thief replies, "Sir, it is my fixed opinion that if ever the same be done, your friend the City Marshall will be the man that doth it, for that he is entirely free from all these evil practises."

But Hitchin is so insistent upon his own virtue as well as upon the vice of "his skittish and baboonish majesty," Jonathan Wild, that he awakes suspicion, and in "An Answer to a Late Insolent Libel" (1718), by Wild himself, is heard the retort discourteous: "When a reformation is to be begun by the devil, it is high time for persons of all denominations to be upon their guard." Wild, indeed, reports such roguery of Hitchin, taking up his pamphlet satirically section by section, and giving so good a Roland for each of Hitchin's Olivers, that the only wonder is that the Marshal was not silenced. Undaunted, however, he shortly issued "The Regulator," a *rifacimento* of the former work, to which was appended a vocabulary of flash terms, an account of those keeping thieves' resorts, and "a list of thieves that are now at liberty that are Jonathan Wild's weekly pensioners." This was undoubtedly the last expedient at self-justification of a desperate man.

That thief-taking was not obsolete by the middle of the century is shown by an extensive tract issued in 1756 by Joseph Cox, High Constable of the Hundred of Black Heath. It is devoted to the doings of four rogues who contrived to secure rewards offered for apprehensions by accusing innocent boys and adducing false testimony to convict them. So late as 1816 George Vaughan of the Horse Patrol and others were sentenced for inducing a burglary in order to secure pay for capturing the offenders.

As for Wild, he long fought off his enemies, escaping with his life when Blueskin, or Joseph Blake, a recalcitrant pupil, stabbed him in the neck. But at last he was fairly caught in his own toils three months after Blueskin's hanging, and for three months more contended vainly in the courts for freedom. Then after an ineffectual attempt at suicide he was strung up May 24, 1725, amid general rejoicings.

Defoe, the year previous, had written in his "Great Law of Subordination Consider'd," "I have been told our famous Thief-taker (as they call him) has a list of seven thousand Newgate-Birds now in services in this city and parts adjacent, all with intent to rob the houses they are in." At Wild's imprisonment he hastened to procure an interview and communicated to the anxious public his exclusive information through notices in "Applebee's Journal," and by means of a pamphlet — "The True, Genuine, and Perfect Account of the Life of Jonathan Wild" — issued by Applebee in three editions after the execution. Other writers were similarly inspired. "Newgate's Garland," a ballad preserved in Swift's "Miscellanies," appeared after the Blueskin affair; a "Life of Jonathan Wild from his Birth to his Death" was compiled by a clerk of the court, H. D. (1725); and a poem in imitation of "Hudibras," entitled "Weighley, alias Wild," was accompanied by a prose biography, "also Jonathan's last farewell and epitaph, with a song never before printed" (1725).[1] A quarter of a century later the demand for information concerning Wild and his intimates induced still another pamphlet, which included a canting dictionary professedly by Jonathan himself.[2]

Defoe, who had shown so much interest in Wild, had been equally interested in other rogues of reality. His life of Captain Avery, "The King of Pirates" (1719), rivaled a "Life and Adventures of Captain John Avery" (1709), apparently composed by Adrian Van Broeck, a Dutch super-cargo captured by that buccaneer. His "Account of the Conduct and Proceedings of John Gow the Pirate" (1725) celebrated another sea-thief; and land-thieves were considered in "A Brief Historical Account of the Lives of Six Notorious Street Robbers Executed at Kingston" (1726). Cartouche, the famous French picaro, claimed the attention of Defoe, who has been credited with a translation (1722) "relating at large his remarkable adventures, desperate enterprises, and various escapes, with an account of his behaviour under sentence and upon the scaffold; and the manner of his execution." A sequel,[3] more certainly by Defoe, and professing to be a translation, described circumstantially the crimes of Cartoucheans led by Bizeau and Le Febvre.[4]

[1] The provinces rejoiced in accounts of Wild, e. g., *The Life of Jonathan Wilde* (Northampton, 1725), and *An Authentic History of the Parentage . . . of Jonathan Wild* (Stamford, 1725 ?).

[2] *History of the Lives and Actions of Jonathan Wild, Thieftaker, Joseph Blake, alias Blueskin, Foot Pad, and John Sheppard, Housebreaker* (1750).

[3] *A Narrative of the Proceedings in France, for Discovering and Detecting the Murderers of the English Gentlemen* (1724).

[4] For fresh light upon the authorship of these tracts I am indebted to Professor W. P. Trent, whose forthcoming *Daniel Defoe* promises a complete revision of the Defoe canon.

It was Jack Sheppard, however, the most distinguished member of Wild's circle, that Defoe chose for his special protégé. Sheppard, an insignificant cane-chair mender, apprenticed to a carpenter, ran away from his master, fell into bad company with Edgeworth Bess and Poll Maggot, took to thieving, but only when imprisoned evinced any talent. His speciality lay in escapes, and these Defoe chronicled in "Applebee's Journal" in sixteen articles. Defoe or another had in press a "History of the Remarkable Life of John Sheppard," when that anti-hero once more disappeared, this time making his way through six strong rooms and over the top of Newgate. When four days later the "History" appeared, it included a description of this last exploit. Upon Sheppard's recapture he became the lion of the town, received the visits of the best people, and sat for his portrait to Sir James Thornhill and to Hogarth. Defoe, who had already interviewed him, and who, posing as Applebee, received Jack's "kind love" by letter after his final escape, now seems to have been distinguished by an invitation into the cart, and by the presentation there of a pamphlet before a crowd estimated to have numbered two hundred thousand persons. This honor is also claimed for Applebee in person, but in any case the advertising trick served its purpose; for Defoe's pretended autobiography of Sheppard, issued the next day, ran through seven editions within a month.[1]

[1] It was published Nov. 17, 1724, as *A Narrative of all the Robberies, Escapes, etc. . . of John Sheppard. . . . Written by Himself.* It saw eight editions in one year, and from the sixth was derived the *Vie et vols du fameux Jean Sheppard* (Amsterdam, 1725). *The Authentic Memoirs of John Sheppard* (1725) furnished matter for a German account (Leipzig, 1765). At the time of Jack's hanging the *British Journal* published a *Dialogue between John Sheppard and Julius Cæsar*, and from Dublin (?) was issued a versified *Epistle from John Sheppard to the late L—d C—ll—r of E—d.* In 1786 appeared *Particulars of the Very Singular and Remarkable Trials, Convictions, and Escapes of John Shepherd* (*sic*). His fame would not down during the nineteenth century. Editions of his

Rob Roy was another picaro glorified with less of reportorial and more of fictional style in "The Highland Rogue" (1723), a piece occasionally attributed to Defoe, yet declared to be no romance, and so "not the adventures of a Robinson Crusoe, Colonel Jack, or a Moll Flanders." Here the writer, whether Defoe or another, assailed for lack of originality his greatest competitor in picaresque biography, — Captain Alexander Smith, author of the "Lives of Highwaymen," — saying with some justice: "If you find a story, or but one sentence in all his scribbling that is even tolerable, depend upon it, he stole it." As Rob Roy, or Robert Macgregor, survived until 1733 and probably five years longer, this account of his deeds broke off abruptly after a narrative no closer to fact than the collected knaveries of Captain Smith.[1]

It was reserved for the mendacious Captain, however, to portray Wild's whole circle. This was done in the "Memoirs of the Life and Times of the Famous Jonathan Wild" (1726). Wild's career and the lives of twenty-two of his companions in iniquity are here set forth, and although the biographies are generally overcircumstantial, yet in the account of Richard Shepherd occur eight tricks derived from "Eulenspiegel," and of Will Chance is told a story from Skelton and the Master

Life and Adventures hail from Devonport (1820 ?), London (1830 ?), and Manchester (1840 ?); of his *Adventures and Exploits* from Derby (1830 ?) and Sydney, N. S. W. (1845 ?); and of his *Life* from London (1830 ?) and Newcastle (1850 ?). Manchester noticed him in the *Lives and Adventures of John Sheppard, D. Morris, W. Nevinson, and S. Beane* (1839), and London in *The Real Life and Times of Jack Sheppard* (1866).

[1] Scott in the introduction to his *Rob Roy* calls *The Highland Rogue* a catch-penny publication, and discredits its attribution to Defoe. He expressly says: "It is great pity so excellent a theme for a narrative of the kind had not fallen into the hands of DeFoe, who was engaged at the time on subjects somewhat similar, though inferior in dignity and interest." William Lee accepts this pamphlet as by Defoe, but G. A. Aitken and Professor Trent reject it.

Thief legend of a corpse dropped through the tiles, supposed to be the thief, and so buried, while the real thief helps himself to booty.

4. *The Longer Criminal Biographies*

By 1730 the popularity of the separate criminal pamphlet was on the wane. Newspaper notices, collected chronicles of crime, and elaborate fictions like those of Defoe tended to supply its place with the vulgar, while to the middle and upper classes literary periodicals offered a more refined and salutary entertainment. Such pamphlets as did appear were generally longer, pieced out by levying upon fiction and reiterating old matter. The "Life and Infamous Actions of that Perjur'd Villain, John Waller" (1732), protests that "Here is no fiction, as is commonly used in pamphlets of this nature, to trepan people under a pretence of entertaining them;" and "The Life, Adventures, and Transactions of Robert Ramsey" (1742) attacks several rival publications for being made from "fictitious stories." Yet this very tract savors of rogue romance in its humor and tricks. Ramsey practices the alchemist dodge quite in the spirit of Garay in the "Garduña de Sevilla," pretends to be a nobleman, dines sumptuously at an inn, and then, taking the drawer home to pay him, walks through the house and embarks on the river from the rear door. He plays the physician, telling a lady she must remain in the dark, but stealing her jewels as soon as her eyes are closed; he joins the Methodists, in order to superintend their collections of alms and to caress the sisters in all brotherly love. In succeeding pamphlets few new tricks emerge, rogues seeming content to repeat traditional devices and to pattern their careers upon those of distinguished elders in the fraternity. So James Maclean, the gentleman highwayman, executed in 1750 and celebrated in several issues,[1] proves the reincarnation of Du Vall with something also of Morrell's delight in fine matches. John Hall, "The Compleat History" (1741) of whose life and death professed to have been written by himself, is a duplicate of more bloodthirsty villains and as lugubrious in his moralizing as an epitaph: —

> Servants take Warning by my fatal Fall
> And shun the Fate of poor unhappy Hall.

The more entertaining pamphlets, as a matter of fact, inclined away from the purely picaresque and tended to become narratives of adventure. An excellent early example of this development was "The Life, Travels, Exploits, Frauds, and Robberies of Charles Speckman" (1763), devoted to a rogue whose meteoric career illumined two continents. He fought under Braddock in Virginia, was whipped out of New York for theft, voyaged to the West Indies, enlisted against the French in Ohio, deserted in Pennsylvania, served as ship's surgeon on the Hudson, and finally returned to England, leaving behind a wake of depredation. The "Life and Adventures of Ambrose Gwynnett" recounted the misfortunes of a wanderer who on circumstantial evidence was hanged, but, reviving after being cut down, nearly perished in Havana prisons, was captured by pirates, rowed in the Spanish galleys, and was enslaved by Algerines. Eventually he reached London short of one leg, and lived as a beggar.

Other accounts of rascals reverted, like "The Discoveries of John Poulter," to the anatomy of roguery or combined such lore with strange adventure as in the "Memoirs of James Hardy Vaux." The need of greater elbow room in the single pamphlet was manifest and, although brief tracts continued to be issued,

[1] Notably *A Complete History*, 1750, and in the same year *An Account of the Behaviour of Mr. James Maclaine*, by the Rev. Dr. Allen.

most separate biographies took on dignified proportions. The first to do so were the narratives detailing the exploits of Bampfylde-Moore Carew.

Carew was born in 1693, the son of the rector of Bickley in Devon. He ran away from Tiverton School to join the Gypsies and became a rogue, wandering about the country under the guise of an unfortunate farmer whose all had been lost in a freshet, or pretending to be mad Tom of Bedlam. Sometimes he masqueraded as a rat-catcher, and at others as a non-juring clergyman, a tin-miner ill from the damps, a burnt-out blacksmith, a ship-wrecked Quaker, the son of a Newfoundland trader, and in petticoats as the grandmother of three infants orphaned by a conflagration.

He not only profited financially from such ruses, but thus gratified his passion for roving and philosophic observation. "He saw servants waste their masters' substance, and that there were no greater nor more crafty thieves than domestic ones; and met with masters who roared out for liberty abroad, acting the arbitrary tyrant in their own houses." Unlike the Spanish picaros he was tender-hearted, melting into tears at the sight of his parents, and waxing sentimental over the daughter of a Newcastle apothecary to whom as his wife he proved a pattern of constancy.

After a voyage to Newfoundland Carew was elected king of the mendicants to succeed Clause Patch. But a justice captured him by guile and banished him to the Maryland plantations. Once in America, to plan and execute an escape was mere pastime for the exiled monarch, who made his way afoot to Philadelphia, New York, and New London, and so sailed home, eluding a press gang at Bristol by feigning the smallpox. New and diverting cheats now occupied him,— beggary as a match-seller and rag-picker, a castaway seaman or impoverished Greek, and pretended discoveries of smugglers to win credit. Two other voyages rounded out his foreign travels, one aboard a man-of-war to the Baltic, and the other a second deportation to Maryland. Having returned to England, Carew undertook fresh rogueries to prove that age had not dulled his faculties, and then abdicated the throne of the mendicants to live in the country "respected best by those who knew him best." His death is variously assigned to 1758 and 1770.

The first of the Carew books appeared in 1745 as the anti-hero's "Life and Adventures," professing to have been related by him "during his passage to the plantations in America." [1] It is a narrative in the third person, and omits the American exploits. Some four years later "An Apology for the Life of Bampfylde-Moore Carew" was printed by R. Goadby, and sold by W. Owen in London. This is a complete rewriting of the previous history. It alters and transposes the incidents, draws upon books of travel for information concerning America, and drops Carew's Newfoundland and Baltic journeys. The same publishers shortly afterward issued, under a similar title, the third and most important biography. This combines both the others, is twice as long as either, and has served as the basis of all future accounts.[2] It is divided into chapters and includes laws of the Gypsies, with a "Gypsy" dictionary drawn in part out of Harman and Dekker, and offers a mild protest against Fielding for the "childish and stupid language" he assigns in

[1] This volume is stamped "Exon; Printed by the Farleys, for Joseph Drew, bookseller, opposite Castle-Lane, 1745."

[2] Both the second and the third biographies are *Apologies* for Carew, but in the former he is qualified as "Commonly known throughout the West of England by the title of King of the Beggars; and Dog Merchant-General;" the latter refers to him merely as "Commonly call'd King of the Beggars." The same preface appears in both. In the latter it is dated February 10, 1750.

"Tom Jones" to a Gypsy. But the animus against Fielding in subsequent editions grew strangely bitter, until in the sixth (*c.* 1765) the novelist was outrageously abused, especially for his realism, — a strange complaint from this source. At least three other editions repeated the attack, but in that of 1779 it was happily abandoned.[1]

Few works have achieved a success so disproportionate to their merit. Without literary pretension or striking originality in substance, no less than thirty editions of Carew's biography were disposed of, some mere chap-books it is true, but others volumes of bulk. In 1825 appeared a romantic melodrama "Bampfylde-Moore Carew, or the Gipsey of the Glen,"[2] and versions from 1871 forward have contained additional matter concerning the vagabonds and their speech, derived from Simson's "History of the Gypsies" (1865). The English love of verisimilitude and adventure insured the fortune of these accounts, which abound in circumstantial references to persons and things at home and abroad in the fashion of Defoe. Yet the reader may be surprised to hear of a white bear prowling through the forests south of Philadelphia, and he will recognize in the Mayor of Bridgewater's ruse to make the halt and the blind recover through fear, an echo of Eulenspiegel's trick upon the invalids of the Amsterdam hospital.

Other extensive rogue biographies followed. Turpin, Eugene Aram, Sixteen String Jack Rann, and Blueskin were celebrated in works of some length, and the "Memoirs of the Northern Impostor, or Prince of Swindlers," describing the rogueries of James George Semple, reached an eighth edition in 1786. America offered a hundred-page "Sketch of the Life of the

[1] The book at this time left Goadby's hands. A new preface reproached the former invective as appearing "more like private pique than candid criticism."

[2] Cf. Duncombe's *British Theatre*, vol. v, 1825.

Notorious Stephen Burroughs" (1810) to offset Josiah Priest's absurdly written pamphlet of the same year, "The Robber, or a Narrative of Pye the Highwayman." Shortly after, an English biography, the "Memoirs of James Hardy Vaux" (1819), won especial favor.

This exhibits an anti-hero who finds his various apprenticeships distasteful, enters the navy, deserts, and after ups and downs as a defrauder of tradesmen gravitates to Botany Bay. By good conduct he there becomes a magistrate's clerk and receives a pardon that enables him to make an eventful homeward voyage around the Horn. But the free life of the picaro still allures him, Newgate opens her arms, and only a reprieve to the hulks saves his neck. In New South Wales he makes alternate attempts to reform and to escape, and the reader will be inclined to pardon his backslidings rather than his lack of humor. Notwithstanding this deficiency, the editor calls Vaux's "Memoirs" "an entertaining and instructive narrative . . . as full of cunning and adventure as 'The Life of Guzman de Alfarache, the Spanish Rogue,' if not so profoundly moralized."

In 1821 appeared a "Life of David Haggart, Alias John Wilson, Alias Barney McCoul," the autobiography of a rogue written, on the eve of his execution, to provide the means for educating his younger brothers and sisters. Haggart was a Scotchman, the companion in boyhood of George Borrow, bolder in attack than Jack Sheppard, and as ingenious in escapes. He frequently hazarded his neck for others, but, having accidentally killed a turnkey in breaking from Dumfries jail, fled to Ireland to put to the blush by his rogueries the old Rapparees. Discovered in an attempt to dig his way out of Kilmainham jail, he was carried to Scotland and hanged at the age of twenty.

Pierce Egan at just this time was issuing from London a series of picaresque tracts, beginning with the playful account of a criminal trial in "The Fancy Tog's Man *versus* Young Sad Boy, the Milling Quaker" (1821), and including "The Life and Extraordinary Adventures of S. D. Hayward" "denominated the modern Macheath" (1822), "A Report of Henry Fauntleroy's Trial for Forgery" (1824), "An Account of the Trial of John Thurtell and Joseph Hunt" (1824), and "The Recollections of John Thurtell."[1] Across the seas "The American Trenck, or the Memoirs of Thomas Ward" (1829) provided a readable account of a dashing robber of the mails, and several hundred pages were devoted to a picara in "Henrietta Robinson" (1855), and to the "first and most celebrated counterfeiter of Connecticut" in "Sketches of the Life of William Stuart" (1854).

But to extend the list is useless. To note that the Edinburgh resurrectionists have received authoritative handling in a "History of Burke and Hare" (1884), or that a notorious swindler has recounted his doings in "Bidwell's Travels from Wall Street to a London Prison" (1897), is of less importance than to observe that all these longer separate biographies fall into three classes. Some are simply social documents, like Joe Bragg's "Confessions of a Thief" or Hutchins Hapgood's "Autobiography of a Thief" (1903); some are tales of adventure, like Langdon W. Moore's "His Own Story" and Stanley Waterloo's "Story of a Strange Career" (1902); and others, like Julian Hawthorne's "Confessions of a Convict" (1893), focus attention upon special phases of criminal life and so expound them as to approach the anatomies of roguery.

[1] It is significant that James Catnach, by the sale of ballads on the trial of Thurtell, made £500. Cf. the curious *Collection of the Books and Woodcuts of James Catnach* (1869).

5. *Collected Chronicles of Crime*

The tendency to combine and organize, made manifest in the world of rogues in the person of Jonathan Wild, was expressed in the literature of roguery by the collected chronicles of crime. Individual rascals had been commemorated in separate pamphlets for more than a century when the possibilities of a union of the best in this kind dawned upon certain ingenious historiographers of iniquity. The result was a "Dictionary of Infamous Biography" compiled by many hands in many volumes and continuing in supplementary issues even to the present day.

Such works hark back to the publications of the Ordinary of Newgate, whose opportunities as a chronicler of crime were deemed a precious perquisite, and to the sessions papers, those official records of the Old Bailey, complete files of which since 1729 are preserved in the British Museum and the Home Office. They further derive from one phase of the anatomies of roguery by an interesting transition which deserves attention.

In 1674 Charles Cotton issued his "Compleat Gamester," a descendant on one side of such picaresque tracts as "Mihil Mumchance" and on the other of Izaak Walton's "Compleat Angler," for the fifth edition of which Cotton himself contributed an article on fly-fishing. The "Gamester" sought not only to describe games and popular sports like riding, racing, and cock-fighting, but to note the cheats to be guarded against in each.

Both elements were taken over in the "Memoirs of Gamesters" (1714), by Theophilus Lucas, who transformed the whole to a biographical record. For the accounts of games he went directly to Cotton, and the cheats were made picturesque by fastening them upon individual gamesters. Thus of the twenty-six anti-heroes portrayed by Lucas, few are confined to card-sharping and dice tricks. Most resemble Major Clancy, whose story is the usual picaresque narrative.

Clancy as a page donned his master's clothes, visited many towns in Ireland, and entertained the Earl of Crawford, although leaving him to pay the bill. In one place he secured a loan on a trunk filled with bricks; at another he received a hundred pounds by telling a servant his lord had ordered its delivery. When apprehended he feigned penitence and was accepted by the Franciscan order, from which he promptly stole, departing to raise a troop for Flanders and making away with the funds provided for their use. He eloped with his jailer's daughter, escaped a bailiff by nailing the latter's belt to a wall, and practiced many other ruses, only to be hanged at Tyburn in 1666.[1]

To pass from the collected biographies of gamesters to those of professional criminals meant but a step, and this was taken in the same year by Captain Alexander Smith, whose "Complete History of the Lives and Robberies of the Most Notorious Highwaymen" (1714) reached a fifth edition by 1719, and in 1720 reappeared with an added volume. Captain Smith's "Lives" is the first notable collection of rogue biographies in English. It comprises the information afforded by whatever criminal pamphlets and last confessions had then been published. Moreover, after the fashion of the "Histoire Générale des Larrons" it contains most of the tricks presented in jest-books and picaresque literature, assigning to real people the stock incidents of fiction. It accepts the scheme suggested by Lucas, but improves upon his practice by departing still further from fact. How large an imaginative leaven there was here

[1] Both Lucas and Cotton borrow verbally from *Leather-More* (1668). Cotton repeats *Leather-More's* statement that "gaming is an enchanting Witchery begot betwixt idleness and avarice," with "gotten" substituted for "begot;" and Lucas says: "It is an enchanting Witchcraft, begotten by those Devils Avarice and Idleness." A late descendant of Lucas is Colonel George Hanger's *Lives and Adventures and Sharping Tricks of Eminent Gamesters* (1804).

will be apparent if any of the hundred and twenty-two lives comprised in the three volumes of 1720 be reviewed.

In the account of Arthur Chambers, for example, it is said that he stole the oxen two countrymen were driving by appearing hanged in a tree at one place and then slipping forward and appearing to hang from another. When the countrymen disputed as to its being the same man, and returned to investigate, Arthur drove off with his booty, concluding a trick recorded centuries before in Don Juan Manuel's "Conde Lucanor" and somewhat later in "Eulenspiegel." He employs, too, the cheat related in the "Desordenada Codicia" of a pickpocket caught in the act, who has a crier call the article as found, at which the victim releases his prisoner. More noteworthy is the plagiarism from Solórzano's "Garduña de Sevilla" in which Chambers is shown holding up a dummy figure upon a ladder against a house, whereupon the proprietor, a miser, comes out and shoots it for a thief. Then while he is burying it in fear, Chambers goes in and helps himself to jewels. He also deceives the miser's wife into thinking him her husband, and she does not discover this until her lord returns, a finale borrowed doubtless from Boccaccio's story of King Agilulf and the horse-courser.

In the account of Claude Du Vall, when that highwayman is being entertained by an actor with a part concerning a bear, a maidservant coming upstairs takes it all in good faith and summons the neighbors, a passage pilfered literally from Quevedo's "Buscon." Du Vall furthermore shows his powers in alchemy by stirring a potion with a stick containing gold, a device used by Garay in the "Garduña" as well as by Chaucer's Canon. More than a dozen rogues practice Eulenspiegel's old trick of promising a creditor he shall be paid at a monastery, and then telling a friar he has come to confess; variants of it, too, are tried by Nan Harris, Dick Low, and Dick Adams.

"The English Rogue" is constantly drawn upon, and Tom Sharp, as there, befools an attorney by passing him a medal, which he in turn passes to another; a confederate walks off with it, and the attorney is held responsible. Again Sharp treats his captor to a shave, and then runs away, whereat the captor leaps up to pursue, but is held by the barber, who fears to lose his pay.

Of Stephen Bunce is told the astrologer-trick from "The English Rogue," in which Stephen, having stolen a tankard while serving as tapster, is sent with a maid to learn from the wonder-worker where it is and by her own mouth forces her to convict another. Will Elby steals a horse from under a man in Smithfield, leaving him sitting on the saddle propped up with sticks, a reminiscence not only of the theft of Sancho's ass in "Don Quixote," but of an incident in "The English Rogue;" and, as there, another knave waxes a cup to the underside of a table, and so is enabled to come back and appropriate it.

Quite as largely borrowed from is García's "Desordenada Codicia," which affords Moll Ruby her adventure of being discovered while hiding under a bed by the chance fight there of a dog and a cat, as well as her swallowing one by one a necklace of pearls in order to conceal them. Dick Morris does the same magic trick related of García's rogue in escaping from the Marseilles galleys, although here the scene is Winchester; and Jack Hall enters a house inside a bale, and cuts a 'prentice sitting on it precisely like the Spaniard. Dick Bauf becomes in turn all the kinds of thieves described in the "Codicia," and Sawney Douglass tries the pearl-swallowing game.

Captain Smith is not without reminiscences, too, of early rogue pamphlets. William Gettings has a victim help him to carry off his own property as in Greene's "Thirde and last Part of Conny-catching," and Tom Taylor has his hand caught by fish-hooks while pocket-picking, as in the "Histoire Générale des Larrons," "The English Rogue," and "Pasquils Jests." Boccaccio furnishes Jonathan Simpson with a method of revenge when he finds his wife has hid a gallant in a chest; and of Thomas Rumbold is told Boccaccio's tale of turning a wife to a mare. Guzman de Alfarache is referred to in the account of Jack Bird, and a merchant in Bristol is shut by Joan Bracey into a court to spend the night half-naked, as was Guzman himself.

To Captain Smith's third volume, "Francion" largely contributes; Walter Tracey teaches a shepherdess to play a new instrument as in the French novel, and, when his master's wife falls in love with him, gets her drubbed, as there and in its probable original, "Marcos de Obregon." So, too, Thomas Houghton repeats Francion's charlatan tricks, and Tom Garret in a village in Sussex has the same experience as Francion in the inn where the hostess tried to persuade her husband he was dead. The opening pages of "Francion" reappear literally in the account of Francis Parquot, who is said to have been executed in 1701. It is notable that Falstaff was in later editions made to lead the procession of rogues in these three volumes. The story of his achievements is of course pieced together from Shakespeare, although it is declared that he really was no coward, and that he "had a countenance in which there appeared so much delicacy and sweetness that there were but few women but would have been glad to have been possessors of the like features." He was born in Potten in Bedfordshire, robbed with Poins, Bardolph, and Peto, and died of grief at being condemned by the king to transportation.

Captain Smith in publishing his "Lives of Highwaymen" had professed the usual moral aim of presenting vice that it might be abhorred, but he was doubtless enamored of his rogues, and in the preface to his second volume he speaks proudly of Steele's having thus noticed his book in the "Englishman:" "There is a satisfaction to curiosity in knowing the adventures of the meanest of mankind; and all that I can say of these great men in their way, recorded by Captain Smith, is that I have more respect for them than for greater criminals."

So much flattered was the Captain by this praise and his book's success that in 1715 he issued the "Secret History of the Lives of the most Celebrated Jilts," and in 1719 published separately the "Thieves' New Canting Dictionary," which had been included in the "Lives of Highwaymen," and which, repeating most of the cant of Harman and Dekker, added many new terms culled from contemporary slang. In his "Comical and Tragical History of the Lives and Adventures of the Most Noted Bayliffs," which saw three editions in 1723, he gave an account of eight bailiffs all of whom had been rogues, but who for policy reversed their profession. These officers show considerable wit in their shifts for taking others. Jacob Broad and a friend, for example, feign to be highwaymen, and so, being brought before a judge who owes a debt, readily capture him. William Cartholick, pretending to be pursued, secures refuge from a kind-hearted victim whom he forthwith arrests. The stories related of the bailiffs, unlike those concerning the highwaymen, are not taken from picaresque literature except in rare instances, but are rather such as invention or the facts might suggest.

In the "Memoirs of the Life and Times of the Famous Jonathan Wild" (1726) Captain Smith returned in a measure to his old manner. But this book was less amusing than its predecessors, and the author seems to have realized that the vein was exhausted. At all events, his next venture in 1730 was of a different character. Its title — "Court Intrigue, or an Account of the Secret Memoirs of the British Nobility" — sufficiently indicates its departure from the picaresque genre.

A certain Captain Charles Johnson posed as Smith's immediate rival and successor. In 1734 in weekly two-penny numbers he issued a "General History of the Lives and Adventures of the Most Famous Highwaymen," to which was added "a genuine account of the voyages and plunders of the most notorious pyrates, interspersed with several diverting tales and pleasant songs, and adorned with the heads of the most remarkable villains in copper." These appended piratical biographies constituted the work's chief original contribution, since the biographies of highwaymen were little more than Smith's "Lives" refurbished. The compilation proved popular and in various forms continued to be reprinted well into the nineteenth century.[1] Johnson had previously issued a "General History of the Robberies and Murders of the Most Notorious Pyrates," containing an account of "their policies, discipline, and government," together with the "adventures of the two female pyrates, Mary Read and Anne Bonny." Captain Avery and a dozen others figured here, and the reports concerning them professed to be delivered by eyewitnesses to their taking. Within two years four editions of this work were called for, the last adding a second volume; and in successive years from 1726 to 1728 French, Dutch, and German versions appeared.

The great original of all such collected chronicles of pirates was Alexander Olivier Exquemelin's[2] "De Americaensche Zee-Roovers" (Amsterdam, 1678), often reissued in Dutch, and translated into Spanish as "Las Piratas" (1681), into French as "Les Avanturiers" (1686), and into English as "The History of the Bucaniers" (1684) and "The Bucaniers of America" (1684–85). Editions of the "Avanturiers Flibus-

[1] Cf. editions of 1742, 1814, 1839, 1840, 1842, and 1853.

[2] The name is variously spelled as Esquemeling, Oexmelin, and Exquemlin.

tiers" from 1726 forward contained Captain Johnson's biographies as an appendix. Johnson's and Exquemelin's rogues continued to figure in new editions and in succeeding collections from the "History of the Buccaneers of America" (1816), by James Burney, "A History of the Pirates" (1834), and G. W. Thornbury's "Buccaneers, or Monarchs of the Main" (1876), to J. S. C. Abbott's "Captain Kidd and Other Pirates" (1874), Howard Pyle's "Buccaneers and Marooners of America" (1891), and F. R. Stockton's "Buccaneers and Pirates of Our Coasts" (1898). Notices of individual pirates have frequently included the biographies of a group of their companions, as, for example, the undated "Davis the Pirate," which professes to give "the true history of the freebooters of the Pacific."

While biographies of fictional or historical interest were being assembled by Smith and Johnson, other chroniclers of less talent were compiling prosaic lives of the miserable many yearly brought to account for their crimes at Newgate and Tyburn. Not long after 1700 a "Tyburn Calendar" was issued from the printing office of G. Swindells, Hanging Bridge, Manchester; in 1720 "The Chronicle of Tyburn" claimed to display villainy in all its branches; and in 1731 Defoe's publisher, Applebee, gratified the public with a "History of Executions," describing the lives and taking off of thirteen desperate characters. His work was continued in later issues and supplemented in 1732 by "The Lives of the Most Remarkable Criminals," which prided itself on having avoided "feigned or romantic adventures, calculated merely to entertain the curiosity of the reader."[1]

If Smith and Johnson and their followers represent the romanticism of rogue biography, books like these represent

[1] This work was reprinted anonymously in 1874, the language of the "original papers and authentic memoirs" being preserved.

its realism. Chief among them all is "The Newgate Calendar." It knows nothing of the amusing picaresque spirit of Captain Smith. It presents only sordid actualities of crime, unrelieved by satire or fiction. It is appropriately subtitled "the Malefactors' Bloody Register," since the two thousand pages of its five volumes offer at best revolting "narratives of the lives and transactions, various exploits and dying speeches of the most notorious criminals of both sexes." Four hundred and thirty wretches are consigned to an immortality of infamy, and the introductory assurance that the regular progress from virtue to vice will throughout be displayed is amply fulfilled. Less satisfactory is the pretense of a moral purpose in this work on the ground that it will serve "to humble the pride of our nature," or the statement that "it will become extremely useful for families and be a fund of entertainment as well as instruction." But positively preposterous is the author's pretended conviction that "parents and guardians will find it one of the most useful books to be put into the hands of the rising generation, before their tender minds have been led astray from the practise of virtue."

Many editions of this cheerful chronicle rejoiced eighteenth-century readers, and inspired imitators and successors. Robert Sanders issued the "Calendar" in six volumes in 1764. The Reverend John Villette, the prison Ordinary, announced his "Annals of Newgate, or Malefactors' Register" of 1776 as "a beacon to warn the rising generation."

Early in the nineteenth century, Knapp and Baldwin, attorneys-at-law, issued a four-volume "Criminal Chronology, or New Newgate Calendar" (1809–10), often reprinted.[1] In 1814

[1] In the edition of London, 1824–28, 4 vols., it was entitled simply *The Newgate Calendar*, "comprising memoirs of the most notorious characters."

George Theodore Wilkinson produced a rival "Newgate Calendar," later continued by William Jackson. In 1815 appeared "The Criminal Recorder, or Biographical Sketches of Notorious Public Characters;" and in 1825 George Borrow assembled in six volumes his "Celebrated Trials and Remarkable Cases of Criminal Jurisprudence," dealing with all the established favorites, but adding foreign rogues, like Cagliostro, and keeping to a higher moral and literary level than most of his fellows. Camden Pelham's "Chronicles of Crime, or New Newgate Calendar" (1841, reissued 1886) is the best of the later collections of biographies. Its five hundred rogues embrace coiners, extortioners, forgers, fraudulent bankrupts, footpads, housebreakers, murderers, mutineers, pirates, smugglers, pickpockets, money-droppers, sharpers, and traitors. Such old friends as Jonathan Wild, Blewitt, Blueskin, Jack Sheppard, Dick Turpin, Jenny Diver, Sixteen String Jack, Captain Kidd, and Galloping Dick Ferguson reappear, together with such subjects of literary treatment as Eugene Aram, Captain Porteous, and Catherine Hayes.

To the same category belong the "Remarkable Trials and Notorious Characters" of Captain Benson, and the "Wonderful Characters" of Henry Wilson and James Caulfield. The former professes to furnish a complete library of sensation-literature as well as the plots for a hundred exciting novels and at least five hundred magazine stories; the latter pillories criminals along with such eccentrics as Old Parr, and Peter the Wild Boy. J. McLevey's "Curiosities of Crime in Edinburgh" and Major Griffiths's anatomies of roguery[1] furnish collected criminal biographies; and "The Lives of Twelve

[1] *Chronicles of Newgate* (1884), vol. i, chs. 8 and 9; vol. ii, chs. 7 and 8; *Mysteries of Police and Crime* (1899), vol. i, pt. 3, "Captains of Crime."

Bad Men" (1894), edited by Thomas Seccombe, and its companion, "The Lives of Twelve Bad Women" (1897), edited by Arthur Vincent, accord distinguished rascals an intensive study.

India has fortified the genre in several histories of the Thugs; Ireland has offered its merrier "Lives and Actions of the Most Notorious Irish Highwaymen, Tories, and Rapparees" (by J. Cosgrave, Dublin, 1839), teeming with matter drawn from folk-tale and jest-book; and America has contributed dozens of collected chronicles of crime, like the "Confessions, Trials, and Biographical Sketches of the Murderers of this Country" (1837), an undated "History of the Vigilantes," Philip Farley's "Criminals of America, or Tales of the Lives of Thieves" (1876), and its late descendant, Inspector Byrnes's "Professional Criminals of America." This in an enlarged edition (1895) presents photographs and concise descriptions of more than six hundred rogues of reality.

6. *Literature and the Rogues of Reality*

The literary significance of the criminal biographies has never been recognized. They have suffered neglect for several reasons. Intrinsically they are of small artistic value; as allied with journalism they are largely and fortunately ephemeral; as catering to the vulgar instincts of the vulgar many, they fall below the dignified historian's horizon line; and, further, they are so widely scattered as to be reassembled for purposes of study only at a cost of pains and patience out of all proportion to their apparent merit. Nevertheless, they have exerted no inconsiderable influence in the shaping of modern fiction. They have been source books of realism, and their narrative method has instructed great story-tellers.

In the nineteenth century alone they have found many admirers. Scott in "Rob Roy" and the "Heart of Mid-Lothian" made use of criminal pamphlets. Bulwer-Lytton, Ainsworth, Borrow, and Reade, Dickens, Thackeray, and Stevenson have not disdained them. Pierce Egan, in the interval between the publication of his popular "Life in London" and its sequel, composed such tracts. In "Eugene Aram" Bulwer turned to account the records of an actual malefactor concerning whom Godwin and Scott had projected romances and much had already been written. Hood in his popular "Dream of Eugene Aram" versified the theme, Bulwer produced upon it two acts of a poetic tragedy, and it was further dramatized by Moncrieff and by Wills. Bulwer, too, in "Lucretia, or the Children of Night" introduced the deeds of Thomas Griffiths Wainewright, the notorious insurance swindler, celebrated also as the anti-hero in Dickens's "Hunted Down." The central rogue of Bulwer's "Paul Clifford" is devoted as a boy to "The Life and Adventures of Richard Turpin," and Ainsworth's "Rookwood" makes Turpin a principal figure, endowing him with amiable qualities scarcely possessed by the original. The same novel abounds in references to rogue chronicles, from the "Life of Du Vall" and the "Villainous Life of John Hall," to the "History of the Rapparees," and an account of Courtenay, the Canterbury impostor, contained in "An Essay on his Character and Reflections on his Trial." Here, too, are sung the praises of Dudley, Hind, Redmond O'Hanlon, Tom King the Gentleman Highwayman, and many others. Ainsworth's "Jack Sheppard" deals not alone with that master of the arts of escape, but equally with Jonathan Wild and with Blueskin, and a rival "romance founded on facts" appeared as the "History of Jack Sheppard" (1839).

Dickens has Fagin present Oliver Twist with a copy of the "Newgate Calendar" by way of entertainment. "It was a history of the lives and trials of great criminals; and the pages were soiled and thumbed with use. . . . The terrible descriptions were so real and vivid, that the sallow pages seemed to turn red with gore; and the words upon them, to be sounded in his ears, as if they were whispered, in hollow murmurs, by the spirits of the dead." Thackeray's "Catherine" is simply an extended and imaginative criminal chronicle based in its facts upon actual pamphlets and upon the later issues of the "Newgate Calendar." Carleton writes entertainingly of Redmond O'Hanlon, the Rapparee chief, and Lever draws upon accounts of John Sadleir, the swindler, in his "Davenport Dunn."

De Quincey's "Murder Considered as One of the Fine Arts" is an ironical digest of rogue biographies, dealing with the crimes of Williams, Alexander and Michael Mackean, Thurtell, Hunt, and Probert. De Quincey declared that Southey in conversation with him had ranked the crimes of the first as "amongst the few domestic events which, by the depth and expansion of horror attending them, had risen to the dignity of a *national* interest." And Egan's praise of the last three was not only echoed in a street ballad by Theodore Hook, but Walter Scott in 1826 could spend "three or four hours over a variorum edition of the Gills Hill Tragedy," and in 1828 made a pilgrimage to its scene.

Charles Reade's "It Is Never Too Late To Mend" introduces the writing of criminal biographies as a salutary occupation for convicts. The prison chaplain "had found out that a bad man's life honestly told is a beacon. So he set roguery teaching by examples," — a notion less seriously maintained in the Spanish picaresque tales from the day when Aleman subtitled his "Guzman de Alfarache" the "beacon of life." Reade's chaplain rebels at all blinking of facts, bidding his convict

". . . write the truth,—do not dress or cook your facts: I shall devour them raw with twice the relish, and they will do you ten times the good. And intersperse no humbug, no sham penitence." The story thus penned received separate publication as "The Autobiography of a Thief," a piece which bears every mark of the genuine criminal pamphlet, even to the absence of literary quality. In issuing it, Reade entered a plea for such picaresque confessions because only the rogue convicted and imprisoned will tell the truth, while the world's undetected scamps are in duty bound to gloze over their interesting traits with insipid lying.

It was left for George Borrow, however, to defend the criminal pamphlets on the ground of their literary excellence. As a hack writer in London he had early been engaged in hunting out works of this class in order to compile his "Celebrated Trials." "What struck me most with respect to these lives," he says, "was the art which the writers, whoever they were, possessed of telling a plain story. It is no easy thing to tell a story plainly and distinctly by mouth; but to tell one on paper is difficult indeed, so many snares lie in the way. People are afraid to put down what is common on paper; they seek to embellish their narratives, as they think, by philosophic speculations and reflections; they are anxious to shine, and people who are anxious to shine can never tell a plain story." Borrow instances as a masterpiece one sentence from a criminal pamphlet dealing with Henry Simms, executed at Tyburn in the middle of the eighteenth century. "So I went with them to a music booth where they made me almost drunk with gin, and began talking their flash language, which I did not understand."

If the rogue biography was a source of Borrow's own art of plain speaking, it gave him delight also in its subject-matter.

He contemplates winning fame by writing the life of an Irish colonel who nearly succeeded in stealing the crown and regalia from the Tower of London. He professes to have actually composed the "Life and Adventures of Joseph Sell," a seemingly fictitious picaro.[1] He has a fancy, too, to immortalize Jemmy, or Jerry, Abershaw, the highwayman, believed by the Gypsies to haunt a certain hill at midnight, and he delights in tales of that rogue and his pal, Galloping Dick Ferguson, as related by the old hostler who had known them both while serving at an inn on Hounslow Heath. He relieves the tedium of his apprenticeship to the law by the pleased perusal, and later by the translation, of the "Mémoires" of the convict-detective Vidocq, and comes to count that worthy as his personal friend.

To the penny-dreadfuls the rogues of reality have proved rare benefactors. Fictions like "Three Fingered Jack,"[2] "Margaret Catchpole,"[3] "Captain Heron," and "Sixteen String Jack"[4] charmed a wide circle; "Claude Duval" en-

[1] Cf. *Lavengro*, vol. ii, chs. 27, 28. Mrs. Borrow denied that her husband ever wrote this *Life*, but it is included in the canon of Borrow's works by his careful biographer, W. I. Knapp, who believes it may yet turn up in some collection of tales of 1825 or 1826.

[2] Cf. *The History and Adventures of that Famous Negro Robber, Three Fingered Jack, the Terror of Jamaica* (Stirling, 1806, and Falkirk, 1822); the *Wonderful Life and Adventures of Three Fingered Jack* (London, 1825); and Benjamin Moseley's *Obi, or the History of Three Fingered Jack.*

[3] *The History of Margaret Catchpole, a Suffolk Girl* (1845), by the Rev. Richard Cobbold, is the best of the type. The historical Margaret stole her master's horse and rode seventy miles in eight hours to meet a lover. Her death-sentence was relaxed to seven years' transportation, but she broke out of Ipswich Jail, March 25, 1800, and being recaptured received a new sentence of death, but was transported to Australia (1801). There she married, lived respected, and died in 1841, after having given Cobbold, who was the son of an early benefactor, permission to tell her story.

[4] *Sixteen String Jack, the Hero Highwayman; or the Dangers and Diversions of the Road* (1877).

joyed great success as issued in weekly numbers by Edward Lloyd and Tom Prest. "Black Bess" and "Blueskin," its sequel, appealed to thousands who were not troubled by perceiving the anachronisms involved in associating Du Vall, Sixteen String Jack, Tom King, and Dick Turpin as the foes of a rather virtuous Jonathan Wild. On the later stage each of these anti-heroes has been liberally hissed or applauded; Jack Sheppard, Blueskin, and Wild, in half a dozen plays derived from Ainsworth; Sixteen String Jack, Margaret Catchpole, Eugene Aram, Du Vall, and Vidocq each in several; Tom King and Dick Turpin in company; and Cartouche, Ambrose Gwynnett, Bampfylde-Moore Carew, Captain Heron, Captain Kidd, and Jerry Abershaw, in separate pieces.[1]

How frequently during the sixteenth and seventeenth centuries the criminal pamphlets furnished matter for literary exploitation has already been suggested. The tendency of the criminal biography both then and in the eighteenth century to appropriate the older jest-book cheats, together with incidents from Spanish and French picaresque story, has also been fully displayed. But the most important influence of the type remains to be indicated. This is not to be seen even in so masterly a work as Fielding's "History of Mr. Jonathan Wild the Great," half of whose satire is directed at the grandiloquence and point of view of the criminal chronicles. It is rather concerned with the direct and vital impulse given by the criminal biography to the making of the modern novel. This impulse was exerted through one man, — Daniel Defoe. For Defoe, when he turned from composing criminal pamphlets upon Wild and Sheppard to write "Moll Flanders" and "Colonel Jacque," merely substituted imaginary for actual beings, and enlarged the scale without altering the method of treatment.

[1] Cf. *infra*, ch. vi, sect. 6, for an account of these plays.

It was not then through the immediate inspiration of jest-book or Spanish romance of roguery that the author of "Robinson Crusoe" became a master of English picaresque fiction, but rather through the native criminal biography. "Crusoe," however admirable in its achievement, remains less a novel than "Moll Flanders;" and the study of character, which appears in the latter and fails in the former, is Defoe's greatest contribution to fiction. By grafting character study upon the low-life realism of the criminal biographies, Defoe produced the first crude specimens of the English novel.

BIBLIOGRAPHY

CHAPTER IV

1

The criminal biographies have never been accorded systematic study, and the literature of the subject is practically covered in the body of this chapter. J. P. Collier's *Illustrations of Early English Popular Literature* (London, 1863–64, 2 vols.) contains several criminal tracts, and his *Illustrations of Old English Literature* (London, 1866, vol. iii) reprints *The Life and Death of Gamaliel Ratsey*, extant only in the Malone Collection of the Bodleian. Of *Ratseys Ghoaste* the single copy surviving is in the John Rylands Library at Manchester. Lodge's pamphlets may be found in his *Complete Works*, edited by Edmund Gosse for the Hunterian Club (Glasgow, 1883, 4 vols.).

An examination of the *Stationers' Registers* reveals the popularity of the criminal pamphlet in the later years of the sixteenth century. In addition to tracts noted in the text the following appear: *A Confession Made by a Preste which Stode upon ye Pyllorye*, 1560–61; *The Confession of Parson Darsy upon his Deathe*, 1566–67; *Doctour Storyes Confession at his Death, Declaryson of Doctour Storye, An Admonyssion of Doctour Storye, The New Newes of Doctour Story*, 1570–71; *A Cruell Murder Done in Kent, The True Historie and Faythfull Relacion of a Moste Horrible Murder Committed by Alphonse Diazius*, 1577; *A Lamentable Confession of Margaret Dorington . . . who was Executed in the Palace at Westminster for Murdering Alice Ffox, A Tragicall Memorye of the Plagues of Adulterye By a Late Example of the Deathe of Ffoure Haynous Trespassers with the Confession of Margaret Dorington, The Mother that Murdered her Children at Kylborne, A Dolefull Discourse or Sorrowfull Sonnet Made by One Edward Ffallows who Lately Suffred Death . . . for a Robberie, The Lamentation of a Yong Man Confessinge his Former Lyfe that he Hath Led*, all of 1578; *A Brief Treatise Conteyninge the Most Strange and Horrible Crueltye of Elizabeth Sule alias Buckingham and her Confederates*

Executed at Abington, A Ballat of ye Fatall Farewell of Captaine Gilbert Horsley Conveied Out of ye Counter in a Clokebag and Notwithstanding Condemned for Pyracy and Executed, 1579; *The Murder Done by Anne Harrison alias Myddelton, A Pastport for Pirates wherein They May Marke, and Shun Their Abuse by the Death of Thomas Clarke, A Dittie of Master Turbervyle Murthered: and John Morgan that Murdered Him: with a Letter of the Said Morgan to his Mother and Another to his Sister Turbervyle,* 1580; *A Ballat of Tyborne Tydings of Watt Foole and his Felloes of the Lamentable End they Made at the Galloes, A True Report of the Late Horrible Murder Commytted by William Sherwood,* 1581.

The Registers are imperfect for the years 1583, 1584, and 1585, and from 1586 to 1589 criminal pamphlets give way to sensational papers against the Spaniards apropos of the Armada. In 1589 was entered *The Execucion of Three Notorious Witches at Chelmisford Assizes Last;* and in 1590 appeared *A Most True Discourse, Declaringe the Damnable Lyfe and Deathe of One Stube Peeter, a Highe Jermayne Borne* and *The Life of Longe Megg of Westminster.* With the publication of Greene's conny-catching pamphlets in 1591 and 1592 the demand for criminal pamphlets lessened, though in 1592 were issued *The Lamentacon of Christofer Tomlinson Horse Corser Commonlye Called "Kytt with the Wry Mouthe"* and *A Ballad Shewing how a Fond Woman Falsely Accused Herself to be the Kinge of Spaines Daughter and . . . was Whipped Through London . . . Being Known to be a Butchers Daughter.* In 1595 another woman, Judith or Dorothie Phillips, was celebrated in two pamphlets, *A Trew Discoverye of ij Notable Villanyes* and *The Notorious Cousenages.*

2

For criminal pamphlets of the seventeenth century I have relied on my reading of miscellaneous originals in the Bodleian and British Museum. Moll Cutpurse, however, is amusingly set forth by Charles Andrews in *The Lives of Twelve Bad Women* (1897); *The Roaring Girle* may be read in A. H. Bullen's edition of *Middleton's Works* (1885); and *Hollands Leagver* appears in Maidment and Logan's edition of Shackerley Marmion's *Dramatic Works* (Edinburgh, 1875), and in William Paterson's *Dramatists of the Restoration* (London, 1875). The *Memoirs of Du Vall* is reprinted (*Harleian Miscellany,* vol. iii).

3

Swift's *Last Speech and Dying Words of Ebenezer Elliston* is reprinted with an explanatory note in Scott's edition of *Swift's Works*, vol. vii, p. 47. The best account of Jonathan Wild is Arthur Vincent's in *The Lives of Twelve Bad Men* (1894). Wild is further discussed in Jackson's *Newgate Calendar* (1818), Villette's *Annals of Newgate* (1776), Borrow's *Celebrated Trials* (1825), Thornbury's *Old and New London* (1873–78), in the *Lives of the Most Remarkable Criminals* (1874), the *Chronicles of Crime* (1886), and Major Griffiths's *Chronicles of Newgate* (1884). Sheppard, Blueskin, and the rest of Wild's circle figure in these books, and George Paston's *Side Lights on the Georgian Period* (London, 1903) studies the eighteenth-century felon (sect. 4). Cf. also A. Andrews's *Crime in the Eighteenth Century* (*Colburn's New Monthly Magazine*, 105: 78). Defoe's connection with the rogues of reality is considered in the biographies and criticisms noted in the bibliography appended to chapter vii.

4

Of the anti-heroes of the longer criminal biographies James Maclaine is best described by G. Thorn Drury in the *Lives of Twelve Bad Men* (1894). Bampfylde-Moore Carew is briefly noticed by John Ashton (*Dict. of Nat. Biog.*, vol. ix), and by *Notes and Queries* (2d series, iii, 4; iv, 330, 441, 522). In the text I have endeavored to set straight the much-muddled Carew bibliography.

5

Most of the collected chronicles of crime are noted in the text, but several of the volumes included among the anatomies of roguery contain biographies of criminals: e. g., C. Sutton's *The New York Tombs, its Secrets and its Mysteries, Being a History of Noted Criminals* (San Francisco, 1874); A. C. Campbell's *Insurance and Crime* (N. Y. and London, 1902), "a consideration of the effects upon society of the abuses of insurance, together with certain historical instances of such abuses;" Thomas Plint's *Crime in England . . . from 1801 to 1848* (London, 1851); and George Barrington's *Voyage to New South Wales* (1795, 1800), which includes "anecdotes of notorious convicts." So far as I know, the genesis of Captain Smith's *Lives of Highwaymen* has not before been pointed out. Nor have such matters as the relation of Lucas to Cotton been investigated. The

Dict. of Nat. Biog. (vol. xxxiv, p. 242), for example, erroneously asserts that Lucas owes nothing to Cotton. Burney's *Buccaneers of America* has been reprinted (1902), and H. Powell has furnished an introduction to an edition of *The Buccaneers and Marooners of America* (London, 1893, 1898). The best account of the Newgate Calendars is given in Major Griffiths's *Chronicles of Newgate.* Excellent incidental notices of English rogues of reality appear in Charles Gordon's *Old Bailey and Newgate* (N. Y. and London, n. d.). To the collected chronicles may be added T. Dunphy and T. J. Cummins's *Remarkable Trials of all Countries* (N. Y., 1870), the *Impudent Imposters and Celebrated Claimants from Perkin Warbeck to Arthur Orton* (London, 1876), and such American works as D. Jardine's *Criminal Trials* (Boston, 1832), the *Celebrated Trials* (Philadelphia, 1843), and Emerson Hough's *The Story of the Outlaw* (N. Y., 1907), and Bancroft's exhaustive *Popular Tribunals* (vols. xxxvi and xxxvii of *The Works of Hubert Howe Bancroft,* San Francisco, 1887), dealing with desperadoes of the West. Notices of the Thugs began to appear in 1820 in vol. xiii of the *Asiatic Researches. Ramaseeana, or a Vocabulary of the Language Used by the Thugs* (1836) discusses their jargon. Their traits and history are presented in four works: E. Thornton's *Illustrations of the History and Practice of the Thugs* (1837), Sir William Sleeman's *Thugs or Phansegars of India* (1839) and *Report on the Depredations Committed by the Thug Gangs* (1840), and J. Hutton's *Popular Account of the Thugs and Dacoits* (1857).

CHAPTER V

ROGUES OF ELIZABETHAN AND RESTORATION FICTION

1. "*The Unfortunate Traveller*"

EFORE the advent of Defoe, the last decade of the sixteenth century and the sixth of the seventeenth were alone fruitful for the English romance of roguery. Each decade was signalized by a characteristic work, the first by "The Vnfortvnate Traveller" of Thomas Nash, the second by "The English Rogue" of Richard Head and Francis Kirkman. Between these two periods the picaresque tradition was kept alive only by native anatomies of roguery, criminal biographies, and plays, and by foreign rogue novels in translation.

Robert Greene, who had brought the anatomy of roguery to perfection in his conny-catching pamphlets, was on the verge of devoting his pen to fiction pure and simple when in 1592 he died. But he left the "Groatsworth of Wit" and "Blacke Bookes Messenger" as an earnest of what he might have done in this direction. Nash, Chettle, and Breton promptly followed his pointing, and Nash at least was able to clasp hands in creative excellence with Defoe. Had he but cultivated fiction as assiduously as he wooed controversy with Gabriel Harvey and in the Martin Marprelate affair, he might have been the magic midwife to have delivered the English novel a century and a quarter before Defoe.

Thomas Nash was a realist. He began his literary career

with a protest in favor of the vernacular prefixed to Greene's "Menaphon." In his "Anatomie of Absurditie" he laughed at Greene's early romances and "the fantastical dreams of those exiled abbie lubbers" concerning King Arthur, Sir Tristram, Huon of Bordeaux, and "infinite others." He was further a satirist. In "Pierce Pennilesse His Svpplication to the Divell" he scourged London vices; in "Christs Teares Over Iervsalem" he lamented the woes of the wicked town afflicted by the plague. In "Lenten Stuffe" his English realism and good humor produced a panegyric upon Yarmouth and its red herring; in "Dido Queene of Carthage," a play composed with Marlowe, he voiced that love of the sensational that allies him with the writers of the tragedy of blood.

But it is in his single fiction, "The Vnfortvnate Traveller, Or the life of Iacke Wilton," twice printed in 1594, that all Nash's qualities unite. Here must be noted his use of the terrible, his love of low-life, his burlesque of romance, his chastising of follies through laughter, his *penchant* for practical jests, and his anti-Italianate spirit. Of all his works this is the most important in literary history. It is the earliest English fiction of pretension in the picaresque genre. It is also the last of literary merit for more than a century. It ranks with "Euphues" as one of the few long Elizabethan tales of value, and it foreshadows the realistic development of the English novel.

Jacke Wilton is a light-hearted, adventurous page, who spends his time winnowing his wits to live merrily. His chronicle, dedicated to Shakespeare's friend and patron, Southampton, and to his dapper fellow pages of the court, opens with an account of four practical jests.

The camp of Henry VIII before Turney and Turwin is the scene of the first, and the cider-seller to the soldiers is its victim. In size and cowardice and feigned nobility, the cider-seller prefigures Falstaff. He is a "cauelier of an ancient house, as it might appeare by the armes of his ancestrie, drawen very amiably in chalke, on the in side of his tent doore." When Jacke insinuates that he is suspected by the King of treason, "he bounst with his fist on the boord so hard, that his Tapster ouerhearing him, cried anone anone sir, by and by, and came and made a low leg and askt him what he lackt." But the poor cider-seller in his fright demands counsel of Jacke, and is advised to distribute all he has amongst the soldiers, for "I would let them burst their bellies with syder, and bathe in it, before I would runne into my Princes ill opinion for a whole sea of it." The result is gratifying to the camp. Soon "euerie vnderfoote soildiour had a distenanted tunne, as Diogenes had his tub to sleepe in." The King discovers the trick and Jacke Wilton is whipped, but many a winter's evening after is made merry with it, so what cares he?

His second exploit concerns a captain who by false dice has secured the better part of Jacke's earnings. The page compasses revenge by sending this officer to the French as a spy to pretend that he is disaffectioned against the English and wishes to go over to the enemy. Jacke eggs him on with classic instances of spies grown famous, and the captain declares that his return shall be short and successful. "Shorter by the necke," muses Jacke; "in the meane time let this be thy posie, I liue in hope to scape the rope." As a suspicious character the captain is examined by the French; and confessing all, is whipped home for a fool.

This only whets Jacke's appetite for new rogueries; a Swiss officer is his next dupe. To him the merry page goes disguised as a girl, simpering "lyke a porredge pot on the fire when it first begins to seeth." But with a prize of six crowns he disappears from the disappointed lover, never to return in that guise. Success leads him to practice in another fashion upon a company of dandy clerks, with "nere bitten beards bedewd euerie daie with rose water." These he puts to flight by warnings of treason afoot, and then appropriates their desks and ink-horns as plunder.

Such tricks, akin to, but not borrowed from, the jest-books, are followed by what may be genuine reminiscences of travel in Germany and Italy.

After witnessing a battle between the Swiss and the French, Jacke makes his way to Munster and sees John Leiden hanged. "Heare what it is to be Anabaptists, to bee puritans, to be villaines; you may be counted illuminate botchers for a while, but your end wil be, Good people pray for me." Returning to England, Jacke is taken into service by Lord Henry Howard, Earl of Surrey, and is made a confidant in his master's love for the stately Geraldine, just come from Italy to wait upon the Dowager Queen Katherine.

Presently the Earl and his page, blessed by Geraldine, set forth upon their travels. At Rotterdam they encounter that "abundant and super-ingenious clarke, Erasmus, as also . . . merrie sir Thomas Moore." At Wittenberg they attend a scholastic reception to the Duke of Saxony, Luther's supporter. Luther himself is seen in disputation with Carolostadius; and a "comedie handled by scollers" whiles away the hours. Cornelius Agrippa, the greatest conjurer of Christendom, journeys with them, and in a glass shows to Surrey and Jacke the Lady Geraldine weeping for her love.

As they approach Italy, Jacke and Surrey change clothes and stations, the better to be prepared against the wiles of that land of false practices. And need they have of this device, for their first adventure leads them into the toils of Tabitha the Temptress and her confederate, Petro de Campo Frego, who plan to murder the Earl. His supposed servant is let into the secret and the plot fails. But Jacke and Surrey are imprisoned for passing counterfeit coin given them by Tabitha. Then Petro, pretending to befriend them, indites their confessions, and "by a fine conny-catching, corrupt translation, made vs plainely to confesse and crie Miserere, ere we had need of our neck-verse." In the same prison is confined a jealous magnifico's wife, Diamante, to whom Surrey offers no harm, only at times fancying her his Geraldine, kissing her hand, and addressing her passionately. Jacke's affection she reciprocates more materially, and together they pleasantly repay her husband for his jealousy. The magnifico dies, and Jacke is invested with his goods and Diamante's person; they are all released from prison; their accusers are hanged; and Jacke runs away from his master to masquerade through Italy as the Earl.

At Florence, however, page and master encounter. Surrey's reprimand cannot ruffle Jacke's serenity, for like Falstaff he has ever a ready reply. "My money," he explains, "I knew not how better to imploy for the honour of my country than by spending it munificently vnder your name. No English-man would I have renowned for bounty, magnificence, and curtesie but you: vnder your colours all my meritorious workes I was desirous to shroud." Against such flattery there is no argument, and with Jacke once more his servant, Surrey visits Geraldine's birthplace and challenges all comers to a tourney in defence of the lady's beauty. Of course he out-tilts every rival, but realistic Jacke will not let his feet be carried off the earth in describing the contest. He pictures Surrey's armor in mock-heroic style, pointing to "his helmet round proportioned like a gardeners water-pot."

When Surrey is recalled to England, Jacke and Diamante proceed to Rome. The grandeurs of the Eternal City impress the roving page less than the horrors of the plague. "All day and all night long carre-men did nothing but goe vp and downe the streetes with their carts and crye, Haue you anie dead to burie?" This doleful wail is the key-note of the latter portion of the novel, which departs from the light-hearted picaresque spirit.

Esdras of Granada, a Spaniard, and Bartol, an Italian, plan to plunder houses ravaged by the plague, and reaching Jacke's lodging, they ravish and kill the inmates and steal away Diamante. An outraged matron stabs herself and dies upon her plague-stricken husband's body, and Jacke is mistakenly seized upon as author of these crimes. Only at the gallows is he saved by a banished English earl, who embraces this opportunity to read the wayward rogue a sermon against the folly of seeking in other lands what England already bountifully possesses. But the page's misfortunes are not at an end, for that very night he tumbles down a cellar-way to find there his Diamante toying with an apprentice, and all three are pounced upon by the wicked owner of the house, Zadoch a Jew. The latter sells Jacke to the Pope's physician for the yearly anatomy, and the page is nigh to dissection when his handsome person catches the eye of the Pope's mistress, Juliana. She obligingly secures from the Pontiff an act of banishment and confiscation against all Jews. Zadoch at this sends Diamante as a present from the synagogue with instructions to poison Juliana, but she reveals the plot, and Zadoch is tortured. Then Jacke and Diamante run away with the treasures of Juliana, who expires after a dose of the physician's poison has been administered to her by mistake. Thus luridly end the Roman villainies.

In Bologna Jacke is present at the execution of Cutwolfe, a brother of Bartol. The latter had been killed by Esdras upon whom Cutwolfe has avenged the murder in the following manner. He bound the Spaniard in bed, made him abjure God and swear oaths of self-commitment to the devil; then, thrusting a pistol into his victim's mouth, Cutwolfe shot him ere he could repent, hoping thus to destroy his soul as well as his body. "No true Italian but will honour me for it," says Cutwolfe; "all true Italians imitate mee in reuenging constantly and dying valiantly. Hangman to thy taske."

By this execution the hitherto incorrigible Jacke is moved to amendment. "To such straight life did it thenceforth incite me, that ere I went out of Bolognia, I married my curtizane, performed manie almes deedes; and hasted so fast out of the Sodom of Italy, that within fortie daies I arriued at the King of Englands Campe twixt Ardes and Guines in France." On the Field of the Cloth of Gold, accordingly, Nash leaves his rogue reformed.

This is the story so often proclaimed an outright imitation of the Spanish romance of roguery. But by 1594 Spain had produced only her first picaresque tale, — "Lazarillo de Tormes," — from which "Jacke Wilton" differs widely. Jacke serves but one master in lieu of Lazarillo's seven; he makes no attempt to satirize that one. Ere long he becomes a victim or a mere spectator of the adventures he recounts. His story grows complicated in plot, and comedy gives way to tragedy, jauntily presented yet none the less gruesome. This tendency to celebrate the villain, not the rascal, has marked English fiction as no other. In later works of the picaresque type it is pronounced, but even here, so close to the days of the jest-book, it has a larger place than in any Spanish story except the "Conde Matisio" of Zavaleta, written during the decadence of the picaresque novel in Spain.

On the other hand, "Lazarillo de Tormes" may have afforded suggestions to Thomas Nash. The rollicking, free and easy wit of the narrator, his delight in roguery for its own sake, the fact that he is a wanderer in service, his observation and description of actualities, all associate the English with the

Spanish fiction. Occasional references to Spain and the portrayal of the arch-villain, Esdras, as a Spaniard who at home had cast the dice a hundred times for the galleys, who had broken his own mother's neck down a pair of stairs, and sold his sister, may be accepted for what they are worth. Nash himself need not have read "Lazarillo" in the original, inasmuch as the English version was already popular. At the same time, there is little or nothing in Nash's novel that may not be indigenous. Those who have remarked the analogy between it and the Spanish tales have usually exaggerated the analogy, and have interpreted it as necessarily the result of causal connection.

The vexed problem of the story's pedigree is of less consequence, however, than an appreciation of its qualities. "The Vnfortvnate Traveller" is distinguished by the freshness and sparkle of its diction, by its narrative power, by its swift and vivid character sketching, by its humor, its realism, and its Puritanism. Although Jacke is allowed in his speeches a tang of euphuism to comport with his court connections, Nash in the main avoids Lyly's mannerism. He is as original in matter as in style. For the crude realism of the beggar-book he substitutes the realism of art. He gives the illusion of fact rather than fact itself. His chronology fails to square with history in regard to John of Leiden's death. His account of Surrey's knight-errantry in Italy is charmingly mythical. The mistakes into which he has led the poet's biographers would have gratified roguish Jacke himself. In short, "Jack Wilton's is such a traveller's tale as Jack Falstaff might have spun in his youth." [1] It deserves the credit of infusing into English fiction the comic spirit, largely lacking since the versified tales of Chaucer, but destined to signal conquests.[2]

[1] Henry Morley, *English Writers*, vol. x, p. 202.
[2] Cf. J. J. Jusserand, *The English Novel*, p. 294.

2. *Tales by Chettle and Breton*

Although there are picaresque touches in other writings by Nash,[1] and nobody knows how many in his lost comedy, "The Isle of Dogs," the portrayal of roguery now devolved in the main upon Henry Chettle, the reviser and publisher of Greene's "Groatsworth of Wit." That Chettle was acquainted with some of the deceits which Greene knew so intimately is apparent from his "Kind-Harts Dreame" (licensed 1592), "conteining fiue apparitions with their inuectiues against abuses raigning." The pamphlet is best known as carrying Chettle's apology for having allowed the printing of Greene's supposed thrusts at Shakespeare in the "Groatsworth."

Kind-Hart, a street dentist, while asleep in a Finsbury inn is interviewed by the spirits of Anthony Now-now, a fiddler, Tarlton of farce and jest-book fame, the juggler William Cuckoe, Doctor Burcot, the charlatan, and Robert Greene, revealer of cosenage. These worthies condemn the vices of the age, from illiterate ballad singing to downright knavery. In the second invective against "the impudent discreditors of Phisickes Art," a charlatan causes his patient to stand with open mouth beside a fire looking into a basin of water. Henbane seeds are cast into the fire, and as the worms they contain sputter out from the blaze into the basin, the credulous patient is persuaded that he has yielded them up from his mouth. The fifth invective reveals the more familiar trick of finding by conjury an article previously concealed.

The perpetrator of this fraud is described as "Your Maship upon a horse whose hire is not paid for, with your page at your stirrop, like a Castilian caualier lighted penilesse at a pretie Inne." But this is not the only evidence of information as to Castilians and roguery possessed by Chettle, for "Piers Plainnes seauen yeres Prentiship," published in 1595, entitles

[1] Cf. his Defoe-like *Terrors of the night, Or a Discourse of Apparitions* (1594).

him to be reckoned as one of the earliest laborers in the picaresque field.

This fiction was more certainly fathered by "Lazarillo de Tormes" than was Nash's "Vnfortvnate Traveller." Yet its hero is no rogue. When urged to do ill by his masters he refuses, and he never has known the rogue's ambition to forge his way in the world by outwitting others. He seems to have less purpose than any Spanish picaro, to be blown hither and thither by every gust with no notion of profiting by the changes of fortune. In its central figure, then, the little novel might be innocent of Spanish influence, but the proof of the latter is to be noted here in the form rather than in the subject-matter.

The hero tells his own story; he has been in the service of a series of masters; their number is precisely that of Lazarillo's, and the servant portrays the foibles and vices of these masters with humor and as a corrective. It is said of him that he is "of speech not altogether rude, but exceedingly satyrical," and if he fails to be as caustic as the Spaniards, it is because his narrative is tempered with other elements, notably the pastoral. For Piers is a shepherd found discoursing to Menalcas, his seventh master, and to Corydon, a plough-swain, in "Tempe the pleasure of Thessalie, and Paradice of Greece." The main story, with which the service of masters has little to do, is a romantic fiction such as Greene might have written or Sidney pastoralized. Piers himself plays a minor rôle, although as narrator he describes much that he could not have known except through the convenient convention of omniscience. If his seven masters figure but incidentally, it is nevertheless about them that the picaresque elements cluster.

The first was a flatterer, fool, braggart, and coward, who nearly perished of fear when obliged to bear arms at the usurpation of Celinus. The second was a spendthrift courtier ruined by a broker, a baylie, and a usurer, so that poor Piers was forced to go about as a packman from fair to fair, and finally was sold to the broker to be his bookkeeper. This third master he describes as "a man of meane stature, with a sulphurous face richly beset, his eyes sanguine, his breath strong, his gate stately; for he would scarcely haue gone his owne length in an hower he was so well timbered beneath." With the broker Piers observed all manner of deceits, for the fellow had legions of familiars, dice players who made light purses and heavy hearts, and others to fit the humors of young gentlemen new-come from the university. But Piers himself was so little a rogue that his sensibilities were soon offended; and he says, "for I could not sweare, forsweare, lye, deceiue, and cog, I lost my service." The broker had determined to cheat his rival the usurer, and desired Piers to play the nobleman and go bail in another's name. Piers refused, and revealed the plot to the usurer. So the latter took him into service. But "thinking to hold God by the hand, I tooke the diuell by the heele."

This Ulpian, indeed, is the veriest rascal, and his native traits have been accentuated by others derived from Spain. His daughter, Ursula, stole from him, to be soundly beaten when she had "plaid one part of a true penetenciary, and made open confession; marrie, restitution she could not otherwise make but with promise to cousen for him as manie gentlemen as she might." The house was one where a long Lent was kept, and Piers going to the apothecaries each morning for ointment to salve poor Ursula came home to hear a sermon on thrift, and other breakfast had he none. "At dinner," he says, "my allowance was two anchovies, sheere water my drink; and at night drie ryce (or rather rye bread) my best repast; my master pretending solemn fast, till Vrsula were recouuered, without whose helth he assured me our commons must needes faile, for that she was the common vpholder of the house." And as summary, he declares that "to describe our diet, were inough to fill all the countrie with a dearth; with remembrance thereof, Famine itself hath seazed on me, and except I here feed I can proceed no farther." In substance and manner this description of famine in the usurer's house tallies with that portraying the sufferings of little Lazarus in the house of the hidalgo, and forecasts the miseries of Pablos of Segovia at the boarding school. In spirit it is wholly Spanish. For hunger was the especial province in fiction and fact of the Spaniards, whose early picaresque novels abound in such passages.

Upon the recovery of Ulpian's daughter, she had her father accused of clipping coins, for which "he blessed the beholders with his goutie heeles, being hanged and dying desperate as he had lived detestably." Then Piers became servant to the Baily of the King, with whom "corne, leather, mettall, any forbidden commodities might passe if he were paid." Having tried his best to undo the country, living by bribes and the favor of the usurper, this base Baily sought finally to sell Celinus himself in his misfortune, only to be duped and deservedly killed. Piers, coming to Crete, served there an honest fisherman, and last of all the Menalcas to whom he tells his tale. Thus of his seven masters only the last two have proved anything but rogues.

Although Piers himself is no rascal, "Piers Plainnes seauen yeres Prentiship" in its picaresque incidents compares not unfavorably with Spanish tales of the kind. Probably Chettle lacked the courage to make his hero a rogue, fearing to alienate sympathy or to be identified himself with such a character. Jest-books and popular tales seem to have exerted no influence upon this story, but so far as it adopts the picaresque scheme Spain is its source as certainly as its pastoral and heroic portions derive from Italy through Sidney, Lyly, and Greene. Its little success was due to the endeavor to combine incompatible elements.

Nicholas Breton, who did not die until thirty-four years after Greene although born eighteen before him, lived long enough to turn his hand to everything, — lyric, masque, satire, pastoral, epistle, dialogue, moral essay, character-book, and fiction. As Greene's disciple in story-writing, he was bound to follow his young master's lead in forsaking the romantic for the realistic; but, lacking Greene's acquaintance with low-life, he failed to achieve distinction in this vein, and did not long cultivate it.

Breton's first realistic experiment was "The Miseries of Mauillia" (1599), but it is the obverse of the picaresque genre. Mavillia experiences villainy passively not actively. She suffers five great miseries instead of visiting them upon others. Her parents early perish in the sacking of a town, she is abused by a cruel laundress, wanders through a wilderness with a kind-hearted page, is seized upon and robbed by a shepherd and his wife, suffers accusation of theft from a jealous serving-maid, and when happily married is abused by a malicious old suitor. But Breton soon after essayed realism of a less passive kind.

"A Mad World my Masters" (1603) is a dialogue between two travelers, the taker and the mistaker, verging upon punning. Lorenzo, the mistaker, is ever in error. Dorindo, the taker, has a fondness for others' property. To him, accordingly, is assigned the roguish account.

At an ordinary he was taken for "a fine fingered companion" and entrusted by rogues with their money for play. He was no sooner master of it than he took ship to "Roane," where, smiling "to thinke how I had overtooke my takers," he confesses to having set up for the cunning man that had a cure for all diseases.

When he had lined his pockets with gold, he shipped for Antwerp, but was overtaken by a pirate. Having paid his ransom and come to land, he was taken with a mistress who stole away his heart with a vain affection, draining him dry of money till he found himself forced to take to a pretense of the law. "With a multitude of clients and golden fees, I made such a gaine of dissembling that neere a Lawyer of my standing, but I carried it cleane from him." His next ruse was "to counterfeit a diseased creature," and "with the ruefull countenance that I framed for the purpose, I would so move the hearts, and peck the purses of kind people, that I doubted not in time to grow a wealthy begger." But one who was more cunning to pry into the knavery of his dissembling than to cure his disease wished the counterfeit to go home with him, and the rogue, seeing danger ahead, ran off, a reminiscence possibly of a passage in "Guzman de Alfarache," where the Spanish picaro similarly disguised proves less fortunate.

In "Grimellos Fortunes" (1604) the youth of that name tells his story to a prospective master to show that by being honest he has remained poor. His adventures, however, seem to have been waggish enough.

He went to school to one more furious than wise, who, growing jealous of his scholars and "imagining by his studie in astronomie that the sign of his Fortune stood too straight vpon Capricorne," removed all his boarders from the house where dwelt his pretty young wife. Grimello then took service with a knight and devoted himself to perpetrating tricks. His best jest was played at the expense of a lovesick gallant. Grimello's fellow pages, who would haunt this fellow at dinner "and with a song or a Galliard nibble on his Purse for a piece of gold," dressed one of their number like a woman, — Grimello will only half confess it to have been himself. Then this rascal ogled the gallant from a window, while the other pages fell in ecstasies over the supposed beauty. "Oh what an eie! what a lippe! what a forehead!" They secured for the lover a poet to make verses to her, and encouraged him to provide a supper for the lady and themselves. On this occasion the disguised page "had the kisse of the hand, vowes and protestations" to feminine perfection. The gallant was captivated and agreed to escort his charmer on a journey next morning. But the pages drugged his wine, and he never woke till noon. He was then so chagrined that he kept his chamber for a day or two; whereupon, seeing his favors worn by the page who had fooled him, and "fearing his folly to be knowen in the court . . . he got him in ye cuntrie, where wee never heard more of him."

Grimello next turned to arms and served under the governor of a town, who kept himself in his castle "as close as a Flea in a flocke-bed." He slept with his gold-bags on one side and a poor page on the other, and one night he awoke from a dream crying, "Arme, arme!" and took it for prophetical. When he fell asleep again, the volley fired by the watch to salute their captain put him into a cold sweat. One saint's day Grimello and his companions tricked this coward by warning him that the enemy was at hand. In the meantime the country people with drums and fifes and a few shots "came toward the towne to make the gouvernour merrie with a Maie-game and a Morris." He hid in a room behind twenty yards of stone, and even crawled into an earthen furnace used for casting ordnance, from which the people's messenger had hard work to persuade him to issue. But he finally ordered his sword and target that his neighbors should see how ready he was upon the least alarum. This cowardly governor is not unworthy to rank with such valiant Spaniards as Estevanillo Gonzalez and Sancho Panza.

The other incidents related by Grimello are slight and echo the jest-books. One is a version of the third story of the "Defence of Conny catching." Another concerns a witty magpie which informed its master how his wife had filched and eaten his pet eel. In punishment the lady picked its poll bare; and one day when the master brought home a bald guest the magpie caused embarrassment by asking if he too had told of the eel. "I thinke I haue heard it long agoe, but not as thou hast told it," says the gentleman to whom Grimello has recounted his adventures. And so well pleased is the listener that he takes the rogue into service forthwith.

The service of masters, indeed, which allies this story, more closely than anything else by Breton, with the Spanish picaresque fictions, may have been suggested by "Piers Plainnes Prentiship" and "The Vnfortvnate Traveller." The latter's influence is especially noticeable in the incident of the disguised page, and in the sprightly tone of the narrative. Both Grimello and Jacke Wilton are able forerunners of the Continental page of reality, Tristan l'Hermite.

3. *An Interval of Translation*

With Breton, Chettle, and Nash celebrating rogues of fiction, and with Awdeley, Harman, Greene, Dekker, and Rowlands picturing low-life tricks and environment, no picaresque literature out of Spain was so rich by 1610 as the English. But just when the romance of roguery seemed fairly established in England it somehow went bankrupt, and for fifty years no one would again venture faith in it.

In the meantime, however, the drama of roguery flourished; the Spanish picaresque novels were translated, and were read in plural editions, while allied fictions, French or Castilian, found ready acceptance. "Don Quixote," which a century later was to inspire the new English novel, was first Englished by Shelton in 1612 and 1620, to reappear in 1652 and 1675, and to be crudely paraphrased in 1687 by John Phillips. James Mabbe translated Cervantes's "Novelas" in 1640, and the "Celestina" as "The Spanish Bawd" in 1631. "Reynard the Fox," which Caxton had Englished as early as 1481, saw half a dozen editions in the seventeenth century, and Rabelais, earlier translated in part, was read in Urquhart's version in 1653 and 1694.

Of the picaresque novels proper, "Lazarillo," between 1622 and 1680, went through a dozen editions, and "Guzman," Englished by Mabbe, had, by 1656, seen five. The "Desordenada Codicia" was issued in 1638 as "The Sonne of the Rogue," reprinted in 1650 as "Lavernæ, or the Spanish Gipsy," and in 1659 as "A Scourge for a Den of Thieves." Quevedo's "Buscon" was "put into English by a person of honour" in 1657, reprinted in 1670, and abridged in 1683; while at least ten editions of his "Visions," translated in 1667 by L'Estrange, were called for within thirty years. "La Garduña de Sevilla," thanks to John Davies of Kidwelly, in 1665 became "La Picara, or the Triumphs of Female Subtilty," and in 1670 Philip Ayres presented "El Necio Bien Afortunado" as "The Fortunate Fool."

Nor were the French imitations of the Spanish romances neglected, from Barclay's satirical "Icon Animorum," translated in 1631 by Thomas May, to Scarron's "Roman Comique," turned into English in 1676. In 1657 Davies of Kidwelly had published three tales out of Scarron, including "The Hypocrites," derived from Barbadillo's "La Hyia de Celestina." To these he added, in 1662, the four from the "Roman Comique." The seven were issued together in 1667, and were increased by an eighth three years later. In the meantime, in 1653, he had produced a version of Sorel's imitation of Cervantes, the "Berger Extravagant," which saw a second edition in 1660. Sorel's picaresque masterpiece appeared in 1655 as "The Comical History of Francion," Englished probably by Robert Loveday.[1]

Between 1610 and 1665, accordingly, there was no dearth of picaresque fiction to gratify English readers, even though original essays were wanting. The latter lack, indeed, is to be attributed less to the rising tide of Puritanism than to the superabundance of dramatic roguery and of the foreign article. The imported picaresque novel for a time killed all competition, and when at last, in "The English Rogue," an attempt was made to vie with the foreign variety, there resulted a cheap imitation of its defects instead of a development of the original excellence of native productions like those of Greene and Nash.

If this be one principal cause of the decline of the English picaresque novel in the seventeenth century, there was also another: romantic fiction of a peculiar type became increasingly popular. The old tales of chivalry — "Amadis," "Palmerin," "Belianis," and "Guy of Warwick" — did not perish from the earth, but descended by degrees to modernized, vulgarized chap-books, leaving the cultivated to seek fresh sources of romantic inspiration abroad.[2]

[1] The influence of these works may be noted in many degenerate English publications at the beginning of the Restoration. A case in point is the impudently indecent *Wandering Whore* (1661), a dialogue in which figure "Francion, a Lascivious Gallant, and Gusman, a Pimping Hector." The title reads "The Fifth and Last Part;" but Anthony à Wood in his Bodleian copy has noted, — "I could never see any other part but this."

[2] In Kirkman's *English Rogue* (pt. iv, ch. 23), a rascal is described who knew all the stories from *Tom Thumb* to *Amadis de Gaule* and the *Mir-*

At first such sentimental histories as Cervantes's "Persiles y Sigismunda," or Cespedes y Meneses's "Gerardo," were translated, the former in 1619, with a reprint in 1639, the latter in 1622, with a reprint in 1653. Then the translators laid hands upon French heroic romance, and even upon d'Urfée's pastoral, "L'Astrée." The latter, six years before it was Englished, fathered Leonard Williams's shepherd play, "Astrea, or True Love's Mirrour" (1651). During the decade just preceding, half a dozen heroic romances were received with acclaim, familiar as they must earlier have been among the cultivated. "Polexandre," "Cléopâtre," "Cassandre," "Ibrahim," "Le Grand Cyrus," and "Clélie" shed lustre upon their translators, Sir Charles Cotterel, John Phillips, John Davies, Robert Loveday, and Henry Cogan. Such new issues as "Scipion," in 1660, "Almahide," in 1677, Voiture's "Histoire d'Alcidalis et Zélide," in 1678, and even Mlle. de Scudéry's "Conversations," Englished by Spence in 1683, were the talk of the town. Bluestockings like Catherine Philips and the Duchess of Newcastle sought to reproduce the French salons; men of fashion sought to counterfeit French romances. The future Earl of Orrery, Roger Boyle, published in 1654 his "Parthenissa" in five parts, with a sixth a dozen years later. Crowne, the dramatist, dropped into fiction with his "Pandion and Amphigenia" (1655). Fortunately, however, the English heroic drama caught most of this French bombastic lightning, and so saved the novel from being struck lifeless.

In native realism practically the only fictional experiments

rour of Knighthood, as also the *Palmerins*, *Primaleons*, and *Don Bellianis of Greece*. A version of the latter was issued by Kirkman himself as *The Famous and Delectable History of Don Bellianis of Greece* (1671-73). Such heroic tales as *The Famous History of Montelion* of 1633 and the sixteenth-century *History of Parismus* saw editions in 1687 and 1696 respectively, the latter being the eleventh.

between Dekker's "O per se O" (1612) and Richard Head's "English Rogue" (1665) were a few satires, the character-books, a didactic novel in Latin, and the criminal biographies. Slightly associated with the latter was Thomas Cranley's prose and verse story, "Amanda" (1635). This professes to be the narrative of a prisoner in the Fleet who falls in love with a girl whom he first spies at a window across Fleet Lane. He discovers that she is no better than she should be, but sends her verses through a friend. Receiving no response, he begins a fresh poetical assault upon her heart: —

Reade againe my second letter,
See if now my phrase be better.

If possible, his phrase is worse, but the lady does not realize it, for she returns his affection by blushing and submits to a thousand lines, describing the daily round of a courtesan and urging her repentance. This rhymed tract goes unanswered, and the prisoner, on his release, finds the lady dying, and is edified by a hundred stanzas of her last love and contrition.

Another experiment in doggerel, and one of the most curious of many satires upon the Welsh, was Humphrey Crouch's "Welch Traveller, or the Unfortunate Welchman" (1657). Taffie, a rogue, early falls a victim to an innkeeper whose practices parallel those of Guzman de Alfarache's first hostess. Taffie steals a ring, but it is claimed by a picara who gets him set in the stocks. When he exposes her and causes her to be put beside him, she torments him. He climbs a chimney to steal bacon, but falls in the fire and is mistaken for a devil. He hobnobs with Gypsies who use him as an assistant in thievery, letting him down chimneys by a rope, and finally abandoning him thus suspended. By acting the devil, he again escapes, but hiding in a church is routed out by a mob and pilloried. In these rapid rhymed adventures there is a marked resemblance to many exploits in Spanish novels as well as to tricks later practiced in the German "Simplicissimus."

Roguery further played a part in "Nova Solyma" (1648), a Latin romance but recently brought to light, done into English, and ascribed on extremely doubtful evidence to John Milton.[1]

Here in one chapter[2] Alcimus, a prodigal, having joined a robber band in Sicily unwittingly captures his own father, Apollos, who is traveling through the country. The father recognizes his long-lost son, reveals his identity, and Alcimus in attempting his release is obliged to fight a fellow bandit, who retaliates by accusing the pair of having slain two of the band. Apollos has been wounded by this rascal with a poisoned scimitar, but Alcimus saves his father's life by sucking out the venom, and the robbers hurry away from their romantic cave when warned by a corrupt governor that he is obliged to make a feint of sending soldiers against them. Apollos is seized by the troops as a bandit, but Alcimus escapes by disguising as a beggar and in this garb witnesses his father's trial and exoneration. Beggary, however, proves difficult, for the young man runs afoul of a republic of mendicants with laws as strict as those of Athens, Sparta, or Rome. The society's chief, a pretended blindman, beats him over the shins with a stick, extorts his promise to abstain from beggary within the society's bounds, and then invites him to attend a carousal of its members. Alcimus refuses, however, and repenting of his wildness, returns to Nova Solyma.

There may here be a reference to the Company of St. Elizabeth, a begging guild that flourished in Italy from 1613 to 1790, but the passage is brief, and in its lack of picturesque detail contrasts with the conny-catching pamphlets. If the tragic complications and the disguises and journeys of the main

[1] *Nova Solyma, the Ideal City; or Jerusalem Regained;* "an Anonymous Romance Written in the Time of Charles I, Now First Drawn from Obscurity and Attributed to the Illustrious John Milton. With an Introduction, Translation, Literary Essays, and a Bibliography," by the Rev. Walter Begley (N. Y., 1902, 2 vols.). The work is reviewed and the editor's claims for Miltonic authorship are discredited by W. A. Neilson in *Modern Philology*, April, 1904.

[2] Bk. i, ch. 4.

plot recall those of "The Vnfortvnate Traveller," their treatment is not realistic, and "Nova Solyma" must be classed with didactic fictions like "Euphues" or with the Latin "Satyricon" (1603) of Barclay. The latter, indeed, in its account of Euphormio's meeting with a vagabond and joining a crew of rogues, provides a possible model for this picaresque episode.

4. "*The English Rogue*"

Such trifling essays as "The Unfortunate Welchman" and "Amanda" may well be forgotten in the face of so remarkable a work as "The English Rogue." This was begun by Richard Head, added to by Francis Kirkman, and further continued by both together. Lacking in art and feeling, never finished, yet of bewildering extent, it is less a novel than a chaotic collection of all the picaresque tricks on record at the moment of its publication. It knows no unity; it attempts no study of character or manners; it imitates but one phase of the Spanish romances of roguery, and neglects everything that made them a link in the development of the modern novel.

Head and Kirkman were poor-devil hacks who set pens to paper for hire alone. Kirkman declared of his design that it was "first and foremost to gain ready money, the second was to gain some reputation by being in print, the third was to advantage the reader." Neither possessed talent or even skill. While Head may have been only half disreputable, Kirkman was beneath contempt, and his treatment of Head is indicative of what his other dealings doubtless were. The world of roguery set forth by Head became with Kirkman a world of villainy and crime, and the same decadence that has marked picaresque literature as a national development was here manifest within a single work.

If "The English Rogue" remains the most considerable of

the avowed imitations of the Spanish romances of roguery in any language,[1] it is a mere debased copy that stole right and left three fourths of its matter from what was of least worth in its models. That it failed to reproduce more than the crudities was due to the brutality of its authors. They thought they were writing the adventures of an English rogue as Aleman had written those of a Spanish rascal. They could not see that by making all their characters knaves they sacrificed artistic contrast, the opportunity for satire, and even all color of reality. They argued that the more concentrated the roguery the greater must be their rogue romance.

In 1665 Richard Head issued the first and best part of this work as "The English Rogue Described in The Life of Meriton Latroon, a Witty Extravagant." Had it been concluded in the same vein and in a second part as Head intended, it might not have been deserving of unqualified blame. Meriton tells his story with considerable humor, and it possesses sufficient unity to hold the reader's interest.

As a child Meriton practises the usual rogueries, stealing books at school, playing truant, capturing geese by whirling a bullet-weighted string about their necks, and when advanced to boarding-school indulging in tricks correspondingly wilder. Then he runs away and joins a company of Gypsies met in a barn.[2] An apt rogue instructs him in the arts of begging and stealing; and in London he employs such familiar jest-

---

[1] Its line of descent is noted in commendatory verses signed N. D., addressed to Head, and prefixed to his Part One: —

> Guzman, Lazaro, Buscon, and Francion,
> Till thou appear'dst did shine as at high Noon.
> Thy Book 's now extant; those that judge of Wit,
> Say, They and Rablais too fall short of it.

[2] Suggested by Harman's *Caueat*, which described a Gypsy barn bivouac. The hierarchy of canters and their vocabulary are drawn from Awdeley and Harman. The canting song is that in Dekker's *Lanthorne and Candle-light*, whence also comes an account of the Gypsies. Dekker's *O per se O* furnishes a description of sore-making.

book devices as cutting the purse of the woman who at his request is putting his purchase of bacon down his back to conceal it from a master.[1]

Like most picaros Meriton enters service. But he consorts with other cheating apprentices who pool their gains. His time is divided between thieving and erotic adventure. One victim of the latter he contrives to send to Virginia by embarking with her in the ship, but slipping away at the last moment. He describes prison life, tours the London dives, and hires himself out in disguise as maid in a young ladies' seminary, a trick inspired by Boccaccio.[2] He eludes kidnappers, gambles, intrigues with the wife of his master, and declares, "I only studied by what means I might raise my fortune, intending to build my future estate upon the ruins of other men."

Now, having married for money, Meriton finds himself outwitted, visits Ireland only to starve, and returns to England to secure a loan under false pretenses. Set upon by robbers, he feigns to be a fellow-highwayman, joins their band, and in his first encounter proves a coward. After deceiving a milkmaid into thinking she is to become a fine lady, he worsts a bandit who proves to be a woman in disguise. Several of her Amazons recount their adventures, and from a lawyer Meriton hears a narrative of new rascalities related in twelve chapters as "The Life of a Law Abusing Cheat." This is merely a jumble of tricks and jest-book lore. A prisoner escapes while his keeper is being shaved; a physician, being called to attend a wag's wife for the flux, finds the patient to be an empty purse; a trinket is passed from one to another for inspection until finally it can be run away with; and a trunk filled with stones is left with an innkeeper as security.[3]

Meriton, reconciled with his wife, turns pimp; but Bridewell receives the lady and Newgate her lord. In repentance the latter composes a paper warning the unwary, most of which is Clavell's "Recantation" (1628), or, more precisely, its prose *rifacimento*, "The Catterpillers of

---

[1] *The English Rogue*, pt. i, ch. 8. This trick in the *Histoire générale des larrons*, pt. i, ch. 21, is done with a straw; in Greene's *Second part of Conny-catching* with flour; and in Rowlands's *Greenes Ghost* with cheese. It reappears in Kirkman's *English Rogue*, pt. ii, ch. 6.

[2] *Decameron*, day iii, *novella* 1; *The English Rogue*, pt. i, ch. 13.

[3] The first had appeared in William Fennor's *Compters Common-Wealth;* the second in the *Histoire générale des larrons*, pt. i, ch. 4; and the fourth in Dekker's *Belman*, 4th jump.

this Nation Anatomized" (1659). The king grants a reprieve, and by a double shipwreck, in the course of transportation, the rogue passes from a Spanish captain to Turkish pirates, to a Jewish merchant, and then to a Greek, with whom he visits the East Indies.

Such in outline is the story of Meriton Latroon, inferior in every way to the Spanish novels, but amply attesting their influence. The "Desordenada Codicia" furnishes the incident of the thief discovered beneath a bed by a cat and dog quarrel there.[1] The "Buscon" supplies the trick of counting and recounting the same sum of money as a pretense of wealth.[2] Quevedo, too, inspires the frequent tone of burlesque and such episodes as Meriton's fasting in Ireland and his experience with the kidnapped in a den that resembles hell. When the rogue has lost all and his landlord grows cold, he will accept aid of none, proudly declaring that he has just dined, an obvious souvenir of the hidalgo in "Lazarillo de Tormes," since it is far enough removed from Meriton's conduct on every other occasion. Even "Don Quixote" is not forgotten in the account of the Gypsy barn in terms of a castle, and the turning knights-errant of the rogue and a pilfering cavalier.[3] Further reminiscences of the Spanish novels are often in evidence, but Head's story presents three notable variations from their type: it exaggerates the erotic element; it fails to observe and portray manners; and it is deficient in satire.

When, in 1668, Francis Kirkman, the bookseller, emboldened by the success of Head's unfinished narrative, undertook to supply for it a second part, he merely emphasized these differences. He, too, was a student of the Spanish and French novels, but the erotic element was for him supreme, and in this and in his later additions obscenity rules. His story is related

[1] *The English Rogue*, pt. i, ch. 55; *Codicia*, ch. 8.
[2] *The English Rogue*, pt. i, ch. 23; *Buscon*, pt. ii, ch. 5.
[3] *The English Rogue*, pt. i, chs. 4, 12.

in thirty-eight chapters that have little to do with Head's anti-hero. Meriton gives some account of his East Indian travels, but an English fleet arrives, six English adventurers disembark, two prove to be women in male disguise, and the rest of the volume is occupied by their cheating autobiographies and that of one of the men.

Mrs. Mary proves to be an old flame of Meriton's at the young ladies' seminary. Mrs. Dorothy is the milkmaid Meriton once deceived. She has proceeded with but one adventure when the author exclaims, "And this shall be the last I shall relate to you in this part, referring the prosecution of hers and the others' adventures to a third part." Of course this method destroys even the unity of person maintained by Head, and the reader's interest flags on being shifted from narrator to narrator. Nor is there any difference between these disagreeable people; the deeds ascribed to one might as well be those of another.

The bulk of Kirkman's Second Part is given over to the Englishman's account of himself.

His mother is a Gypsy, his father a transmogrifier of shoes. Together they rob shop-keepers, the boy at night entering to ask a light for his link, then putting out the candle handed him, and running off with the first goods available, while the father gleans after as the victim pursues.[1] He practices on orchards, uses the bacon trick already related by Head, puts fleas down ladies' necks, lays trains of gunpowder, and in a crowd sews the coats of neighbors together. In serving a surgeon barber, he learns to increase rather than to heal wounds, and then finds employment at an inn. Here he froths the ale with chalk, snatches away flagons before they are empty, greases the horses' teeth to keep them from eating,[2] and employs a hundred other devices, most of which had been

[1] *The English Rogue*, pt. ii, ch. 5, from *The Catterpillers of this Nation*, and the third story of Rowlands's *Greenes Ghost*.

[2] *The English Rogue*, pt. ii, ch. 9, from Dekker's *Lanthorne and Candle-light* and Wilson's *Three Ladies of London*.

exploited half a century before in the "Pícara Justina." Next he serves a cook, observes his cheats and those of nurses, and like Estevanillo Gonzalez kills a patient by giving him water during a fever.[1]

Successive terms of service with a locksmith, a tailor, a baker, and a plasterer afford him opportunity for describing the illicit practices of each. He joins the Gypsies, and embroiders Head's account of the orders of rogues with passages stolen *verbatim* from Dekker's "Belman of London."[2] Included in his further narrative are the rogue autobiographies of a drugster, a scrivener, and a bookseller, the tricks of the two latter echoing Kirkman's own experience in those trades.

As for Mrs. Mary's story, it describes her fall from grace, and her meeting with the drugster; while Mrs. Dorothy's account is limited to befooling three lovers. When this miserable performance breaks off, it has accomplished nothing beyond accentuating the Spanish scheme of the service of masters already imitated by Head.

There must have been readers for the extended "English Rogue," since, in 1671, there appeared a Third and a Fourth Part with prefaces signed by Head and Kirkman together. The rivals, after some bitterness, had shaken hands, and although, from Head's own statement in his "Proteus Redivivus," it is evident that he must still have nursed resentment, he probably thought it more profitable to join with Kirkman than to oppose him. But if Head possessed greater ability than Kirkman, the leaven was lost in the lump, and the Third Part proved worse than even the Second. Sixteen of its twenty-four chapters are given to a continuation of Mrs. Dorothy's story. She recounts also the life of a Celestina employed by her, and tells a hodge-podge of jests.

[1] *The English Rogue*, pt. ii, ch. 11; *Estevanillo*, cap. 3.
[2] *The English Rogue*, pt. ii, ch. 15.

Only after a new rogue has rehearsed his exploits in France does Meriton Latroon reappear. His wife has fallen in love with Mrs. Mary and Mrs. Dorothy in their male disguise; and now in a fit of jealousy she kills the former and then herself. Meriton and the rest, unmoved by the tragedy, sail to Surat, where the anti-hero discovers Mrs. Jane, the girl he had once lured aboard a ship for Virginia. When the reader has listened to her story, she robs a lover, embarks for England with Meriton, and they have proceeded as far as Saint Helena before the Third Part closes.[1]

Villainy is as prominent here as roguery, especially in Mrs. Dorothy's account, and the borrowings are manifold. The "Garduña de Sevilla" is drawn upon in the episode of the procuress outwitted by a gallant who secures the return of a borrowed gown, and in her device for disposing of two lovers by having them fight and destroy each other.[2] The "Desordenada Codicia" furnishes several incidents, one a robbery done by a boy in a bale, another a cheat with boots, of earlier use in "Eulenspiegel" and "Scoggins Jests."[3] Here, too, reappear the Italian *novella* employed in "Lazarillo de Manzanares" of the one-eyed husband whom his wife blindfolds while her lover escapes, and the trick of a judge who declares in a crowd that the thief he is seeking is the man with a straw in his beard, whereat the thief reveals himself by trying to brush out the

[1] The journal of the voyage anticipates the manner of Defoe: "The fifth from twelve to six (per compass) east five leagues, having at four of the clock had ground sixty four fathoms oazy sand, then set more sail and stood in north, north-west till six in the morning, our depth in running the course of seven leagues was fifty-five, sixty, and sixty-four fathome in latitude, about 20 degrees, seconds 42, and longitude 30 degrees, seconds 3 digits west." *The English Rogue*, pt. iii, chs. 22, 23.

[2] *The English Rogue*, pt. iii, chs. 4, 5; *La garduña*, caps. 2, 3. The former trick figures also in the *Decameron*, day viii, *novella* 1; in Chaucer's "Shipmannes Tale," and in *L'histoire générale des larrons*, pt. ii, ch. 19.

[3] *The English Rogue*, pt. iii, ch. 14; *La desordenada codicia*, cap. 4.

fictitious straw.[1] The device of waxing a silver cup to the underside of a table is hackneyed, as is that of a cheater attending uninvited a banquet, the host thinking him a friend of his guests, the guests believing him a friend of the host.[2]

The story itself has become a mere vehicle for the recital of jests, few of which fail to be brutal, stupid, or indecent.[3] Yet Kirkman says in his preface, "I hope all persons who make use of this book to practice debaucheries will be induced to forbear and decline their wickedness, lest a just judgment overtake them, as they will find it hath done these extravagants."

That the authors appreciated the nature of their work is apparent from their preface to the Fourth Part. "From the actions of others we gather'd matter, which materials we methodized, and so formed this structure." The fresh addition shows the wanderers proceeding by way of Messina to Naples. During the journey Mrs. Dorothy completes the story of her checkered life, the captain tells the story of his, and includes in it the account of a gamester's career, and Mrs. Jane gives a

[1] A variation of a trick in *Marcos de Obregon*, rel. i, des. 16; in *Alonso, moço de muchos amos*, parte ii, cap. 3, and in *Francion*, liv. ix.

[2] *The English Rogue*, pt. iii, ch. 18, from *L'histoire générale des larrons*, pt. i, chs. 6, 24.

[3] Other borrowings are the following: *The English Rogue*, pt. iii, ch. 12, a version of Awdeley's ring-faller trick with a brass chain, and the story of an innkeeper beguiled within the enemy's lines by two soldiers, his creditors, from *L'histoire générale des larrons*, pt. i, ch. 16; *The English Rogue*, pt. iii, ch. 16, two pickpockets sit in the stocks while a third plies through the crowd, slightly varied from *Pasquils Iests; The English Rogue*, pt. iii, ch. 17, a master thief peaches on his acolyte in order to victimize the onlookers, from *L'histoire générale des larrons*, pt. i, ch. 17; *The English Rogue*, pt. iii, chs. 18, 19, and 20, a robbery by two rogues in religious garb, the account of a machine for catching pickpockets, the device of artificial hands that the genuine may be free to undertake rogueries, the hiring of rascals by a lawyer to steal his too confiding brother's purse, which is then served up to the victim at dinner, and the trick of robbing a merchant as he tries on a priest's cape, drawn from *L'histoire générale des larrons*, pt. i, chs. 13, 18, 21, 22, and 14, respectively.

list of cheats loosely connected by their ascription to a single rogue.

Her auditors were pleased, "as we hope the reader will be," say the authors, "and now we shall put an end to this fourth part. And if (as we hope) you are pleased with what is already written, we shall in short time give you greater pleasure and satisfaction in the continuation of our extravagants' adventures, which shall be fully finished in a fifth and last part."

As a mercy to all concerned, the promised Fifth Part never appeared, though later editions professed to embrace it; and so ended without an end "The English Rogue." The Fourth Part contains little worthy of mention. The advice concerning gaming and the list of the frequenters of an ordinary was stolen from "Leather-More" (1668).[1] Many tricks were versions of those it had earlier celebrated. The device of the straw in the beard recurs in the trick of a woman who declares to the probable thieves that she has just found her stolen ring, whereat the thief reveals himself by his sudden search for it.[2] Several characters are given after the example of Head, whose First Part had included the Character of a Bottle of Canary and the Character of an Hector or Trepan. The episode of the widow bent upon marrying none but the wealthy, yet deceived into wedding an impoverished rogue, resembles a familiar piece of Spanish intrigue.[3]

As for the central story of Meriton Latroon, it has remained at a standstill from the moment of Kirkman's rivalry and collaboration. Everything since the close of the First Part has

[1] *The English Rogue*, pt. iv, ch. 18.

[2] The Smithfield horse courser's cheat of giving an old nag a live eel to swallow (*The English Rogue*, pt. iv, ch. 13) occurs in *Robin Conscience, or Conscionable Robin, his Progress through Court, City, and Country* (1635).

[3] Cervantes's *Casamiento engañoso*, which was shortly after translated by Kirkman in *The Wits, or Sport upon Sport* (1672).

been told reminiscently by people in whom the reader can have mustered small interest. In construction "The English Rogue" reverts to a primitive type of fiction. It is little more than a collection of traditional tales deficient in characterization, and at a tangent with the main plot.[1] Morally it is without meaning. Its fifteen hundred pages do not mention a kindly deed, a generous sentiment, a genial impulse, or a decent person. Not only has the light-hearted rogue of Spain turned a miserable pervert, but the world at which he laughed has become a cesspool of iniquity. This rank growth of the Restoration has neglected the artistic contrast between witty roguery and honest stupidity, the satire and irony of the Spanish scheme, as well as the relief afforded by sentimental tales embodied in such narratives as "Guzman de Alfarache" and the "Roman Comique." It not unnaturally induced in its readers a feeling of sick satiety, and, although it continued to be read by the lowest, by rakes, vagabonds, and thieves, nobody of taste regarded it. Yet, in 1672, Kirkman furnished a revision of Head's First Part, making twenty-one changes, altering the phraseology, adding a few chapters and incidents, and, despite his own lubricity, toning down improper passages. There were editions of the whole in 1674 and 1680, after which, until the elaborate reprint of 1874 by Pearson, none but abridgments appeared. Of these there were the following: in 1679 and toward 1700 a brief "Life and Death of the English Rogue, or his Last Legacy to the World;" in 1688 a black-letter chap-book and a "Life and Death

[1] Occasional resemblances to *Simplicissimus* may be noted, e. g.: the burlesque account of Meriton's simple home (*The English Rogue*, pt. i, ch. 1, and *Simplicissimus*, i, ch. 1); the devices of Gypsies for coloring the face with walnuts (pt. i, ch. 5, and *Trutz Simplex*, ch. xxvii); the moralization upon God as all-seeing (pt. i, ch. 9, and *Vogel-Nest*, i, ch. 19); a rogue's hiding in a mill and spying on the miller and his wench (pt. iv, ch. 9, and *Simplicissimus*, ii, ch. 1); and the general shift of scene to the East

of Young Lazarillo," appended to "The Pleasant Adventures of the Witty Spaniard, Lazarillo de Tormes," and containing a *rechauffé* of Meriton's tricks; in 1689 a curtailed and repentant "English Rogue, or Witty Extravagant" in "Five Parts," reissued in 1723 for one shilling as the seventh edition, and without date at Gosport as the fourth edition, and again in still briefer form in 1759. In 1786 was published "The Original English Rogue" in "Two Parts," and in 1776 appeared in three volumes "The English Rogue, or Life of Jeremy Sharp," labeled the eighth edition. This version, a complete rewriting of Kirkman, keeps the anti-hero as the centre of events, attributing to him many exploits heretofore distributed at random among other personages. The rogue returns to England, and as in the abridged adaptations of 1689, 1723, and 1759, repents in old age, wetting the paper with his tears. "Therefore," says he, "let me return thanks to the Almighty, who hath given me grace to see my errors, and sincerely beg pardon for them." [1]

In all these reissues of "The English Rogue," and in the occasional undated abridgments of the nineteenth century,[2] it is noteworthy that the most outrageous passages were not revived, and that the tendency toward moralizing the most immoral of English fictions was constant.

5. *Minor Restoration Fiction*

When the last volume of "The English Rogue" had appeared, and Head's first volume had been revised by Kirkman and himself, each attempted separately a similar work. Kirkman's "Unlucky Citizen" (1673) proved as unliterary as

[1] To this version was added "A Narrative of an Extraordinary Delivery of Mary Toft of Eighteen Rabbits," a fraud assigned to the year 1726, and without connection with *The English Rogue*.

[2] I have one labeled "Printed for Fras. Kirkman, 1671, reprinted by M. Metford, 19 Little Queen St., Holborn."

Head's "Proteus Redivivus, or the Art of Wheedling or Insinuation" (1675), but it possessed more interest. Its anti-hero refuses to describe the misfortunes of his parents, "as is usual in books of this nature, viz. 'Gusman,' 'Lazarillo de Tormes,' or our late 'English Rogue.'" He gives, however, an account of the first twenty years of his life. This sets forth his roguery at school and his apprenticeship to two masters. The first is a scrivener who obliged him to "cleane the shooes, carry out the ashes and dust, sweep the shop, cleanse the sink (and a long nasty one it was), draw the beer, and at washing times to fetch up coals and kettles."

After a beating, he decamps, meets a party of story-tellers, and is outwitted by a blind rogue at gaming and also in a race. Then he meditates joining the Gypsies,[1] but instead enters the service of a new master. "I would not have you think that I should have as many as the unlucky Spaniard, Lazarillo de Tormes; no, I had but two and he seven." This employer is a cheating bookseller, whose shifts, together with those of the anti-hero and the latter's step-mother, are duly exposed. The translation of romances "that treated of old impossible knight-errantry" brings success, and after suffering wrongful arrest at the hands of a blackmailing catch-pole, and retaliating upon society with fresh rogueries, the Unlucky Citizen establishes a shop of his own. At this point the story disintegrates into eight irrelevant anecdotes.[2] Several derive from the French, as does one of earlier recital in which two brothers, each informed by a rogue of the other's death, and journeying to act as his

[1] "But I think our *English Rogue* hath sufficiently described the various humours of that sort of people," says Kirkman, who never lets slip an opportunity for advertising.

[2] The tale of a Cordelier dropping into a river a Jacobin who refused to pay him for portage, harks back to the Spanish *Alonso* (parte ii, cap. 2), and appears in *The English Rogue* (pt. iv, ch. 20).

executor, meet by night at an inn. They mistake each other for ghosts, but in the meantime their deserted houses have been pillaged by the rogue.[1] A promised continuation of this poor piece of book-making failed to appear.

Richard Head, who had been defeated in his plan of prosecuting his rogue theme as a novel, broke from that form in "Proteus Redivivus" and wrote a series of characters. The art of wheedling, or deceiving, and the qualifications of the wheedler are first considered. Then "the private and publick practicers of this mysterious science" receive attention, and the tricks of rakes or town-shifts, vintners, and drawers are detailed. The rake is studied in each of his haunts, — the coffee-house, the ordinary, the theatre, the inn, his lodgings, with the watch, and on the road. The wheedles of the quack, the shop-keeper, the apothecary, the country-attorney, the catch-pole, the ship-master, the handsome hostess, and even the "self-edifying non-conformist" follow. The treatise ends with an account of the cheats of the scrivener, a worthy already anatomized "in a character not long since printed."[2]

In witness of the plagiarism rampant at this time, it may be noted that when Head asks why we should not match the knaves of classic antiquity "with a pair of as lusty rogues, one Spanish, and the other English; not but that other countries have as large a stock of each, but only want recording," he is stealing literally a passage from Nicholas Goodman's "Hollands Leagver" (1632). All his efforts to add to what notoriety he had already gained through "The English Rogue" proved ineffectual, and later editions of "Proteus Redivivus" testified to the popularity of the character-book rather than to that of the romance of roguery.

[1] *L'histoire générale des larrons*, pt. iii, ch. 6.

[2] No doubt a reference to Kirkman's *Citizen* of two years before.

As for Head's "Nugæ Venales, or a Complaisant Companion," which reached a third enlarged edition by 1686, it was simply a collection of most ancient "new jests, domestick and foreign; bulls, rodomontados, pleasant novels, and miscellanies." This meritless compilation contains an abridged version of the "Rodomontades Espagnoles," and attempts self-justification on the ground that literary thievery has become the fashion.

Fortunatus of legendary fame [1] received partial picaresque treatment in "The Right Pleasant and Variable Tragical History of Fortvnatvs" (1676), probably by Thomas Churchyard.[2] Like the anti-heroes of the romance of roguery, Fortunatus embarks upon his adventures as a poor boy in service. He becomes his master's favorite, but envious fellow servants frighten him into believing the master jealous and about to take revenge. He flees away, falls into riotous company, and having squandered his all, takes service again, entering the household of a rich Florentine. Here a rascally domestic practices such knaveries that Fortunatus narrowly escapes hanging.

Then medieval magic enters the story, which henceforward bears some analogy to Grimmelshausen's "Vogel-Nest."

Fortunatus becomes possessor of an inexhaustible purse and an infallible wishing-cap. He visits the Purgatory of St. Patrick, exploited to Spaniards by Calderon, as well as the realms of Prester John, and on dying leaves to his sons, Ampedo and Andalocia, the two mysterious gifts. But they prove no blessings. Andalocia runs through roguish adventures only to perish in prison as a result of the envy aroused in

---

[1] *Fortunatus* proper had appeared in a German edition, Vienna, 1509, and in English before 1600. It is mentioned in the dedication of Meredith Hanmer's translation of *Eusebius* (1577), and in Henry Crope's *Vertues Commonwealth* (1602). An edition of 1682 is one of the earliest now extant.

[2] An imperfect black-letter copy in the British Museum may date from 1650.

two earls by his purse. Ampedo in grief burns the cap and expires; while the earls, finding the purse to have lost its charm, reveal their perfidy through a quarrel, and are executed.

This fiction is picaresque in its use of the service of masters and in its tricks. Of the latter, the first at Fortunatus's expense slightly resembles a similar incident in Barclay's "Euphormio;"[1] the second involves the jest-book device of taking to a gentleman's wife his ring as a token for the delivery of jewels; and the third is an innkeeper's theft from a guest through a secret aperture in a wall, reminiscent, perhaps, of a deceit in "Marcos de Obregon."[2] Espinel's novel, indeed, may have further suggested Andalocia's curing a princess of an ailment he himself had occasioned. Here, however, the disease is induced by magic apples, while in "Marcos" its source was love.[3]

Four years later from an unexpected quarter issued a Puritan romance of roguery. This was John Bunyan's "Life and Death of Mr. Badman," a blast to sinners, blown in degenerate times, and no conscious echo of the merry music of Spain. Bunyan's preface, nevertheless, strikes the same chord as Aleman's preface to "Guzman de Alfarache." Where one sets up a beacon, the other fires a shot of warning to the wicked. "I have put fire to the pan," cries Bunyan, "and doubt not but the report will quickly be heard." The task has been no easy one, he admits, for "The man also that writeth Mr. Badman's life had need to be fenced with a coat of mail. . . . To conclude, let those that would not dye Mr. Badman's death, take heed of Mr. Badman's ways."

Despite the dialogue form, the allegory, and the absence of humor, Bunyan has here subscribed to the picaresque scheme in setting up an anti-hero as antithesis to the hero of "The

[1] *Euphormio*, liv. i, ch. 2. [2] *Marcos de Obregon*, rel. i, des. 13.
[3] *Marcos de Obregon*, rel. ii, des. 10.

Pilgrim's Progress." "It came again into my mind to write, as then of him that was going to Heaven, so now of the Life and Death of the Ungodly, and of their travel from this world to Hell." Mr. Wiseman's description, to Mr. Attentive, of Badman's youth, his robbing of orchards and gardens and other mischievous pranks, is in the true roguish vein. But Badman, who among his deplorable traits "could not endure the Lord's Day," turns villain, and only in the moralizings, anecdotes, and frauds do picaresque hints remain. One of the frauds parallels the Angel Gabriel story in Boccaccio, Massuccio, and Grimmelshausen,[1] for a lover bids his lady, should worst come to worst, ". . . say (saith he) when you come before the judge that you are with child by the Holy Ghost."

Two dramatists, the witty Congreve and the improper Mrs. Behn, neither of Bunyan's congregation, showed some acquaintance with Spanish intrigue. Congreve's single fiction, "Incognita, or Love and Duty Reconciled" (1691), was labeled "a novel." Its preface made a plea for realism, distinguished the novel from the romance, and exploited a theory of a fictional unity of contrivance, suggested by the dramatic unities. But "Incognita" scarcely matched the principles it purported to illustrate. Mrs. Behn, who died in 1689, exhibited less familiarity with picaresque literature than might have been expected from her acquaintance with Spanish gained through residence in Antwerp and the West Indies. She often lays her plots in Spain, yet in only one of her stories is rascality prominent. This is "The Fair Jilt," which narrates the life of a wanton, who as a nun practiced her wiles upon a young priest, falsely accused him, and then, allying herself with a Belgian prince, conspired against her own sister, and at last repented.

Here and in her longest and most successful work, "Oroo-

[1] Cf. *ante*, p. 29.

noko," Mrs. Behn insists that "every circumstance to a tittle is truth." If in "Oroonoko" she anticipated Rousseau by her doctrine that "simple nature is the most harmless, inoffensive, and virtuous mistress," in her other tales — "The Perjur'd Beauty," "Agnes de Castro," "The Lucky Mistake," and "The Court of the King of Bantam" — she imitated Spanish intrigue. Of her plays, the only one that approached to the picaresque was "The False Count." Here a lover, rejected because his lady will have nobility or nothing, gains revenge through a chimney-sweep secured to masquerade as a count. At the proper moment the sweep reassumes his proper shape, to her complete distraction. The scene is Spain, as it is in "The Dutch Lover" and in "The Moor's Revenge," while in the "Banished Cavaliers" it is Spanish Naples.

Earlier attempts at realistic writing, like "Zelinda" and "English Adventures," of 1676, retained the interest in intrigue, and may be associated with the genre. "Zelinda," whose author was Thomas Duffet (or another T. D.), satirizes the heroic romance by giving a half-cynical version of Voiture's unfinished "Histoire d'Alcidalis et Zélide," which, out of sheer roguery, his title-page declares to be "translated from the French of Monsieur de Scudéry." "English Adventures," from the pen of Roger Boyle, author of England's most successful heroic fiction, "Parthenissa," is frankly anti-heroic. "Love which terminates in marriage is not of the essentials of my history," says Boyle, who, besides providing Otway with the plot for his "Orphan," in the story of Brandon, describes the wiles of the picaresque Isabella and of her maid Leticia, the one an English Celestina, and the other the mistress of Henry VIII.

Less intrigue and more realism marked two fictions of 1699, "The Adventures of Covent Garden," depicting bourgeois life, and "The Compleat Mendicant," aiming to moralize the romance of roguery. The former declared itself composed "in imitation of Scarron's 'City Romance,'" a blundering allusion to Furetière's "Roman Bourgeois," which it remotely follows. Peregrine, a town gallant, is torn in his affections between two ladies of Bow Street, the fair Selinda and a jilting coquette, Emilia. But the vignettes of London life, rather than the plot, give the story value. Its descriptions of Bartholomew Fair and its discussions of the drama echo the gossip of Will's Coffee-House, to whose ingenious frequenters it was dedicated.

Another Peregrine is the chief personage in "The Compleat Mendicant," doubtfully attributed to Defoe.

This orphan of a cavalier family attends school and the university as servitor to a nobleman's son. Setting forth to wander, he falls in with a charlatan who removes artificial cancers from confederates, and eventually picks Peregrine's pocket and leaves him the inn-reckoning to settle. A kindly landlord provides him with introductions to others of the fraternity, and a gentleman recommends him as usher to a schoolmaster in Northamptonshire. On the way thither, Peregrine is induced by a pretended divine to turn vagabond. His begging letters and poems reap a harvest of silver until a constable interferes. But on being released from jail he is installed in the school, and is finally ordained deacon.

The schoolmaster's sister falls in love with him, and to escape her attentions, he takes to the road once more. After arrest for a highway robbery committed by another, he becomes curate, but failing to secure preferment turns shepherd. The curiosity of a neighboring squire alarms him, so, having composed tedious essays upon the calamities of life and the desirability of death, he wanders forth. Here the story breaks off, although a second part is advertised to be in press.

So pale an imitation of the picaresque novel could exert no influence. It is significant, however, as a reaction against the immorality of "The English Rogue." It affects realism and vouches for the truth of every incident. "But after all," says the author, "supposing the worst that can be, that the whole should be a well-contriv'd fable; I can see no reason, why the fabulous life of a vertuous mendicant should not be as acceptable to the world as an English Rogue, a Gusman, Lazerillo, or any other Romantick History of Villanous Tricks." In its accounts of the charlatan and of shepherd life the little novel resembles "Francion," but the sprightliness, wit, and immorality of the French work have disappeared.

Thus English picaresque fiction reached the eighteenth century after two chief experiments. The first was Elizabethan and combined adventure with artistic realism; the second was of the Restoration and forsook observation in reverting to jest-book and *fabliaux*, sifting unrelated tricks out of foreign story. "The English Rogue" stood at a further remove from the modern novel than "The Vnfortvnate Traveller," and so far exhausted its special type that the continued cultivation of it was impossible. Henceforth he who would run English life into the picaresque mould must employ some new procedure. As this was not at once forthcoming, the romance of roguery languished, to be revived only in the second decade of the eighteenth century by two forces. One was the naturalism and character-drawing of Defoe; the other was the literary inspiration of Le Sage.

BIBLIOGRAPHY

CHAPTER V

1

J. J. Jusserand's *English Novel in the Time of Shakespeare* (London, 1890, trans. by E. Lee) offers the best account of sixteenth-century fiction. The same author's *Literary History of the English People* (N. Y., 1906, vol. ii) deals less fully with this matter. Robert Palfrey Utter's *The Beginnings of the Picaresque Novel in England* (*Harvard Monthly*, Apr., 1906) demonstrates the futility of assuming Spanish influence upon Nash. Martin A. S. Hume's *Spanish Influence in English Literature* (London, 1905) is inadequate and untrustworthy in its treatment of picaresque fiction and Spanish inspiration. It owes, moreover, an unacknowledged debt for most that is not inaccurate to John Garrett Underhill's authoritative *Spanish Literature in the England of the Tudors* (N. Y., 1899). Much slighter is Ludwig Bahlsen's *Spanische Quellen der Englischen Litteratur besonders Englands zu Shakespeares Zeit* (in the *Zeitschr. f. vergl. litteraturgeschichte*, n. f., vi, 1893). Other notices of Spanish influence in England for this period almost exclusively concern the drama.

The *Complete Works of Thomas Nash* was edited in the Huth Library by Alex. B. Grosart (London, 1883–85, 6 vols.). Edmund Gosse has reprinted *The Vnfortvnate Traveller* separately with an introduction (London, 1892), and Ronald B. McKerrow has issued four volumes of Nash's *Works* (London, 1904–05). Here *The Vnfortvnate Traveller* (in vol. ii) reproduces the Bodleian text of 1594, which differs slightly from the earlier text of the British Museum used by Gosse and by Grosart (in vol. v).

2–3

Chettle's *Piers Plainnes Prentiship* survives in a unique copy in the Bodleian. His *Kind-Harts Dreame* is edited by E. F. Rimbault (vol. v, *Percy Soc. Publ.*), and appears together with *England's Mourning Garment* (*New Shakspere Soc. Publ.*, series 4, pt. 2). Grosart has edited the *Works in Prose and Verse of Nicholas Breton* (London, 1879, 2 vols.). Breton's poetry is noticed by E. M. Tappan (*Publ. of the Mod. Lang. Ass. of America*, 1898, xiii, pp. 297 ff.); and his prose fiction is studied by Theodor Kuskop in a dissertation entitled *Nicholas Breton und seine Prosaschriften* (Leipzig, 1902). Jusserand's *English Novel* and Chandler's *Romances of Roguery* provide an account of picaresque translations into English. L. Charlanne's *L'influence française en Angleterre au xvii siècle* (Paris, 1906) confines its attention almost wholly to the transplanting of heroic fiction in England; cf. especially chapter vi, pp. 158 ff. Crouch's *Welch Traveller* is reprinted by J. O. Halliwell (London, 1860) and by W. C. Hazlitt (*Remains of the Early Popular Poetry of England*, London, 1866, vol. iv).

4–5

The English Rogue should be read in the anonymous reprint by Pearson (London, 1874, 4 vols.). The only detailed discussion it has received is that by Wilhelm Kollmann in *Nashs Unfortunate Traveller und Heads English Rogue, die beiden Hauptvertreter des englischen Schelmenromans* (*Anglia*, 1899, vol. xxii). Here, however, the significant feature — its dependence upon jest-books and foreign picaresque sources — receives no notice. I have endeavored to supply this lack. Of Head himself, the best account is by Sidney Lee (*Dict. of Nat. Biog.*, vol. xxv). Kirkman is noticed at greater length in the same work (vol. xxi) by Gordon Goodwin. The best reprint of *Badman* is *The Life and Death of Mr. Badman, and the Holy War*, edited by John Brown (Cambridge, 1905). Mrs. Behn's *Plays, Histories, and Novels* are reprinted (London, 1871, 6 vols.), and she has recently been studied by P. Siegel in *Aphra Behns Gedichte und Prosawerke* (*Anglia*, 1902). *The Compleat Mendicant* is assigned to Defoe in the British Museum catalogue, but Lee, Aitken, and Trent reject it.

CHAPTER VI

ROGUERY IN THE DRAMA

1. *Shakespeare and Jonson*

HE exploitation of low-life in the drama was chiefly the work of the early seventeenth century. Roguery had played a slight part, as has been shown,[1] in the miracle and morality plays, the interludes, and "Ralph Roister Doister;" but with Shakespeare's predecessors it found little favor. Lyly's "Mother Bombie" portrayed the cunning old woman of Rochester, his "Endimion" satirized the watch, and his "Gallathea" in a brief underplot took occasion to wing a shaft at astrological and alchemical pretenders. Peele's "Famous Chronicle of King Edward the First" dealt with a Welsh Robin Hood. Similar matter was developed by Greene, if he be the author of "George-a-Greene the Pinner of Wakefield," and by Munday and Chettle in their "Downfall" and "Death of Robert Earl of Huntington;" yet such plays were romantic, not anti-heroic, and Greene and Lodge's "A Looking Glasse for London," although it displayed the vices of Nineveh satirically, could by no means compare in realism with Greene's own conny-catching pamphlets. Chapman's "Blind Beggar of Alexandria" proved honest enough, while Kyd and Marlowe reveled in sanguinary horrors and conjured up villains pure and simple.

It was left for Shakespeare, therefore, to take the lead in the

[1] Cf. *ante*, pp. 50–54.

creation of rogues, as in all else. If low-life is most realistically exhibited by him in the two parts of "Henry IV," and the picaro is best portrayed in "The Winter's Tale," roguery is not forgotten in his other plays. The bandits of "The Two Gentlemen of Verona," who swear "by the bare scalp of Robin Hood's fat friar," are romantic figures, and Parolles, in "All 's Well That Ends Well," is justly accounted "a notorious liar, a great way fool, solely a coward." When exposed in his treasonable confession to the supposed enemy, he nonchalantly asks, "Who cannot be crushed with a plot?" but perceiving the uselessness of further pretense, abdicates his captaincy, exclaiming with picaresque philosophy: —

> Rust, sword! cool, blushes! and, Parolles, live
> Safest in shame! being fool'd, by foolery thrive!
> There 's place and means for every man alive.

Edgar, in "King Lear," disguises as the Abraham Man of the beggar-books, and in the precipice episode while masquerading as leader to blind Gloster varies ingeniously Lazarillo's trick upon his blind man. This is more directly referred to when Benedick, in "Much Ado About Nothing," says to Claudio, "Ho! now you strike like the blind man: 't was the boy that stole your meat, and you'll beat the post;" [1] and Launcelot Gobbo, in "The Merchant of Venice," may owe a hint, too, to Lazarillo in the practical jest at his blind father's expense, and in his desire to flee from the miserly service of Shylock and take as master, Bassanio, who "gives rare new liveries." Constables, the picaro's butts and enemies, are laughed at by reference in "The Comedy of Errors," and in person in the delightful Dogberry and Verges of "Much Ado," who with their fainter copy, Elbow, in "Measure for Measure," make forever ridiculous the Elizabethan watch; while Abhorson, in the last-named

[1] Act ii, sc. 1.

play, provides a commentary on the custom of transforming criminals into executioners. Timon of Athens, to the banditti that assail him, proclaims the universality of theft, instancing the sun, moon, sea, and earth, and concluding: —

> All that you meet are thieves: to Athens go,
> Break open shops; nothing can you steal,
> But thieves do lose it.

Such misanthropy, however, is not shared by Shakespeare's clowns and jesters — often half picaros — or by Falstaff and Autolycus, who surpass all other comic rogues. Neither is of the Spanish type, in so far as neither is a rascal in service satirizing his masters; but in volatile humor that disarms reprehension, both are essentially picaresque, and as living personalities, they outrank any Spanish picaro. Especially is this true of Falstaff. His appearance in a series of plays gives scope not merely for a rare variety of jesting cheats in peace and war, but for the unfolding through inimitable dialogue of a many-sided character. There is no moralizing concerning him, or by him, as with Guzman de Alfarache, but the moral values are more perfectly preserved, and his gradual degradation is as impressive as it is inevitable.

In his cowardice, real or assumed, his infinite yearning for capons and sack, his notions of honor and love, his ready shifts and wonderful lies, relished though he knows they can never pass muster, even in his proneness to self-delusion, Falstaff shares the common picaresque traits. What but a picaro is he when he robs on the road at Gadshill, or hacks his sword and tickles his nose with a straw for blood as proof to the prince of his valor? when he misuses the king's press damnably, or in battle counterfeits death at one moment and then at the next stabs the corpse of Hotspur to pose as his vanquisher? The cruder scenes of boisterous quarreling and mirth at the Boar's-

Head in Eastcheap, even his misadventures with the buck-basket, and his escape as the fat woman of Brentford are not without parallel in the Spanish romances. Of his friends, Ancient Pistol and Corporal Nym are English *valientes*, and Doll Tearsheet is a more tangible Justina or Rufina. Bardolph of the fiery face, who is ultimately hanged for stealing a pyx, garrulous Dame Quickly, and once wicked, senile Shallow are close enough to the picaresque family; yet to hold them or Falstaff immediately related to their cousins of Spain would be folly. They are at most a collateral branch, joint heirs with the Spaniards of the perverseness, ingenuity, and sensuality of unregenerate human nature.[1]

Shakespeare certainly needed no foreign tutelage. Ready to hand, he had good English matter in jest-books, beggar-books, and actual life, and his was the genius of all others for transferring this matter to art. Small wonder then that his rascals remain vitally distinct and individual; for where Spanish novelists and their Continental followers are intent upon society seen through the eye of the rogue, Shakespeare in Falstaff has anatomized the rogue himself.

No slip of a threadbare page is Sir John, devising sly schemes

[1] They antedate all save two of the Peninsular romances of roguery. *Henry IV*, *pt. i*, was licensed February 25, 1598; *pt. ii*, August 23, 1600; *Henry V* was entered August 14, 1600, and *The Merry Wives of Windsor*, January 18, 1602, though it may have been written in 1598. Shakespeare probably knew *Lazarillo de Tormes* (1554) through David Rowlands's translation (licensed 1568, printed 1576, and extant in editions of 1586 and 1596), known also to Spenser. There is no evidence of his acquaintance with *Guzman de Alfarache* (Aleman's pt. i, 1599), translated into French by Chappuys (1600). *The Winter's Tale* was played not later than May 15, 1611, when Simon Forman saw it at The Globe. In the meantime, Spanish picaresque literature had produced only Sayavedra's (Martí's) *Guzman* (1602), Aleman's *Guzman*, pt. ii (1605), and the *Pícara Justina* (1605). To none of these does Autolycus owe anything. Klein somewhat plausibly suggests (*Geschichte des Dramas*, vol. viii, p. 916) that Ancient Pistol is inspired by the Centurio of the *Celestina*.

to get on in a world which has fooled him at first, and which presently he will learn to flatter and trick and laugh at in turn as he paints it minutely. He is rather the picaro grown old in iniquity, full-blown, mellower, lazier, less ambitious, a genial, selfish, forgivable mountain of flesh and desire, comic to the end, yet falling more and more surely a victim to his own gross nature and the chastisements bestowed by others. The Spanish rogues could at best do no more than amuse, but Falstaff is so human that he moves to indulgent affection, nay, almost to tears as at last Nell Quickly relates how dying he fumbled with the sheets and played with flowers, and smiling upon his fingers' ends, babbled of green fields.

A bird of another feather is Autolycus, in "The Winter's Tale." Swaggering into the pretty pastoral world of Bohemia, he is perhaps more of the typical picaro than Falstaff, just because so lightly sketched. He is the simple, fun-loving "snapper-up of unconsidered trifles," pilferer of sheets bleaching on hedges,[1] caroler of airy, canting songs, haunter of wakes, fairs, and bear-baitings, peddler of golden coifs and stomachers, and pitiful true ballads. He has led an ape about the country; he has been a bailiff; he has served the prince, and though whipped out of court, he treasures no resentment against his master. On his own confession, he resembles the Spanish picaro in that he has flown over many knavish professions to settle only in roguery. He knows that to have an open ear, a quick eye, and a nimble hand is necessary for a cutpurse, together with a good nose to smell out work for the other senses. He refuses to inform on the king's runaway son because he holds it the more knavery to conceal it. But even if he had a mind to be honest, Fortune would forbid, for she drops booties in his mouth. "I see this is

[1] In Dekker's *Belman*, 1608, thieves are instructed "where to strike down geese, where to steale hennes, and from what hedge to fetch sheetes." Cf., also, *The Three Ladies of London*, *ante*, p. 53.

the time that the unjust man doth thrive," he cries; "sure the gods do this year connive at us and we may do anything extempore." His eyes twinkle as he insinuates to the old shepherd and his son the tortures they shall suffer for receiving the prince as Perdita's lover; and his picking of the clown's pocket, while being helped to his feet after a feigned beating and robbing, is as much for the jest as for gain. This trick, indeed, is an improvement upon a familiar beggar-book device, just as the cant terms that drop so glibly from his tongue are drawn out of Harman and Greene.[1] In sprightliness and wit, however, Autolycus excels all the beggar-book crew or the rogues of reality, and unlike them he can no more repent and reform than can Falstaff. As for the life to come, he sleeps out the thought of it.

Ben Jonson, the realist, who joined with Fletcher in contributing laudatory verse to Mabbe's translation of "Guzman de Alfarache," was predisposed to deal with roguery in his comedy of humors. His business lay, not with romantic bandits or a light-hearted Autolycus, but with manners and types of character to be observed in any corner of the London he knew so well. Although "Every Man in his Humour" (pl. *c.* 1598) pilloried the dignified coward Captain Bobadil together with the usurer Kitely, and although "The Case is Altered" (pl. *c.* 1599) drew a miser out of Plautus, and "The Poetaster" (pl. 1607) gave scope to Captain Tucca's canting braggadocio, it was not until the appearance of "Volpone, or the Fox" (pl. 1605–06) that Jonson devoted himself seriously to the exposure of rascality.

[1] Cf. for this trick Greene's *Second Part of Conny-catching* (1592). Under "The Discovery of the Nip and Foist" is told the story of a foist who pretends to swoon in Paul's that he and others may pick the pocket of the countryman who aids him to rise. Cf., also, Greene's *Thirde Part of Conny-catching* (1592), 8th story.

Here the rich and licentious Volpone victimizes those who would victimize him, and falls at last a prey to his agent, the parasite Mosca. The plot derives from Petronius, but the elaboration of its rogues is Jonson's own. Volpone, with his disguises as mountebank and *commendatore*, with his pretended illness and promised bequests, extorts from his deceived beneficiaries every concession. Corvino agrees to lend him his wife; Corbuccio signs over his property; the advocate Voltore perjures himself to oblige the magnifico, and then must feign madness to cover his tricks. And Mosca, though he conspires in outwitting the others, turns on Volpone at last and is himself whipped and sent to the galleys. Sir Politick Wouldbe, the English projector tricked by a fellow countryman into believing himself under arrest, may be the source of laughter less bitter, but the satire throughout is almost too savage for the picaresque vein.

In "The Alchemist" (pl. 1610), however, better humor prevails, and its master-rogue, Face, escapes without punishment. He is a rascal in service, left to care for the house of his master, and leagued with Subtle, a charlatan, and Dol Common, a courtesan, to bilk the gullible. Sir Epicure Mammon and the Puritans, Ananias and Tribulation Wholesome, prove alchemical dupes, and Kastril the "angry boy," Drugger the aspiring tobacconist, Dapper the gaming lawyer's clerk, and Dame Pliant, assured that she shall marry a nobleman, are victims of other tricks. It is the folly of these dupes quite as much as the roguery of the dupers that is chastised, hence poetic justice is not greatly outraged by allowing Subtle and Dol to make off at the catastrophe, leaving their plunder to be enjoyed by Face's master and by the knavish valet himself. Here, although Jonson's indebtedness to Plautus is obvious, the life of the time provides most of the matter. Simon Forman, the notorious quack, then at the zenith of his career, posed as the principal model for Subtle, for whom John Dee furnished still other traits. Edward Kelley contributed to Face, and in every detail Jonson drew upon a fund of curious learning acquired by minute observation.

Five years later he reëntered the lists against alchemy in a masque acted before King James. "Mercury Vindicated From the Alchemists" shows the god emerging from a charlatan's furnace to proclaim his independence of such masters and to vanquish them in word and deed. It is perhaps significant that shortly before this the King had witnessed at Cambridge a comedy, "Albumazar," adapted from Gian Battista della Porta's "L' Astrologo," satirizing astrology as practiced by a band of rogues accustomed to sound their victims by fortune-telling as a preliminary to theft.

Rascality in Jonson's "Bartholomew Fair" (pl. 1614) centres in Ezechiel Edgeworth, a cutpurse, who plies a brisk business at the Fair, and bestows especial attention upon Bartholomew Cokes of Harrow. This gull, after losing one purse to Edgeworth, boasts of possessing another which no one can come at. As he listens to a ballad sung by a confederate rogue, and releases his purse to scratch the ear that Edgeworth is slyly tickling with a straw, the purse disappears. Then Edgeworth steals Cokes's marriage-license from a servant, and secures his hat, sword, and cloak by offering to hold these articles while the innocent conny assists an apple-woman to recover her wares, dropped to entrap him. Captain Whit, a bawd, in whose company Edgeworth gallants Mistress Littlewit and Dame Overdo, Wasp, the servant of Cokes, who escapes from the stocks by inserting his wrists in a pair of shoes in lieu of his legs, Nightingale the ballad-singer, and Joan Trash and Lanthorn Leatherhead, who sell their wares only to snatch them again when the customer has turned his back, are adjunct picaresque figures in a comedy that teems with the scenes and folk of real life. The rollicking humor is reinforced rather than hampered by the satire upon Puritans directed against Zeal-of-the-Land Busy, and roguery is treated with picaresque indulgence when Justice Overdo, who in disguise has observed all these wiles, tenders a dinner to Edgeworth and his accomplices, purposing to reform them by moral suasion rather than by severity.

The "Historie of Friar Rvsh," already considered as allied with the literature of roguery, partially inspired Jonson's "Devil is an Ass" (pl. 1616), which presents Satan's offspring, Pug, "the less devil," taking service with a silly Norfolk squire, Fitzdottrel. If the master be a fool, the diabolical servant is an ass, outwitted from the moment of his assuming the body of a hanged cutpurse. In his attempts to engage the affections of his master's wife and the wench Pitfall, and in his theft of a gallant's garments and his delivery of a diamond ring to a sharper's man, Pug comes to grief. Then, recognizing his inability to cope in roguery with this roguish world, he escapes from prison through an appeal to Satan, and is borne back by Iniquity to the commonwealth of hell.

Pug's master is the victim of a more expert rascal, the projector Meercraft, who with his accomplices, Engine, Trains, and Ever-ill, plays upon Fitzdottrel's ambition to become Duke of Drownlands. The gull doubts his wife's capacity to play the duchess, and in his endeavor to educate her up to it, loses both wife and estate, and is prevailed upon to feign madness. In the end, Meercraft is exposed, and Fitzdottrel regains what he had lost. The array of projects here satirized embraces schemes for providing the state with tooth-picks, for making wine out of raisins, for dressing dogskins, draining waste lands, and establishing a court of arbitration for private differences.

In the decline of Jonson's dramatic powers the portrayal of roguery suffered. "The Staple of News" (pl. 1625) might suggest the establishment of a Canter's College; "The New Inn" (pl. 1629) might comment on the decay of chivalry and the substitution of roguery for loyalty in the attitude of the page to his master; "The Magnetic Lady" (pl. 1633) might draw a loquacious feminine parasite in Polish; and "The Sad Shepherd" (*c.* 1637) might revive Robin Hood and Robin Goodfellow; but the vigorous realism of the earlier plays was lacking.

Of Jonson's masques few were really roguish. Alchemy was laughed at in one, as has been shown; Robin Goodfellow figures in "Love Restored;" the "Dame" proved a powerful witch in "The Masque of Queens," and Howleglass acted the jester in "The Fortunate Isles;" but "The Gipsies Metamorphosed" (1621) was the chief picaresque essay in this form. It introduces a troop of Gypsies who enter to tell the fortunes of the king, his court, and a company of dancing clowns and wenches. When the Gypsies have exhibited their prowess in pocket-picking and the devising of satirical fortunes, they restore their pilferings, and one of them sings a coarse popular song, explaining the origin of the term applied to the Derbyshire resort of vagabonds (the so-called Devil's-Arse-Apeak), and celebrating Cocklorrel their rascal leader, deceased in 1533. At the request of the clowns, the Patrico describes the ceremonies attendant upon the initiation of candidates for the fraternity, whereupon the Gypsies throw off their tatters and stand revealed as courtiers. Needless to say, the Patrico and the Jackman, or forger of seals, are figures drawn from the beggar-books, and the cant so abundant here derives from the same source and has nothing to do with Romany speech.

2. *The Middleton Group*

While Jonson was dealing with low-life in these various phases, Thomas Middleton and a group of fellow dramatists, including Chapman, Marston, and Dekker, were contributing liberally, if with less distinction, to the literature of roguery. George Chapman's principal offering in this kind was "Eastward Hoe" (pr. 1605), written with the aid of Marston and Jonson himself.

Sir Petronell Flash, a knight-adventurer, pretending great wealth, marries the vain daughter of a goldsmith, sends her off on a progress to his imaginary castle in the East, and lays hands upon her dowry. He then plans to elope with the wife of his confederate usurer, and is about to embark on a gold-hunting expedition to Virginia in company with such choice spirits as Seagull, Spendall, and Scapethrift, when, falling drunk, they are all wrecked in a small boat on the Isle of Dogs. Among them is the cheating apprentice Quicksilver, who, having made free with one master's money and acquired the art of coin-clipping, has entered the service of Sir Petronell. He and his new master are now arrested and imprisoned, but Quicksilver turns hymn-singing Puritan, and with Sir Petronell and the usurer Securitie is bailed out by the soft-hearted goldsmith.

The comedy is excellent in its lashing of folly in the goldsmith's family, in its exposure of rascality in the apprentice and the knight-adventurer, and in its satire upon bribe-taking jailers and feigned conversions. Chapman's other plays were not without a tang of roguery, as witness the pranks played by Lemot in "An Humerous Dayes Myrth," the knavery that recoils upon its practicer, Rinaldo, in "All Fooles," and the jest of the courtiers who prevail upon a conceited coxcomb to think himself exalted to the post of ambassador in "Monsieur d'Olive."

John Marston's "Dutch Courtezan" (pr. 1605) is picaresque

less in its main plot than in the subordinate action. This is concerned with the wiles of Cocledemoy, "a witty city jester," who delights to victimize a Puritan vintner.

Having pilfered three bowls from Mulligrub's inn and escaped by the window, Cocledemoy returns in the guise of a barber's boy, shaves the unsuspecting vintner, pulls his cap over his eyes, and makes off with a bag of money. When the vintner presents his wife with a cup, Cocledemoy secures it from her by Scoggin's old trick of offering a fish as token for its delivery, alleging that the jeweler desires to engrave it. Then he returns and claims the fish itself. When the incensed vintner lies in wait for his tormentor, the latter lets fall his cloak. The vintner catches it up and pursues, but Cocledemoy, accusing him of theft, has him clapped into jail, visits him disguised as a sergeant, and extorts from him a confession of his cheating practices, and the promise of immunity. Then he discloses his identity and restores the booty which he professes to have taken "but for wit's sake."[1]

Franciscina, the courtesan, and Mary Faugh, the bawd, are repulsive figures, although used to good purpose in showing "the difference between the love of a courtesan and a wife."

A more sympathetic courtesan is presented in Thomas Dekker's two-part play, "The Honest Whore" (Part I, pr. 1604; Part II, pr. 1630).

Bellafront repents of her evil courses out of love for Count Hippolito. But he is already enamored of the noble Infelice, and plans to marry her despite the opposition of the Duke, her father. Bedlam madhouse is to be the scene of the secret union, and though the lovers disguised as friars are there exposed by Bellafront herself, who has feigned madness for this purpose, the Duke forgives, the lovers marry, and Bellafront is united, by the Duke's order, with Matheo, a courtier, who had first

---

1 Somewhat similar in its reversion to the tricks of the jest-books is a little-known play of later date, *The Knave in Grain*, whose anti-hero, Julio, buys satin and plush of a mercer, and sends the mercer's man to a barber for payment, the barber believing that he comes to apply for surgical aid. *The Knave in Grain, or Jack Cottington* was entered 1639. In the next year appeared *The Knave in Grain New Vampt*, by J. D. Fleay holds J. D. to have been merely the "vamper" of the first play.

wronged her. In the Second Part of this play, Bellafront continues steadfast in virtue, despite the poverty to which she had been reduced by the profligacy of her husband. She rejects the advances of Hippolito. And when Matheo, after pawning most of her garments, is jailed for the theft of a quantity of linen and denounces her publicly, her devotion does not waver. If Bellafront is patient heroically, Candido, a linen-draper, shows himself but comically patient, and serves as the butt for shrewish first and second wives and for the schemes of a pander and a bawd. The two latter are haled to Bridewell, along with Matheo, after a scandalous drinking-scene, and here four impressive processions of the wicked and their guardians appear. Bots, the pander, is accompanied by a constable and beadles bearing hemp and a mallet. Dorothy Target "swells with a wanton rein," but is brought a wheel for spinning, and a blue gown as a badge of her shame. Penelope Whorehound, trailing by, begs bail of the bystanders vainly, and Catherina Bountinall and Mistress Horseleech are haled to judgment by five men of the law.

Dekker in other plays touched half-picaresque themes, — Friar Rush, in "If It Be Not Good, the Divel Is In It," and Fortunatus, in "Olde Fortunatus."[1] Further he collaborated with Webster in producing two coarse studies of low-life — "Westward Hoe" and "Northward Hoe" — and with Middleton in the delightful "Roaring Girle" already described.[2] It was Thomas Middleton, however, rather than Dekker, or even Jonson, who proved the most persistent cultivator of roguery for the stage, and the master spirit of this group. At least five comedies of his unaided composition demand attention in this connection.

[1] A Fortunatus unrelated to the *Volksbuch* hero and a Robin Goodfellow figure in *Wily Beguiled* (pr. 1606), whose chief actors are "a poor scholar, a rich fool, and a knave at a shift." The true picaro here is Churms who has been "at Cambridge a scholar; at Calais a soldier; and now in the country a lawyer, and the next degree shall be a coney-catcher." Fleay thinks that Churms stands for Lodge, Fortunatus for Jonson, and Robin for Drayton (*Chronicle History of the English Drama*, vol. ii, p. 158).

[2] Cf. *supra*, p. 145.

In "The Phoenix" (pr. 1607), a prince, supposed to be abroad on a journey, observes in disguise manifold knaveries at home. He discovers a political plot against his father's life, is engaged to compass his own murder, defeats a piratical captain's scheme of selling his wife to a nobleman, exposes an unjust judge in league with a band of thieves, rescues a young lady from durance, and rebukes a wife anxious to barter her honor for an introduction at court. The social satire that results from this "Measure for Measure" device is especially vigorous in assailing the legal monomaniac, Tangle, and the roguish Justice Falso. The former receives a commission from attorneys for inducing the unsophisticated to go to law; the latter sits in judgment on the servant he has instigated to highway robbery, and whose accomplices assist in his examination and are allowed to bear him away as if for punishment.

While "The Phoenix" centres interest in a keen-witted observer of frauds, Middleton's "Michaelmas Term" (1607) fixes attention upon their simple victim.

Easy is a country gull who falls into the toils of a money-lending linen-draper, Quomodo. On his arrival in London, Easy is entertained with dice at an ordinary, and when he loses to Quomodo's confederate, Shortyard, the latter procures him fresh funds. Then having won these back, the rogue induces him to sign a bond for the loan of certain linens to be used in raising more money, and as the unhappy conny is about to be apprehended for inability to discharge his indebtedness, offers, with another rascal, to supply his bail on the pledge of Easy's whole estate as security. Thus far, roguery has triumphed, but the tables are suddenly turned. Quomodo, fancying himself already a landed proprietor and the founder of a line, circulates a rumor of his demise in order that, disguised as a beadle, he may enjoy observing the conduct of his wife and his son, a Cambridge graduate. But the former hastens to accept Easy as second husband, and the latter is delighted at his father's death. The mock beadle, by a trick, is induced to sign a paper releasing Easy of all obligations, and on proclaiming his identity, is declared insane. When, in order to relieve himself of this charge, he confesses his cheats in court, he is banished, along with his accomplices and with Andrew Lethe, the seducer of a country girl.

The Quomodo type reappears in duplicate in "A Trick to Catch the Old-One" (pr. 1608). Here rival usurers, Lucre and Hoard, contend to lay hands upon the hypothetical fortune of Widow Medlar, who turns out to be a penniless courtesan engaged by the gay young Witgood to pose as his intended bride, and so raise his credit in the world.

When the young man by this means has regained title to the estate he had mortgaged to his greedy uncle Lucre, and has further led old Hoard to propose marriage to the lady, he allows himself to be bought off as her suitor. Dampit and Gulf, two "tramplers," or law-sharks, are involved in the intrigue, and the first proves especially comic in inebriation as he assails his servant-maid with Falstaffian invective.

Although "Your Five Gallants" (lic. 1608) is one of the slightest of Middleton's comedies, it teems with roguery. Five rascals pay court to a lady, whose one honest lover joins their ranks in disguise, determined to expose them. This he does at the end of a month by means of a masque performed before the lady, who requites him with her hand, while the rogues are forced to marry their courtesans. These rascals are abstract types of iniquity, from Primero, the bawd-gallant, Tailby, the whore-gallant, and Frippery, the broker-gallant, to Pursenet, the pocket-gallant, and Goldstone, the cheating-gallant.

The last two are accomplished thieves who operate with the assistance of light-fingered servants. Pursenet, for example, feigns a swoon before a gentleman and is assisted to rise, while his boy picks the victim's pocket thus left unguarded. Goldstone games at "The Mitre," in collusion with his man Fulk, using false dice, attempting to substitute two "alchemy knaves," or counterfeit goblets, for mine host's genuine beakers, and concealing a gilt goblet to be later made off with by Fulk. When the landlord misses his property, Goldstone suggests that all the company contribute to make good his loss, and so escapes suspicion at small cost to himself. In the meantime, Pursenet's boy has been deftly emptying the pockets of the players, while Frippery, the broker-gallant, has supplied them with uncurrent coins — washed angels and rose-nobles cracked in the ring — in return for the pawn of their wearing apparel. Pursenet himself goes upon the pad, playing highwayman at Combe Park, whose keeper, according to Middleton's "Blacke Booke" (1604), is a "high thief on horseback." Other cheats cluster about the theft of a necklace of pearls, which goes its dishonest rounds from gallant to gallant; Primero cloaks his establishment for a frail sisterhood under the guise of a boarding-school in music; and Goldstone, while dining out, confiscates his hostess's salt-cellars as if in jest.[1]

The society here exploited by Middleton is no whit superior to that exhibited in "The English Rogue," although the author's moral intention is somewhat more apparent.

Morality remains at a sufficiently low ebb, however, in "A Mad World My Masters" (pr. 1608), which sets forth a young gentleman's ruses for outwitting his gay old grandfather.

Dick Follywit disguises as a lord, and with friends in the rôle of servants visits his wealthy relative, Sir Bounteous Progress. In burglar's vizards, the rogues rob the household at night and are so little suspected that their host begs especially that they will spare his guests. Next morning, when they are all discovered tied by their own hands, he insists that they accept compensation for the sums they profess to have lost. But Dick, not content with these gains, dons the garb of a wench, wheedles a gold chain from his grandfather's steward, and rifles the old gentleman's treasure-chest while concealed as if in furtherance of an intrigue. Dick's confederates are arrested, but the rogue poses as a justice and orders their release, the bystanders believing this a play got up for their entertainment, and the constable assuming it to be a judicial rebuke to his blundering. After the picaro has been trapped into marrying his grandfather's mistress, he confesses his tricks, and the old man is so elated at the misalliance that he forgives, and the courtesan promises amendment.

---

[1] This trick is the thirteenth of Rowlands's *Greenes Ghost Havnting Conie-catchers*, the story of a Lift who, pretending to know the master of a house, stole a salt and told the guests it was done as a joke.

Several other comedies by Middleton are more remotely associated with the literature of roguery. "The Mayor of Quinborough," of doubtful date, employs the device noted above, whereby what seems to be a play proves a piece of actual knavery used by feigned comedians to cheat the simple mayor. "Blurt, Master Constable, or The Spaniards Night-Walke" (pr. 1602), introduces "Lazarillo de Tormes in Castile, cousin-german to the adelantado of Spain," whose titles illiterate Blurt bids his man Slubber write down as "Lazarillo in torment at the castle." If constable and clerk hark back to Dogberry and Verges, the Spaniard recalls Holofernes, and bears no resemblance to his namesake, the first picaro of Spain, unless it be in the hunger that he shares with his starveling page, Pilcher. "A Chaste Maid in Cheapside" (pr. 1630) employs a brace of informers or "promoters"[1] engaged in supplying their ladies with the profits of blackmail. Their speciality of the moment consists in detecting such as buy and sell meat during Lent. In this business they reap bribes in cash from the butchers and rich customers, and bribes in commodity from those too poor to pay other toll. All goes well until, seizing a country girl's basket to be retained till she can fetch her master to settle the indemnity, they discover that it holds a superfluous infant, thus ingeniously left on their hands.

Middleton's "The Widow" (pr. 1652), doubtfully assigned in part to Jonson and Fletcher, introduces a roguish crew, who first practice as highwaymen and then, in the dull season for travelers, take up quarters at an inn to cozen as quacks. Latricino, their chief, prescribes for the sore eyes of a justice, and while salving them with one hand picks his patient's

[1] Defined in Cowell's *Interpreters* (ed. 1637) as "those which in popular and penall actions do deferre the names, or complaine of offenders, having part of the profit for their reward."

pocket with the other. Occulto, another rascal, draws the teeth of a victim, and his purse as well, while confederates, dressed as tradesmen, increase the charlatans' vogue by feigning sundry ills and announcing their miraculous cure.

In two comedies, written by Middleton in collaboration with William Rowley, picaresque features are of diminished importance. "The Spanish Gipsie" (pl. 1623) combines the plots of Cervantes's "La Gitanilla" and "La Fuerza de la Sangre," but, like Jonson's "Gipsies Metamorphosed," its low-life is merely assumed. The chief personages for one reason or another have sought concealment in the guise of Gypsies, "no red-ochre rascals umbered with soot and bacon as the English gipsies are, that sally out upon pullen, lie in ambuscado for a rope of onions, as if they were Welsh freebooters; no, our stile has higher steps to climb over, Spanish gipsies, noble gipsies." Indeed, the only characters of less than high-life here are a young hostess to the Gypsies and the amusing *gracioso* Soto.[1]

In "A Faire Quarrell" (pr. 1617), Chough, a rough Cornishman, the heroine's preposterous suitor, completes his education in a roaring-school conducted by a rogue at the sign of the Cheat-Loaf. Here he selects as his special form of roaring the modern Londonian, preferring it to such types as the Sclavonian, Parthamenian, Barmeothian, Tyburnian, and Wappinganian. So well does he learn his lesson that he excites the envy of a pander, a bawd, and a courtesan, whom he bullies on the street.

Middleton was not only a master of literary roguery, but a model for others, and his "A Trick to Catch the Old-One" partially inspired Philip Massinger's "A New Way to Pay Old

[1] Act ii, sc. 1, contains cant derived from Harman, Dekker, *et al.*, and is notable for its early use of the term "pickaroes." Middleton's *More Dissemblers Besides Women* (wr. before 1622) shows Dondolo, a comic servant, in a Gypsy camp vainly endeavoring to learn the language.

Debts" (pl. 1625) and Lodowick Barry's "Ram Alley, or Merry Tricks" (pl. 1611). In the last named, William Small-Shanks conspires with a mistress to hoodwink his creditor, the sharping lawyer Throat. The lady, by impersonating an heiress, lures Throat into marriage, and the lawyer, in return for Small-Shanks's withdrawal from rivalry, turns over the mortgage held on his property. Yet the jubilant trickster weds a widow scarcely more virtuous than his victim's bride.

Similarly, in Massinger's masterpiece, when Sir Giles Overreach, the most extortionate and prodigal of usurers, has ruined his nephew, that clever young man schemes to get even by feigning a match with the wealthy Lady Allworth. She allows the use of her name, however, simply out of kindness, and the wretched Sir Giles is further cozened by his "term-driving" tool and secret enemy, Marrall, who, in drawing up a deed, has made use of a fading ink. The usurer's devices for luring his victims into law-suits and suborning justice come to naught; his self-seeking scheme for his daughter's marriage miscarries, and his shameless rascality is punished by madness. Indeed, Massinger's moral emphasis is so great that roguery is as much obscured here in the reprobation of villainy as it is in Jonson's "Volpone." Even in Massinger's other plays it figures little, notwithstanding the Robin Hood outlaws of "The Guardian," the intriguing courtiers of "The Picture," and the comic servant, Calandrino, of "The Great Duke of Florence."

The less sophisticated drama of mild roguery had early found an exemplar in "The Blind Beggar of Bednal-Green" (pl. 1600), by John Day and Henry Chettle. This presented beggary as a disguise assumed in adversity by Lord Momford, thus enabled to defeat his enemies and defend the honor of his daughter. Tom Stroud, full of proverbs and bluster, but cozened of his satin suit by a pretended Gypsy, turns castaway in London, yet saves Lord Momford's life, and reappears in further plays by Day and William Haughton.[1]

It was Thomas Heywood, however, who brought most talent to the dramatization of popular themes. He celebrated the Tanner of Tamworth, the Four Prentices of London, Besse Bridges the Faire Maid of the West, and competed with other makers of witch-plays in "The Late Lancashire Witches," composed with Richard Brome. His chief contribution to the literature of roguery was less the "Fortune by Land and Sea," which recalls criminal pamphlets in recording the deeds of the pirates, Clinton, Purser, and Arnold, than "The Wise-woman of Hogsdon" (pr. 1638). This glories in an anti-heroine who acts as bawd, midwife, disposer of offspring, fortune-teller, and quack. She declares her superiority to all rivals, from Mother Bomby, Mother Nottingham, Hatfield of Pepper Alley who conjures the lost, and the lady of Coleharbour, skilled in the planets, to Mother Shirton in Golden Lane, an adept in fore-speaking, and Mother Phillips on the Bankside, the curer of weak backs. When victims resort to her house, the Wise-woman, ensconced in a secret closet beside the door, takes note of their talk and readily hoodwinks them. Here, as in most of the dramas produced by the Middleton group, realism was rampant; but this alone could not satisfy. Roguery of a romantic strain accordingly found sponsors, chief among whom was John Fletcher.

3. *Fletcher: his Collaborators and Successors*

Of the plays in which Fletcher had a hand, "The Beggars' Bush" (pl. 1615?) and "The Night-Walker" (pl. 1634) were especially roguish. The former was written in conjunction with

[1] Cf. The *Second* and *Third Part* of *Thomas Stroud* (pl. 1600, 1601).

Massinger, and probably with Beaumont.[1] It resembles "The Blind Beggar of Bednal-Green" in exhibiting a lord's retreat to beggary when driven out of his kingdom by a traitor, but it is far more elaborate.

Gerrard, ruler of Flanders, dwells at Beggars' Bush with his daughter and his lords, enjoying the companionship of such gentry as Snap, Ferret, Prigg, Ginks, and Higgen, orator and singer of the jolly crew. When Gerrard has been chosen the mendicant's leader he is installed with due ceremony, and his rascal band sets about defeating the plots of the usurper. In a tavern they pick the pockets of boors sent to spy upon them, and, pretending to restore what they have stolen, foist counterfeit coin upon their victims. They lead the enemy's soldiers astray, and rally at last to seize the treacherous Wolfart. Then Gerrard is restored to his rights; his son emerges from disguise to marry the Duke of Brabant's daughter, who has long been supposed a mere burgher maiden; and the beggars conclude to emigrate to England to continue their free life as actors.

The local color of this comedy is borrowed from the anatomies of roguery (Dekker's principally), and shows no first-hand knowledge of low-life; but the piece is excellent for all that, and resembles the romantic comedies of Shakespeare, with the substitution of the beggars' commonwealth for a pastoral Arden or Bohemia.

The same lightness of fancy marks "The Night-Walker, or The Little Thief," written by Fletcher and corrected by James Shirley. Here, however, bits of amusing realism are mingled with absurdest farce.

Alathe has been betrayed by the usurer Algripe. On the night of his wedding to another, she invades his bride's house in male disguise as "The Little Thief," and with her brother, wild Tom Lurcher, steals a supposed treasure-chest, which proves to be a coffin. This contains the person of the bride, who has swooned on being discovered by her

[1] When first printed, in 1661, it was ascribed to Beaumont and Fletcher; but Massinger's share in it is now admitted by scholars.

husband engaged with a lover, and is thought to be dead. After the thieves have frightened off old Algripe by setting the coffin on end and hiding behind it, they take to their heels as the bride revives groaning.

Later they practice upon the usurer by posing as ballad-sellers, and while his servants are absorbed in reading their pitiful songs, bind and rob him. Again, Alathe disguises as a constable, and by pretending to know of a band of robbers whom Algripe as justice desires the honor of apprehending, gains entrance to his stronghold. This time Algripe is drugged, and awakes in a vault to believe himself in the presence of furies, and to promise reparation of honor to Alathe, and of a misappropriated fortune to Tom Lurcher. "The Little Thief's" final trick is played at the expense of certain bell-ringers, induced to try ringing in the dark to prove that they are guided by their ears rather than by their eyes. Of course, as soon as the lights are out, Alathe and Lurcher appropriate their victims' cloaks and purses.

Such pranks savor of the jest-books, and while the moral tone of the comedy is low, the piece is harmless because preposterous.

Other plays by Fletcher and his collaborators are more slightly related to the literature of roguery. "The Little French Lawyer" (pr. 1647), for example, in which Massinger seems to have had part, elaborates a *novela* interpolated in "Guzman de Alfarache" and originally derived from Massuccio.[1] "The Woman Hater" (pr. 1607), which has been assigned now to Fletcher and now to Beaumont, includes among its *dramatis personæ* a "voluptuous smell-feast Lazarillo," associated with the first Lazarillo de Tormes only in his insatiate desire for food. "The Bloody Brother" (pl. 1637) reveals the hand of Jonson in a characteristic scene introducing well-known rogues of reality in a company of astrologers. "Love's Cure, or The Martial Maid" (pr. 1647) presents in Bobadilla a jesting rogue in service, and a constable of distinguished dishonesty in the sharking alguazier; and "The Noble Gentleman" (pl. 1626), in its trick of convincing a foolish fellow that he has

[1] *Il novellino, novella* xli, used by Scarron in *La précaution inutile.*

been raised to high station, echoes Chapman's "Monsieur d'Olive," and recalls its most delightful analogue in fiction, the trick played upon the Pedant Hortensius in "Francion."

A similar device is used in James Shirley's "Constant Maid, or Love Will Find Out the Way" (pr. 1640). Here the usurer, Hornet, is made to believe himself about to be knighted; but, when royally clad he attends the audience of a mock king, his keys are stolen, and his niece is released from durance and married to her lover. Shirley was inclined to romantic roguery; and, although his "Gamester" (lic. 1633) draws a dicing-scene at an ordinary and laughs at a sporting uncle's ambition for his nephew to learn the art of roaring,[1] the main plot merely varies a *novella* of intrigue from the "Heptameron," employed also in "Greenes Newes both from Heauen and Hell" (1593); and "The Sisters" (lic. 1642), his typical contribution to the picaresque drama, is even less realistic.

Outlaws range the Parmesan forest and capture a clown, Piperollo, who, professing to have been a pickpocket from childhood, and for many years a house-thief, begs admittance to their fraternity. To prove his fitness, he leads the bandits to the home of his parents and binds and robs them. But the bandits, offended by his inhumanity, restore part of their booty and deliver him over to be chastised by his mother. In the meantime Frapolo, their leader, has conceived a scheme for securing the wealth of an heiress Paulina, and, with his fellows disguised as astrologers, visits her castle to tell fortunes and pick pockets. The delighted lady is assured that she shall marry a prince; her steward is promised a robbing; and Piperollo, who has taken service here, is told that his pate will be broken. The clown and the steward when encountered by bandits next day are only too glad to be beaten and robbed, since the fulfillment of so much of the prophecy argues that of the rest. Nor are they wholly disappointed in hopes of their lady's fine match, for Frapolo undertakes the rôle of Prince Farnese, and with his

---

[1] Cf. Nathaniel Field's *Amends for Ladies* (pl. 1611), in which Lord Feesimple takes a lesson in this art.

rogues clad as lords, pays court to Paulina, and it is only when the real Prince appears that Frapolo is caught on the point of absconding with the jewels and plate. He protests that at least he is a prince of rogues, but the bubble bursts when the ambitious Paulina turns out no heiress at all, but the sister of Piperollo.

Still pleasanter in its romantic roguery was Richard Brome's "A Joviall Crew, or The Merry Beggars" (pl. 1641), one of the best of the comedies that celebrate cheerful vagabondage.[1]

Its central figure is Oldrents, a sort of fictional Harman, who welcomes to his estate all tatterdemalions. His daughters share his tastes, and even run away with their lovers to become "stark, errant, downright beggars, I, without equivocation statute beggars," and his steward every spring finds himself irresistibly called to go roving with the canting crew. Among those who dance and sing in a jolly circle in the good squire's barn are a decayed poet, an attorney "pitch'd over the bar," a soldier who "ran away from his colours and was taken lame with lying in the fields by a sciatica; I mean, Sir, the strapado," an ex-courtier to whom begging comes easy, and musicians fled away from London and the lash for singing libelous ballads.

See in their rags then, dancing for your sports,
Our clapper dugeons and their walking morts.

These folk have their Patrico whose autem mort carols a drinking-song, after which, in true Harman lingo, they all join in a roaring chorus. A poor-spirited clerk who has eloped with a justice's niece presently joins the vagabonds, but growing tired of his bargain, informs on them. His lady, however, has fallen in love with the roving steward, who now turns out to be Oldrents's son by a beggar-girl, and all ends merrily in reconciliation, after a little play within the play, presented by the beggars.

In "The Court Beggar" (pr. 1653), Brome was less romantic than realistic, affecting the manner of Jonson, his master in more senses than one. The comedy exposes the folly of Sir Andrew Mendicant, ambitious to win advancement by means

[1] Day and Chettle's *Blind Beggar of Bednal-Green*, Jonson's *Gipsies Metamorphosed*, Middleton and Rowley's *Spanish Gipsie*, and Fletcher's *Beggars' Bush*. The influence of the last is especially potent here, as is that of the anatomies of roguery.

of court suits and projects, among which figure schemes for erecting a theatre upon barges in the Thames, for procuring a monopoly of wigs, for levying a tax upon the coiners of new fashions, and for exacting a fee of parents at the birth of every girl. A rogue picture-drawer, who is seen picking the pockets of his rivals in love, suggests further projects, — one the purchase of the privilege to paint all the heads used as tavern-signs, and another forecasting Jonathan Wild in the proposed establishment of a cutpurse-hall, where thieves may dispose of their booty, and the victims may recover their losses by the payment of a ten per cent commission.

Such a comedy of manners was poor enough, compared with the pieces of Jonson's earlier followers, and William Cartwright's "The Ordinary" (pr. 1651) is scarcely better.

Here Widow Potluck entertains free of charge at her ordinary three rascals from among whom she hopes to pick a husband. They enjoy her hospitality, but evade her advances, procuring an absurd antiquary as a substitute, and practicing profitable deceits. One engages to supply a silly knight with a daughter-in-law, another robs the knight's son of jewels while he is blindfolded, and then poses as a confessor to the old gentleman whose sins he absolves for fifty pounds. When the rogues' knavery is found out, the watch comes to apprehend them, but by disguising as constables, they readily make off to embark for New England where the orthodox will fall their easy prey.

The satire upon the watch recalls the assaults of Middleton's "Blurt," Fletcher's "Love's Cure" and "Knight of Malta," and Henry Glapthorne's entertaining "Wit in a Constable" (pr. 1640), itself indebted to Shakespeare.

With the closing of the theatres by the Ordinance of the Lords and Commons, September 2, 1642, the most vigorous period of the English drama came to an end, less, perhaps, from external repression than from internal decline. The richness of the dramatic literature of roguery throughout this period must be obvious. It has never been approached, and can only be compared with the flourishing of roguery in fiction during the nineteenth century. It was essentially a national growth, rooted in the soil, and but slightly indebted to foreign picaresque sources. The rogue in service, for example, cut little figure here, while the usurer played an important part, though rarely exploited in the Spanish or French picaresque novel. The rogue physician, so generally attacked on the Continent, received trifling notice, and religious imposture, notwithstanding the frequent baiting of Puritans, amounted to scarcely more than negative hypocrisy. No law-cheats were borrowed from abroad, though dishonest attorneys, justices, jailers, and dull-witted constables throve. And if the courtesans were surprisingly numerous, they copied those of Latin comedy or the native article, as in Shackerley Marmion's "Hollands Leagver,"[1] rather than their sisters of Spanish or French romance. The beggars were drawn from English anatomies of roguery, together with the gamesters and swindlers in large part, while cutpurses, burglars, and highwaymen were the creatures of romantic fancy or more often folk of the London streets. Sketches from life were developed in such minor types as the witch, the wise-woman, and the roarer; and though the employment by Cervantes of Gypsies may have suggested their use to English dramatists, the Gypsies themselves were simply the vagabonds of the conny-catching pamphlets.

Thus the drama, with its army of typical home-bred rogues, with its scenes in the tavern, at the fair, in the brothel, madhouse, and jail, and with its tricks based upon observation and the jest-books rather than upon foreign literary precedent, constitutes from Shakespeare's day to the closing of the theatres the most original and fruitful branch of rogue letters.

[1] Cf. *ante*, p. 147.

4. *The Restoration Drama*

During the eighteen years that the drama remained under the Puritan ban, old plays survived either in print or else in episodes adapted as drolls to the crudest popular presentation and acceptance. Typical picaresque examples of such drolls are "The Empiric," derived from Jonson's "Alchemist," and "The Lame Commonwealth," from Fletcher's "Beggars' Bush." Collections were published, in 1672, by Robert Cox, the actor, and by Francis Kirkman, joint author of "The English Rogue." But by far the larger number of old plays continued their vogue through publication, many dramatic favorites achieving the dignity of book-form only when no longer admitted to the stage.

One play of this class, not hitherto noted, was "The Goblins," by Sir John Suckling (pr. 1646), wherein a band of robbers, disguised as devils, live underground, and in the title they bear are possibly reminiscent of the Spanish *duendes*, or "hobgoblins," [1] although these were sneak thieves rather than highwaymen.

> The common people think them a race
> Of honest and familiar devils;
> For they do hurt to none, unless resisted:
> They seldom take away, but with exchange;
> And to the poor they often give;
> Return the hurt and sick recover'd;
> Reward and punish as they do find cause.

Of course such romantic and beneficent rogues are lightly forgiven at the close, along with Tamoren, their king, who proves to be a noble.

With the resumption of public performances in 1660, the

[1] Cf. *Desordenada codicia*, cap. vii.

drama seemed to have lost in part its national character. It was more subject to exotic inspiration, less the entertainment and reflection of the life of the people. It appealed to a class and was largely a matter of fashion and the court. It is not strange, therefore, that Restoration comedy should have contributed little to the literature of roguery. Immoral as it was, it dealt but meagrely with low-life, confining itself to a conventionally rakish society whose chief business was intrigue rather than theft. Yet a few plays on the Jonsonian model still satirized the humors of rascality. John Wilson's "The Cheats" (wr. 1662) assailed a dissenting minister, Scruple, and the astrological quack, Mopus. His "Projectors" (pr. 1664) lashed the schemers who plot against Sir Gudgeon Credulous, as well as the usurer Suckdry, a Plautine miser, and with "Belphegor" (pr. 1691) recalled "The Devil is an Ass" and other variations upon the theme earlier presented in Machiavelli's famous *novella*. Abraham Cowley's "Cutter of Coleman Street" (pl. 1661)[1] combined an attack upon the Puritans with the portrayal of a brace of amusing swaggerers, Cutter and Worm, who work the religious swindle to perfection.

It was Thomas Shadwell, however, who excelled in this line. His relation to Jonson was acknowledged in the Preface as well as in the title of "The Humourists" (1671), and continued to be manifest in such pieces as "Epsom Wells" (1675), "The Virtuoso" (1676), and "The Volunteers, or the Stock Jobbers" (1692). If the last shows small mercy to the scheming projectors for patents, chief of whom is a godly Cromwellian veteran, "Epsom Wells" exposes the licentious folly of city ladies and the tricks of two "cheating, sharking, cowardly bullies," Kick and Cuff, who, among other feats, rob a country-

[1] Revised from Cowley's comedy *The Guardian* (played at Cambridge, in 1641–42 and printed in 1650).

man, and leave him gagged and bound in a sheet to figure as a ghost, and so frighten off possible assistance. "Bury Fair" (1689) pricks the bubble of English preciosity; "The Scowrers" (1693) pillories two groups of roaring rakes, hoodlums who boast of bullying market-people, overthrowing butter-women, defeating the pippin-merchants, wiping out milkscores, pulling off door-knockers, dawbing gilt signs, clearing the taverns, smashing windows, and baiting the constables. "The Libertine" (1676) weakly essays treatment of the Don Juan legend,[1] and "The Woman Captain" (1680) draws upon Fletcher and Shirley's roguish "Night-Walker."[2] But supreme in rascality among the lot is "The Squire of Alsatia" (1688), a comedy worthier in literary affiliations than in literary merit.[3]

Whitefriars, or Alsatia, is the haunt and refuge of debtors, rogues, and gay young blades in quest of debauchery. One of the last is Belfond Senior, who has come up from the country and fallen into the toils of the picaro, Cheatley, developing into a proficient in cant, bullying, and knavery, yet himself thoroughly victimized. His father's matrimonial ambitions for the son present an opportunity for the disreputable to play upon both, and Belfond is about to be wed to a notorious woman by Cheatley disguised in a parson's gown, when his younger and city-bred brother, who has suffered from the same lady, rushes to the rescue

---

[1] Cf. Arturo Farinelli's admirable papers on the various versions of this theme, — *Don Giovanni*, in the *Giornale storico della letteratura italiana* (vol. xxvii, 1896).

[2] Shadwell was precise in his usage of rogue terms. The critics he calls "Those Piccaroons in Wit" (Prologue to *The Libertine*); Nickum in *The Volunteers* he labels "a Sharper, which is a new name for a Rogue and a Cheat;" Shamwell in *The Squire of Alsatia* is a Decoy-Duck; and in the Epilogue of that play the author explains that

> The cant he hopes will not be long unknown,
> 'T is almost grown the language of the Town.

Here and elsewhere Shadwell's cant is distinctly "up-to-date" and no mere copy of the Elizabethan.

[3] It is based upon the *Adelphi* of Terence, and contributes to Scott's *Fortunes of Nigel*, *q. v. infra*, ch. viii, sect. 1, p. 346.

with musketeers, and routs the Alsatian rabble. The complications of the plot, however ingenious, are of less moment than the character-types and the low-life scenes here set forth. In addition to Cheatley, whose business is the leading astray of young heirs, the rogues of Alsatia include Captain Hackum, a blusterer run away from the Flemish wars; his wife, a bawd who lets lodgings and sells cherry brandy; Mistress Termagant, a vindictive courtesan; Mistress Betty, a more agreeable young baggage; Scrapeall, a psalm-singing rascal, who is seeking to dispose of his nieces to the highest bidders; and Shamwell, a profligate cousin of Belfond. The scenes of conflict, when the watch invades the bankrupts' sanctuary, and is driven out by the screaming mob brandishing fire-forks, spits, and shovels, or when the officers return, and with the aid of the Templars treat the ringleader to the pump, are graphic to say the least.

Roguery that was less original and more romantic prevailed, however. In "The Triumphant Widow" (pr. 1677), by William Cavendish, Duke of Newcastle, "The Beggar's Opera" is prefigured in the opening scene and song, while Autolycus is not forgotten in Footpad, the captain of a bevy of rogues. In "The Banditti" (pl. 1686), a lady in distress takes refuge with an old hag whose husband, a bandit, robs and would ravish her, but is foiled by his supposed son, her lover, who turns out a noble. "Guzman de Alfarache" appears to have inspired "The Spanish Rogue" (pl. 1674), "a poor piece in rhyme," dedicated by Duffet to Nell Gwyn.[1] Otway adapted Molière's "Les Fourberies" as "The Cheats of Scapin" (pl. 1677); Crowne's "Sir Courtly Nice" (1685) took over the picaro Crack along with the plot of Moreto's "No Puede Ser;" Southerne's "Fatal Marriage" (1694) borrowed from Fletcher and Shirley's "Night-Walker;" Mrs. Behn altered Middleton's "Mad World My Masters" into "The City Heiress" (pl. 1682); and to her

[1] Cf. Geneste, vol. i, p. 162. *The English Rogue*, a play by Thomas Thompson, "acted before persons of honour" and published in 1668, is noted by F. G. Fleay in his *Chronicle of the English Drama*, vol. ii, p. 372.

facile pen has been assigned a reworking of Chapman's "Dutch Courtezan," entitled "The Revenge, or a Match in Newgate" (pl. 1680), which, under various names, enjoyed a long life on the boards and perpetuated several of Scoggin's "Jests." [1]

Of the more distinguished Restoration dramatists, Congreve gave nothing to the literature of roguery; Wycherley did little more than sketch the amusing valet Jeremy in "Love for Love" (1695), with Maskwell in "The Double Dealer" (1693), who cheats both sides by telling both the truth; while Dryden's portrait of one excellent rogue in the "huge, fat, religious gentleman," Dominick, of "The Spanish Friar" (pl. 1681), a truckling go-between in the intrigues of Don Lorenzo and the usurer's wife, shows what he might have achieved in this field had he deemed it worth his while.

Vanbrugh and Farquhar did slightly better. In "The Confederacy" (1705), by the former, two misers, Gripe and Moneytrap, have fallen in love with each other's wives, and the ladies conspire to make the most of the situation as a means of bleeding their lords of money. Mixed up in these edifying intrigues are Flippanta, the roguish lady's maid, Dick Amlet, a gamester, and his knavish man Brass.

Dick, the son of a church-thief and a female peddler and pawnbroker, poses as a colonel, and is in jeopardy of the law through having cheated at picquet. When presently he steals a necklace pledged with his mother, his valet outwits him of the trinket, and demands further satisfaction for his services in urging Dick's suit with Gripe's daughter. The necklace passes to a jeweler, and is finally restored, bringing to a fortunate conclusion what remains a perfectly unmoral play.

Of George Farquhar's comedies, altogether the best is "The

[1] Revived in 1730; reduced to three acts, in 1715, as *Woman's Revenge*, reproduced in 1739; presented as an opera, *Love and Revenge*, in 1729; as a one-act farce, *The Vintner in the Suds*, in 1739; and altered as *The Vintner Tricked*, in 1746, and *Trick upon Trick*, in 1789.

Beaux' Stratagem" (1707), which shows a rascally innkeeper in league with highwaymen, and introduces a burglary scene. Boniface and his daughter, Cherry, receivers of the thieves' booty, are amusingly drawn, as are the rogues, Gibbet, Hounslow, and Bagshot. Gibbet, when he demands Lady Sullen's trinkets, while standing over her with pistol and dark-lantern, is as polite as Claude Du Vall on the highways, and when the gallant who has been hid in the lady's closet pounces on him, he offers a rich bribe to be allowed to escape. Mild roguery of an unprofessional type marks the ruses of Aimwell to attract Dorinda, for the nose-bleed feigned at church, the fit indulged in before her house, and the reports circulated by his friend, disguised as valet, are those of the matrimonial adventurer.

5. *"The Beggar's Opera" and Other Georgian Plays*

The presentation of roguery suffered in the moral reaction against the lubricity of Restoration Comedy so effectively voiced by Jeremy Collier's famous tract. Steele and the writers of sentimental comedy hastened to provide a harmless substitute, and the rivalry of fiction more and more diverted interest from the drama. Indeed, in the literature of roguery the centre of gravity was shifted to the novel as early as the publication of "The English Rogue," and the only notable play of the genre during the eighteenth century was John Gay's "The Beggar's Opera" (pl. January 29, 1728).

Swift had suggested Gay's writing a Newgate pastoral,[1]

[1] Swift, who had been poking fun at "Namby Pamby" Ambrose Philips's pastorals, wrote to Pope (August 30, 1716), "I believe that the pastoral ridicule is not exhausted, and that a porter, footman, or chairman's pastoral might do well, or what think you of a Newgate pastoral?" Pope to Spence (*Anecdotes*, ed. Singer, pp. 110, 120) denied that he and Swift did more than give Gay "a correction, or a word or two of advice." Cf. Austin Dobson on Gay (*Dictionary of National Biography*, vol. xvi).

adding, "I will, *sub rosa*, afford you my best assistance," but Gay found the pastoral element ill suited to his purpose, and produced instead a dramatic burlesque. The result far exceeded his or his friends' expectations, owing in part to the conditions of the time. For society had been stirred by the dangers of a period of crime unprecedented in English annals. Although Jonathan Wild was dead, the recollection of his villainy remained fresh in the public mind, and he was readily recognized in the delectable Peachum. The political flings at Sir Robert Walpole further gratified the taste for veiled allusion. Satire and burlesque were in their apogee, and this amusing piece was both original in kind and excellent in workmanship.

When Polly marries Macheath, a highwayman, her father, the thief-taker Peachum, is enraged, and Mrs. Peachum complains: "If she had had only an intrigue with the fellow, why the very best families have excus'd and huddled up a frailty of that sort. 'T is marriage, husband, that makes it a blemish." To mend a bad matter, they conclude to forgive the girl and then inform upon Macheath, thus securing the reward for his apprehension and insuring Polly his property at his hanging. Macheath is warned of the plot and takes affecting leave of his followers, — Jemmy Twitcher, Crook Finger'd Jack, Wat Dreary, Robin of Bagshot, Nimming Ned, Henry Paddington, Matt of the Mint, and Ben Budge. But forthwith he falls into a trap laid by some Newgate ladies, who, while hanging on his neck clamoring for kisses, seize his pistols as Peachum and his constables rush in.

Once in Newgate, however, Macheath makes such politic love to Lucy, the keeper's daughter, that she arranges his escape, her sire upbraiding her only because she took no bribe of him. "If you would not be look'd upon as a fool, you should never do anything but upon the foot of interest," he advises. While Peachum and Lockit confer, casting up their thief-taking accounts, Lucy endeavors to poison her rival, Polly, in a glass of spirits, admitting that "brandy and men (though women love them never so well) are always to be taken by us with some reluctance — unless 't is in private." Macheath is recaptured and condemned to immediate execution, lamenting merely that he should have been betrayed by one of his own band. "'T is a plain proof that the world is all alike, and that even our gang can no more trust one another than other people." Four ladies, each with a child, claim him as their own, and Lucy declares that "there is nothing that moves one so much as a great man in distress." The crying of a reprieve, however, prevents a tragic climax, and the expedient is excused on the plea that "all this we must do to comply with the taste of the town."

The rollicking songs and the ironical humor, glancing at high life while ostensibly attacking low, gave this piece remarkable popularity, and laid it open to praise and dispraise alike. Those who felt the Puritan within them professed to be shocked, and Defoe in his "Augusta Triumphans" says of rogues in general: "We take pains to puff 'em up in their villainy, and thieves are set out in so amiable a light in 'The Beggar's Opera' that it has taught them to value themselves on their profession, rather than be asham'd of it." Dr. Herring, Archbishop of Canterbury, preached a sermon denouncing the work, and its evil influence has been repeatedly proclaimed.[1] But such condemnation seems scarcely warranted. Gay's obvious purpose was the scourging of hypocrisy, not the glorification of vice. And to those not deficient in humor, the fun of his libretto is a sufficient antidote to its roguery.

The vogue of "The Beggar's Opera" proved immense. After a run of sixty-odd nights at Lincoln's Inn Fields, it was received with acclaim in the provinces, and performances reached even to Minorca. Macheath, torn between his charmers, was several times painted by Hogarth; ladies of fashion talked Newgate and flirted fans inscribed with rogue lyrics; and for the remainder of the century no piece was so frequently represented as this. Gay and his manager reaped a small fortune, and the former promptly composed a sequel. This was under rehearsal in December, 1728, when suppressed by order of the king. But

[1] Cf. William Lee's arraignment in *Daniel Defoe; His Life and Recently Discovered Writings*, London, 1869, vol. i, p. 443, *et seq.*

curiosity was only piqued, and in book form, "Polly" made its way with ease. When the Duchess of Queensberry was dismissed from the court for peddling subscriptions, a host of elegant champions sprang up, and Gay, the indolent, gained glory as a martyr.

Gay's sequel little deserved the commotion it produced. It shifts the scene to the West Indies, where Polly has come in search of Macheath, now turned pirate. She plays no pleasant rôle, and when seized by the pirates, fails to recognize her disguised lover, escaping instead with an Indian prince, whom she marries after Macheath's execution. The plot is manifestly less picaresque than that of "The Beggar's Opera." If the satire does not flag, romance intrudes, and virtue victorious comes to light where one might least expect it, in the savages as opposed to the Europeans, — a reminiscence of Mrs. Behn's "Oroonoko." Civilized man is portrayed as governed solely by interest, and picaresque philosophy finds frequent expression, from Macheath's "Honest industry! I have heard talk of it, indeed, among the common people, but all great geniuses are above it," to Mrs. Trapes's eloquent exposition of the force of circumstances: "I am forced to play at small game. I now and then betray and ruin an innocent girl, and what of that? Can I in conscience expect to be equally wealthy with those who betray and ruin provinces and countries? In troth, all their great fortunes are owing to situation; as for genius and capacity, I can match them to a hair; were they in my circumstances, they would act like me; were I in theirs, I should be rewarded as a most profound penetrating politician." In the literature of roguery no single idea has been more frequently exploited.

Aside from "The Beggar's Opera," the eighteenth century produced few plays of importance to the genre. To Gay has been ascribed "The Mohocks" (1712), "a Tragi-Comical Farce that was acted near the watch-house in Covent Garden by her Majesty's servants." This mediocre piece satirizes both the disorderly "Mohocks" and the inefficient watch, who, being forced to don the rogues' clothes, are marched off to the judges, and barely escape commitment to prison.[1] Captain Avery got upon the stage in a heroic drama entitled "The Successful Pirate" (pl. 1712), where, thinly disguised as Arviragus, the pirate king of Madagascar, he falls in love with a fair captive, the granddaughter of Aurungzebe, and condemns to death a rival who proves to be his own son. In "Cartouche, or the French Robbers" (pl. 1723), that anti-hero with his gang obligingly victimizes a foolish pretender to the hand of Isabella that a more worthy suitor may obtain her, despite the designs of her worldly papa. Defoe's acquaintance, Jack Sheppard, appeared before the footlights in John Thurmond's "Harlequin Sheppard" (1725), and in a farce, "The Prison Breaker" (1725), which was further adapted to the needs of Bartholomew Fair as "The Quakers' Opera" (1728). Robin Hood was celebrated in a musical entertainment in 1750, in an opera by MacNally in 1784, and in a popular farce in 1797. "The Beggar's Wedding" (1729), a ballad opera by Colley, exhibiting the amours of Tib Tatter and Grigg and the humors of Chaunter, king of the mendicants, was scarcely more realistic than "The Beggar's Pantomime" (1737), which laughed at the quarrel between Mrs. Cibber and Mrs. Clive as to who should perform the part of Polly in "The Beggar's Opera." "The City Ramble, or Humours of the Compter" (1715), though lacking in plot, presented amusing characters in Twang, the turnkey, Ezekiel Prim, the parson, and Justice Hardhead, while

[1] Gay's poem *Trivia, or the Art of Walking the Streets of London* (1716) is noteworthy for its realism.

such trifles as "The Tavern Bilkers" (1733), "Joe Miller's Jests" (1730), and "Humours of the Road, or a Ramble to Oxford" (1738), amused the town with facetious roguery.

Many old favorites reappeared: "The Night-Walker," in 1705, "The Puritan," in 1714, "The Blind Beggar of Bednal-Green," in 1741, and Shirley's "Gamester," in 1751, 1772, and 1790. "Eastward Hoe" was revived in 1751, and altered by Mrs. Lennox to "Old City Manners" in 1775. Jonson's "Alchemist" suggested Francis Gentleman's "The Tobacconist" (1771). Fletcher's "Little French Lawyer," after frequent presentations, inspired Richard Cumberland's Sir Benjamin Dove in "The Brothers" (1769), and was turned into a farce by Mrs. Booth in 1778. Fletcher's "Beggars' Bush" was revived five times, from 1705 to 1760, as "The Royal Merchant," and in 1761 was made into an opera by J. Hall. Brome's "Joviall Crew," its companion comedy, profited by the vogue of Gay's masterpiece and created a furore in operatic form (1731), while its Beggars' Chorus was frequently printed among ballads, and "All the Songs and a Key to the Beggars' Cant" appeared in 1708.[1] An echo of "The Beggar's Opera" was heard in "Macheath in the Shades" (1735); Molière was drawn upon in Swiney's "Quacks" (1705) and in Fielding's "Mock Doctor" (1732); and Sir Robert Howard's "The Committee" was adapted by Thomas Knight as a farce, "Honest Thieves" (1797), satirizing the pious frauds of the Puritans.

The Gypsies were romantically treated in several plays, — "May Day, or the Little Gipsy" (1775), a trifle, attributed to Garrick, wherein a farmer scheming to claim a certain legacy by marrying a Romany maiden is outwitted by his son; Charles

[1] The opera was by Roome, Concanen, and Yonge. It saw editions in 1732, 1760, 1761, 1767, 1774, and 1780, and held the stage till 1791.

Dibdin's "Gipsies" (1778), which lays its scene in Italy and uses noble personages who merely assume Gypsy garb; and "The Norwood Gipsies" (1799). Tom Jones, Tristram Shandy, and other figures of fiction were brought upon the boards, the picaresque novel as a rule inspiring unpicaresque plays. A *novela*, from "Guzman de Alfarache," became the musical romance "Ozmyn and Daraxa," acted five times in 1793;[1] "Jack of Newbury," a farce, was presented in 1795, and "Gil Blas" was adapted by Edward Moore in 1751, and performed nine times with Garrick in the title rôle. Reed's "Impostors, or a Cure for Credulity" (1776) was drawn from the same source; and Samuel Foote gained a small fortune from his dramatization of "Le Diable Boiteux" as "The Devil Upon Two Sticks" (1768).

The graver bourgeois drama, destined to exert its influence upon Diderot and Lessing, found its earliest expression in "The London Merchant," of George Lillo (1731). Here George Barnwell, the apprentice lured into robbery and murder by the courtesan Millwood, is but remotely connected with the anti-heroism of picaresque fiction, and Moore's "Gamester" (1753), in its portrayal of the sins and remorse of Beverley, is even less roguish. Cumberland, who cultivated this vein, mingled more mirth in his "Impostors" (1789), where Harry Singleton, the valet of Lord James, assumes his master's title, and with a confederate as his pretended man of business, nearly captures the heiress whose father favors his suit. But neither classic comedy nor bourgeois tragedy had anything novel to offer in roguery. Goldsmith and Sheridan were not concerned with such matters, unless the pranks

[1] In an advertisement for 1723 of books printed and sold by Thomas Corbett, at Addison's Head without the Temple, there is announced as "Just publish'd, neatly printed in pocket editions in six volumes," *The Loves of Osmin and Daraxa*, together with the *Novelas* of Cervantes.

of the former's Tony Lumpkin be allowed in this category; and at the close of the century Thomas Holcroft's "Road to Ruin" (1792) drew its young prodigal as but faintly roguish, while in the younger Colman's "Iron Chest" (1796) the picaresque features of its original — Godwin's "Caleb Williams" — wholly disappeared.

6. *Roguery on the Nineteenth-Century Stage*

With the nineteenth century the dependence of the drama upon the novel was fully established. Every fictional success found dramatization, and that romances of roguery should have been adapted for the boards was only natural. The "Waverley Novels," for example, were frequently arranged for presentation;[1] Egan's "Life in London" gave rise to several plays, the chief by W. T. Moncrieff; Gilbert A. à Beckett did Hook's "Jack Brag" into a farce (1837); and Ainsworth's "Jack Sheppard" furnished the matter for dramas by G. White, J. B. Buckstone, and Tom Greenwood. Most of Dickens's novels underwent the process, and of the more picaresque, "Pickwick" was exploited by Edward Stirling and Leman Rede in 1837, and by James Albery in 1871 and 1878; while "Oliver Twist" was arranged by C. Z. Barnett (1838), by John Oxenford (1868), by J. B. Johnstone (1868), and by Cyril Searle (1878), by George Almar in a burletta, and in cheap versions like "The Workhouse Boy, or the Scamps of Seven Dials" (1865) and "The Artful Dodger" (1867). Bulwer's "Paul

[1] Roguery figured more or less in the following: Edward Fitzball's *Waverley;* Soane's *Rob Roy;* Isaac Pocock's *Rob Roy Macgregor*, a musical drama (1818); Sydney French's *Rob Roy* (1867); *The Pirate* (1822); *Kenilworth*, by Tom Dibdin; *The Earl of Leicester*, by Samuel Heath (1843); *Kenilworth*, a comic opera extravaganza, by Halliday and Laurence; *Kenilworth*, a melodrama, by William Oxberry; *Guy Mannering, or the Gipsey's Prophecy*, a musical play (1816); *The Fortunes of Nigel*, by Fitzball (1822); and *Nigel, or the Crown Jewels* (1823).

Clifford" was turned into plays by Fitzball (1835) and by Benjamin Webster (1833), and his "Eugene Aram" was dramatized by Moncrieff and long after by W. G. Wills (1873). Thomas Dibdin altered Griffin's "Suil Dhuv, the Coiner" into melodrama, and the latter's "Collegians" was prepared for the stage by T. E. Wilks as "Eily O'Connor" (1831) and by Dion Boucicault as "The Colleen Bawn" (1860). R. B. Peake dramatized Warren's "Ten Thousand a Year" (1841), and Charles Dillon staged Sue's "Mysteries of Paris" (1844). John Palgrave Simpson wrote a play founded on Edmund Yates's "Black Sheep" (1868); Charles Reade's "It Is Never Too Late To Mend" figured theatrically both before and after its appearance as a novel; Isaac Pocock presented a romantic "Robinson Crusoe, or the Bold Buccaniers;" and "Gil Blas" inspired "The Boy of Santillane" (1827).

The last is representative of its class in unreality. Gil Blas, confined with Donna Mensia in the robbers' cave, meets harrowing experiences that reach a climax when a train of gunpowder burns across the stage and blows robbers and mountains to atoms as the hero, with the lady in his arms, escapes through a trap-door. Similar in spirit is "Margaret Catchpole" (1845), Edward Stirling's dramatization of Richard Cobbold's once popular fiction. The anti-heroine, in love with a smuggler, steals a horse and gallops seventy miles to meet him. She is arrested, condemned to death, and reprieved, but escapes from prison to join her lover. Being retaken, she is transported to Australia, where she flings over a cliff the convict who confesses to having murdered her lover and incited her own first crime. An American elaboration of the same theme was known as "The Horse-Thief" (1854).

If melodrama marked these adaptations, it was not lacking in more original pieces, as witness "Hawk, the Highwayman;"

Fitzball's "Red Rover;" N. B. Clarke's "Pirate of the Isles," with its Byronic anti-hero Mavroyeni and its repentant corsair Barozzi; "Captain Spruce, the Highwayman;" William E. Suter's "Robbers of the Pyrenees," "Child-Stealer," and "Felon's Bond;" George Almar's "Rover's Bride;" Tom Dibdin's "Ruffian Boy;" Charles Dibdin's "Smuggler's Daughter," and Stirling's "Ragpicker of Paris" (1847), wherein a desperate outcast poses as a baron on the proceeds of a theft, but twenty years after, being discovered in the crime that has brought him wealth, returns to ragpicking.

The romantic bandit was early in favor, too, in such plays as "The Female Brigand," Fitzball's "Hans von Stein, or the Robber Knight," Almar's "Robber of the Rhine," Isaac Pocock's "Robber's Wife," and J. R. Planché's "The Brigand" (1829), which celebrates Alessandro Massaroni, an Italian Robin Hood. To a miserly steward disguised as a pilgrim the brigand offers two hundred ducats that he professes to have lost at cards to a saint. The mock pilgrim is pleased to pose as the saint's representative, but when he keeps an appointment to receive the money, Massaroni declares that, having played again and won from the saint ten thousand ducats, he must exact that sum of the agent. So the steward is ruefully forced to hand over the treasure he had concealed in his staff. Presently, when a count falls into the brigand's clutches, Massaroni assumes his clothes and title, and attends the festivities given by Prince Bianchi in Rome. Being recognized there, he is shot, and dies after discovering that he is the prince's own son.

Even notorieties of the "Newgate Calendar," when brought upon the stage, were romantically handled. The list of plays conceived in this spirit includes J. S. Jones's "Captain Kyd," J. B. Howe's "Jerry Abbershaw," Suter's "Dick Turpin and Tom King," J. T. Haines's "Claude Duval," Leman Rede's "Sixteen String Jack," J. F. Poole's "Captain Heron, or the Highwayman of Epping Forest," Waldron's "Cartouche, the French Robber," N. B. Clarke's "Adventures of Vidocq" (in rivalry with an anonymous "Vidocq, the Thieftaker"), Douglas Jerrold's "Vidocq," and his "Ambrose Gwinett," concerned with one who was hanged on circumstantial evidence, but survived to meet his supposed victim and to sweep the road at Charing Cross as a beggar. In Suter's drama, King is the comic rogue and Turpin the sentimental one. Each robs a cockney artist, and then holds up the other by mistake. Turpin is captured and King flies to the rescue, but when matters are reversed, Turpin by accident wounds his friend. He springs astride Black Bess, and as the pursuit comes up, his sweetheart intercepts her father's shot and dies.

The plays on Jack Sheppard found a late echo in "Jack Sheppard and his Dog" (1863), "Jack Sheppard on Horseback" (1865), and "London Bridge One Hundred and Fifty Years Ago, or the Old Mint" (1873), professing to be "adapted and rewritten from 'Les Chevaliers du Brouillard,'" a French version of Ainsworth's novel.[1] Here Sheppard becomes Jack Younger, Sir Rowland Trenchard is Sir Rowland Hardman, and Jonathan Wild by inversion is Wild Jonathan, a Police Spy.

As for Rede's "Sixteen String Jack" (1841), it shows the historic Jack Rann gaining entrance to a victim's house by feigning himself a suitor and then, at the plea of a former sweetheart, preventing his band's perpetration of their intended burglary. Jack next masquerades as a French count, games with Beau Brummell and Major Hanger, bets they will be

[1] *Jack Sheppard, ou les Chevaliers du Brouillard, roman traduit de l'anglais* (Paris, 1873).

robbed that night, and in winning his wager is captured. He changes clothes in prison with his devoted Mary Ferrers and escapes, only to be retaken. Then Brummell and Hanger secure a reprieve, which arrives as the cart bearing him to Tyburn crosses the stage.[1] Rede wrote other plays of low-life, his "Rake's Progress" (1833) presenting scenes in the King's Bench Prison and in Bedlam, and his "Faith and Falsehood, or the Fate of a Bushranger" (1837) introducing Charles Graves, accused of robbery and transported as the result of interfering with the plans of a libertine. He breaks jail and escapes to the bush with his sweetheart, but when she is slain by another convict, Graves surrenders to the lord who had ruined her, and dies of a broken heart.

From the twenties to the forties, the most persistent cultivator of roguery for the boards was W. T. Moncrieff. Aside from his adaptations of Egan and Bulwer, and such trifles as "Giovanni in London, or the Libertine Reclaimed," an extravaganza, and "The Rogueries of Nicholas," written for the ventriloquist Alexander, Moncrieff did a number of plays which were original or patterned upon French models. Three of these may be described as typical.

The "Beggar of Cripplegate" contains recollections of the beggar-books, and revives the famous Cocke Lorrell, who figures here as "Prince of Patricos, Chancellor of the Cadgers, and Lord High Commissioner of all the jarkmen, rufflers, and uprightmen in Romeville." The king of the beggars is a gentleman in disguise, who bestows a thousand pounds on the father of his sweetheart, and with the romantic Gypsy,

[1] Thomas Egerton Wilks composed a less amusing piece on the same theme. In his *Sixteen String Jack, or the Knaves of Knaves' Acre*, Jack joins with a gambler and a highwayman to swindle a bridegroom, but the bride, disguised as Gunpowder Dick, rescues her lover, attacks Jack Rann himself, and secures from him a stolen will.

Millicent, protects bluff King Hal from the plots of certain churchmen. The sessions of the cadgers are picturesquely set forth, and when Henry VIII knights the mendicant's monarch, Cocke Lorrell succeeds to office, and a cadger's chorus rings the changes upon the joys of beggar life.

In an amusing extravaganza entitled "Gipsy Jack, or the Napoleon of Humble Life" Moncrieff burlesqued Napoleon's career and an earlier dramatic representation of it.

This travesty shows Gipsy Jack as a brigand on a smaller scale, born of a drab in a Blackheath ditch, and the hero of Fives' Court. He undertakes the siege of Norwood Common, from which the Gypsies have been driven, effects the daring passage of Highgate Hill, is crowned emperor of the Gypsies at South Mimms, attacks the Finchley beggars, ravages Hendon and Barnet, carrying off no end of poultry and linen, fights the constables at Battle Bridge, surrenders at Hampstead Heath, and after incarceration at Newgate, is transported, but escapes by feigning death. Harman (an unconscious reminiscence of Thomas Harman) and Carew appear among the beggars, while the usual tinkers and poachers are enlisted with the Gypsies.

A Parisian original — "Les Bohémiens" — gave the hint for Moncrieff's "Scamps of London" (1843), which exhibits low-life in garret and cellar, in a Bermondsey dance-hall, and among the cadgers lodging for the night beneath the dry arches of Waterloo Bridge. The rogues include Fox Skinner, king of the scamps and greeks; Ikey Bates, landlord of Rats' Castle; and the swindler, Hawksworth Shabner, proprietor of a West End silver hell.

Sheridan Knowles's ill-starred "Beggar of Bethnal Green" (1834) was sentimental and not picaresque, but "Robert Macaire," Charles Selby's popular two-act melodrama of the same year, adapted from "L'Auberge des Adrets," displayed humorous rascality in its two murderers, — witty Macaire and his cowardly companion, Jacques Strop.

The tatterdemalions have escaped from prison, and under assumed names indulge in pocket-picking at an inn. A nocturnal attack upon a wealthy farmer results in his death, and Macaire, after showing great *nonchalance* both before and after the crime is discovered, finds in the innkeeper a son, and in the woman suspected of the deed, his wife, but is shot by the police while endeavoring to escape.

Selby continued this play in "Jacques Strop" (1837), which revives Macaire, "the thief *par excellence*, combining in his own proper person the essence of politeness, the quintessence of impudence, and the most perfect collection of all the interesting qualities that have belonged, do belong, or may belong to the most daring, polished, and accomplished rascal in the world."

Macaire and Strop elude their captors and disguise as noblemen to perpetrate a fraud upon a credulous landlady, after which, clad as old women, they seek refuge with Macaire's son. When the arch rogue is fatally wounded by his pursuers, he exonerates an escaped convict who has suffered for one of his robberies.

Claude Melnotte in "The Lady of Lyons" (1838) proved the typical Bulwerian rogue, with heroism emphasized and rascality condoned.

Out of pique for the scorn bestowed upon him by a merchant's daughter, and egged on by another disgruntled suitor, Melnotte, though a peasant, masquerades as the Prince of Como, and is eagerly accepted by the lady. So far he seems a perfect swindler, presenting Pauline with the gold snuff-box and the diamond ring that are not his, prating of his grandfather, the Doge of Venice, glibly describing the splendors that await her as his wife, and falling in with his confederates' lies that will insure a speedy marriage. But roguery gives place to heroism, the bridegroom reveals his perfidy, refuses to profit by his misrepresentations, and departs to the wars, to return ere long a wealthy colonel and to rescue and wed the heroine.

As a relief from all this sentimentalism came the burlesque of roguery, already attempted by Moncrieff, but first flourishing in the sixties and introduced by H. J. Byron's mock "Lady of Lyons" (1859). That decade saw among others Selby's "Pirates of Putney," F. C. Burnand's "Robin Hood," "Humbug," and "Claude Duval, or the Highwayman for Ladies," Suter's "Highwayman's Holiday," in which three girls in the guise of road-knights rob a stingy old fellow and his man, and W. S. Gilbert's "Merry Zingara, or the Tipsy Gipsy and the Popsy Wopsy." Later pieces in the same vein were H. B. Farnie's "Idle 'Prentice, a Tyburnian Idyll of High, Low, Jack and his Little Game;" Byron's "Robert Macaire, or the Roadside Inn Turned Inside Out;" Robert Reece's "Little Robin Hood;" Burnand's "Robbing Roy, or Scotched and Kilt," and Gilbert's comic opera librettos, "The Ne'er-do-Well," "The Mountebanks," and "The Pirates of Penzance," the last poking fun at the romantic criminal in the familiar lines: —

> When the enterprising burglar 's not a-burgling,
> When the cut-throat is n't occupied in crime,
> He loves to hear the little brook a-gurgling
> And listen to the merry village chime.

Among the more serious playwrights Tom Taylor and Dion Boucicault wrote melodramas associated with the literature of roguery, but such a piece as Boucicault's "Rapparee" (1870) proved heroic rather than otherwise, for Roderick O'Malley is less a bandit than the leader of a lost cause. As for Taylor, he never portrayed roguery for its own sake, although low-life figured in such dramas as "Barefaced Impostors," "Going to the Bad," and "The Brigand and his Banker." His best work — "The Ticket-of-Leave Man" (1863), adapted from the French — introduces a professional criminal, James Dalton, and his inveterate enemy, the detective Hawkshaw.

Dalton's confederate, Melter Moss, furnishes counterfeit notes which their pigeon, Bob Brierly, innocently passes. Hawkshaw and his men, in a general scrimmage, capture Brierly, who is sent to Portland. Prison makes a new man of him, and he returns to be welcomed by the singing-girl he had earlier befriended. He wins success as a clerk, and is about to marry when Dalton, whose swindling scheme he foils, exposes him as a ticket-of-leave man. Although turned away and hounded from master to master, Brierly is finally able to protect his first employer's property from burglary, and with Hawkshaw duly triumphs. Neither the rogue nor the detective is especially astute, but both are apt in disguise, and the crooks are masters of thieves' flash.

T. W. Robertson's classic "Caste" (1867), inspired in part by "Vanity Fair," drew an amusing old scamp in the impecunious Eccles, who frequents the public-house on urgent business, harangues upon the nobility of labor, poses in his cups as a beneficent socialist, yet plays the thief when unobserved. Young Henry Irving first won notice by reciting Hood's "Dream of Eugene Aram," and made his earliest pronounced success as the crime-haunted Matthias in "The Bells" (1871), Leopold Lewis's version of "Le Juif Polonais," by Erckmann-Chatrian. John Lang's "Plot and Passion" introduced the female foreign-office spy. Clement Scott and E. Manuel adapted Sardou's "Dora" as "Diplomacy" (1878), but modified the roguish Countess Zicka so that she no longer emphasized her early career as thief, beggar, and wife of a forger. French influence was equally responsible for Charles Reade's "The Lyons Mail" and "Drink," and for F. C. Burnand's farcical comedy, "Artful Cards" (1877). Here the dissipated Spicer Rumford, squeezing money from his wife by cheats, falls into the net of an adventuress in league with gamblers disguised as foreign noblemen. After a descent of police has been met by transforming the roulette board into a piano and the rogues into respectable musicians, Rumford gets home, half fuddled, to find that his wife has herself succumbed to the wiles of a foreign swindler. So each excuses the other, and Rumford somewhat improbably regains the money he had lost to the countess.

A favorite type of native play is exemplified in a hundred pieces of slight value, such as C. H. Hazlewood's "Alone in the Pirates' Lair," W. Travers's "Boy Detective," Stanley McKenna's "Boy Burglar," Fred Marsden's "Bushrangers," J. C. Foster's "Bob Covey, the Newgate Jester," and J. B. Howe's "Bessy Wild, or the Thief-taker's Daughter," "Handsome Jack," and "Scarlet Dick" (1878). Dick, with his robber band, carries off his sweetheart as she is about to be wed to another, and, sparing the life of George III, is reprieved by that monarch when captured; while Jack, the rightful heir to the Town estates, turns highwayman and is persecuted by the wicked Sir James, who has enlisted the services of Jonathan Wild. The scenes exhibit St. Pancras Workhouse, the den of Wild, a flash ken, the robbers' sanctuary, and Hounslow Heath by moonlight.

More recently G. R. Sims has achieved success in "The Lights o' London" (1881) and "The Romany Rye" (1882), presenting low-life with sympathetic realism, and offering such characters as Old Mother Shipton, Boss Knivett the burglar, chivalrous in devotion to his pal, and Harold the convict, who escapes through the good offices of a showman. Sims and Shirley's "Two Little Vagabonds" (1896), from Decourcelle's "Deux Gosses," affects the same style, and Henry Arthur Jones's "Silver King" (1882) has prepared the way for Raffles and his ilk by popularizing the aristocratic leader of a gang of thieves who does his crimes in evening dress. The rogue of good family, respected by society and by his friends, is further set forth in Sir Charles Young's "Jim the Penman" (1886), based in part upon the career of James Townsend Seward, an accomplished English criminal.

James Ralston has turned forger merely to defeat his rival in love, but upon the craft that has brought him a wife he comes to rely to provide him a livelihood. When, after years of fortunate rascality, he would reform, Baron Hartfeld, his confederate, goads him on to a final crime. This is the forging of an order for the family diamonds of the lord who is about to become his son-in-law. Captain Redwood, a detective disguised as a fop, intervenes, and the old rival learns of the trick by which his sweetheart has become the forger's wife. Although out of regard for her he refuses to prosecute, Mrs. Ralston discovers her husband's true character and her lover's long fidelity, while Jim the Penman, after having made restitution and quarreled with his accomplice, opportunely drops dead.

In three plays by Robert Louis Stevenson and W. E. Henley roguery cuts a prominent figure. "Admiral Guinea" (pr. 1884) revives the picturesque blind rascal, David Pew, exploited less fully in "Treasure Island." A hackneyed picaresque theme is wittily revamped in "Macaire, a Melodramatic Farce" (pr. 1895); and "Deacon Brodie, or the Double Life" (pl. 1884) portrays the downfall of a rogue who, posing as an honest carpenter by day, is leader of a gang of housebreakers by night. Thieves' cant abounds in this piece, and its Bow Street runner proves a second Hawkshaw.

A. W. Pinero's "The Profligate" (1889) shows the traditional seducer, who eventually succumbs to conscience; and the type of social swindler is exploited by Sydney Grundy's two adaptations of Octave Feuillet's "Montjoye," the first entitled "Mammon" (1877), and the second "A Bunch of Violets" (1894). In the latter, Sir Philip Marchant, although he has without scruple defrauded the poor, the public, and his wife, refuses, on sentimental grounds, to give up for a king's ransom the violets that are his daughter's gift. More matter of fact is Bailey Prothero, the charlatan of Jones's "Rogue's Comedy" (1896), who pretends to clairvoyant powers, and, by the aid of his wife disguised as companion to Lady Dovergreen, is able to hoodwink the people of Lord Dovergreen's set. The swindler's son persists in endeavoring to show up his unrecognized father for a rogue; but when the young man's love-match with Lady Clarabut is threatened, Prothero denies the relationship. Then after a last reception in Park Lane, during which the unpaid servants revolt and the creditors descend *en masse*, Prothero and his wife decamp.

Adaptations from fiction have continued to vie with the original drama of roguery. Stage versions of such recent successes as "Sherlock Holmes," "The Amateur Cracksman,"[1] "The Social Highwayman," and "In the Bishop's Carriage," as well as of classic favorites like "Vanity Fair," have received no less attention than so excellent a piece at first hand as C. M. S. McLellan's "Leah Kleschna" (1904), which exhibits the female rogue of professional rank using blackmail as a defense in burglary, but yielding to the generous treatment accorded by a distinguished victim. Indeed, if it be plain that playwrights are prone to lean upon the prop of fiction, with its ready-made characters and situations, it is equally clear that audiences find especial relish in the more tangible stage presentation of scenes and personages whose acquaintance they have already made through the imagination. Whether these facts alone can explain the purely derivative character of so much of the modern drama, certain it is that since "The Beggar's Opera" no distinguished exemplar of the literature of roguery has appeared first upon the stage.

[1] Langdon McCormick's melodrama, *The Burglar and the Lady* (1906), includes both Raffles and Holmes.

BIBLIOGRAPHY

CHAPTER VI

1–4

For the drama from Shakespeare to the eighteenth century, consult A. W. Ward's *History of English Dramatic Literature* (London, 1899, vols. ii and iii); W. J. Courthope's *History of English Poetry* (London, 1903, vol. iv); F. G. Fleay's *Biographical Chronicle of the English Drama* (1559–1642) (London, 1891, 2 vols.); W. C. Hazlitt's *English Drama and Stage under the Tudor and Stuart Princes* (London, 1869); and J. P. Collier's *History of English Dramatic Poetry to Shakespeare, and Annals of the Stage to the Restoration* (London, 1831, vols. ii and iii).

1

Although low-life in Shakespeare is not explicitly discussed, it receives incidental mention in several works. Cf. especially Fleay's *Chronicle History of the Life and Work of Shakespeare* (1886); Maurice Morgann's *Essay on the Dramatic Character of Falstaff* (1777), directed against the assumption of Falstaff's cowardice; Halliwell-Phillipps's *Character of Sir John Falstaff as Originally Exhibited by Shakespeare* (1841), connecting Falstaff with Oldcastle; and J. Thümmel's *Der Miles Gloriosus bei Shakespeare ; Falstaff-Parolles, Armado-Pistol* (*Jahrbuch der deutschen Shakespeare Gesellschaft*, vol. xii, 1877). The same author's essays, *Über Shakespeares Narren* (*Jahrbuch*, vol. ix, 1874) and *Über Shakespeares Clowns* (*Jahrbuch*, vol. xi, 1876); Francis Douce's *Illustrations of Shakespeare* (new ed. 1839); N. Drake's *Memorials of Shakespeare* (1828); J. Weiss's *Wit, Humor, and Shakspeare* (1878); and Josef Kohler's *Die Verbrecher Typen in Shakespeares Dramen* (Berlin, 1903) contain matter germane to this theme. Jonson's *Works* are edited with notes and a biographical memoir by W. Gifford (new ed. London, 1875, 9 vols), and his *Best Plays* are edited by Brinsley Nicholson (London, *Mermaid Series*, 1894). *Volpone* has been issued with a critical essay by V. O'Sullivan (London, 1898), and *Bartholomew Fair*, *The Alchemist*, *The Devil is an Ass*, and *The*

Staple of News appear, with valuable introductions and notes, in *The Yale Studies in English* (N. Y., 1903–05). J. A. Symonds's *Ben Jonson* (*English Worthies*, 1886) and A. C. Swinburne's *Study of Ben Jonson* (1889) are the best critical monographs. E. Koeppel investigates the sources in *Quellen-Studien zu den Dramen Ben Jonsons* (Erlangen u. Leipzig, 1895), and the masques are considered in A. Soergel's *Die Englischen Maskenspiele* (Halle, 1882). Cf., also, Professor J. W. Cunliffe's forthcoming volume, *The Masque*, in the present series.

2–4

Dekker's *Dramatic Works* are edited by R. H. Shepherd with a Memoir (Pearson's Reprints, 1873, 4 vols.), and by E. Rhys (*Mermaid*, 1887). He is discussed by A. C. Swinburne (*Nineteenth Century*, Jan., 1887). Swinburne's essay on Chapman appears in R. H. Shepherd's edition of the *Works* of Chapman (London, 1874–75, 3 vols.). *The Comedies and Tragedies of George Chapman* (London, 1873, 3 vols.) contains reprints of the plays. A. H. Bullen is editor of the *Works* of Marston (London, 1887, 3 vols.) and of those of Middleton (London, 1885, 8 vols.), earlier edited by Dyce (1840, 5 vols.), and edited in part by Ellis (*Mermaid*, 1902). Massinger's *New Way to Pay Old Debts* appears in Gifford's edition (1805), in Cunningham's (1870), and in Symons's (*Mermaid*, 1887). E. Koeppel's *Quellen-Studien zu den Dramen Chapmans, Massingers, und Fords* (Strassburg, 1897) investigates the sources. The *Blind Beggar of Bednal-Green* appears in Bullen's edition of the *Works* of John Day (1887), and is reprinted by W. Bang (Louvain, 1902). The *Wise-Woman of Hogsdon* may be found in Heywood's *Dramatic Works* (Pearson's Reprints, 1874), and in A. W. Verity's *Thomas Heywood* (*Mermaid*, 1888).

The Fletcher plays noted in the text are contained in the Variorum Edition of the works of Beaumont and Fletcher (London, 1904 ff.) and in the Cambridge University Press Edition (Cambridge, 1905 ff.). Dyce and Gifford edited the *Dramatic Works and Poems of James Shirley* (London, 1833, 6 vols.), and Brome's *Dramatic Works* appear in Pearson's Reprints (London, 1873). In writing sections 2 and 3, I have been largely indebted to an unpublished essay prepared under my direction by Mr. Ernest J. Streubel, a former pupil.

James Maidment and W. H. Logan issued *The Dramatic Works of John Wilson* (London, 1874). Shadwell's plays have not been reprinted since the edition of 1720 (4 vols., with a Prefatory Memoir by the author's son). *The Goblins* is accessible in W. C. Hazlitt's *Poems, Plays, and other Remains of Sir John Suckling* (1874, 2 vols.). Vanbrugh's *Plays* is edited by W. C. Ward (London, 1893), and by A. E. H. Swaen (*Mermaid*, 1896). Farquhar's *Dramatic Works* is edited by A. C. Ewald and R. W. Lowe (London, 1892).

5–6

Gay is studied in Johnson's *Lives of the Poets*, in Thackeray's *English Humourists*, by Austin Dobson in his edition of the *Fables* (1884), in the *Dict. of Nat. Biog.* (vol. xxi), and by John Underhill in his standard *Gay's Works, with a Life and Notes* (London, 1893, 2 vols.).

Accounts of the drama after the seventeenth century deal mainly with the stage and the actors, and infrequently with dramatic literature. This is the case with Charles Dibdin's *Complete History of the Stage* (London, 1800, 5 vols.), with P. Fitzgerald's *New History of the English Stage* (London, 1882, 2 vols.), and with Dr. J. Doran's *Annals of the English Stage* (London, 1888, 3 vols., edited and revised by R. W. Lowe). D. E. Baker's *Biographia Dramatica* (London, 1812, 3 vols.) contains notices of playwrights and plays, and J. Geneste's *Some Account of the English Stage from 1660 to 1830* (Bath, 1832, 10 vols.) tabulates the performances of each year at the chief London theatres. Clement Scott's *Drama of Yesterday and To-Day* (London, 1899, 2 vols.) contains as an appendix a list of important plays produced in London from 1830 to the close of the century. The body of this work, however, principally concerns actors and stage life.

Plays themselves are discussed in William Archer's *English Dramatists of To-Day* (London, 1882), in D. Cook's *Nights at the Play* (London, 1883, 2 vols.), and in Augustin Filon's *English Stage, Being an Account of the Victorian Drama* (London, 1897, translation by Frederic Whyte). Consult, also, R. M. Levey and J. O'Rorke's *Annals of the Theatre Royal, Dublin, from 1821 to 1880* (Dublin, 1880); J. C. Dibdin's *Annals of the Edinburgh Stage* (Edinburgh, 1888); Henry Morley's *Journal of a London Playgoer from 1851 to 1866* (London, 1891), and T. Allston Brown's *History of the New York Stage* (N. Y., 1903, 3 vols.). J. B. Clapp and E. F. Edgett, in *Plays of the Present* (Dunlap Society, N. Y., 1902), print the bills of important plays of the past thirty-five years.

END OF VOLUME I